Microfranchising

Microfranchising

How Social Entrepreneurs are Building a New Road to Development

Edited by **Nicolas Sireau**

Routledge
Taylor & Francis Group

LONDON AND NEW YORK

First published 2011 by Greenleaf Publishing Limited

Published 2017 by Routledge
2 Park Square, Milton Park, Abingdon, Oxon OX14 4RN
711 Third Avenue, New York, NY 10017, USA

Routledge is an imprint of the Taylor & Francis Group, an informa business

Cover by LaliAbril.com

British Library Cataloguing in Publication Data:
   A catalogue record for this book is available from the British Library.

   ISBN-13: 9781906093433 (pbk)

Contents

Abbreviations and acronyms

BFA	British Franchise Association
BOOT	build, own, operate and transfer
BoP	base of the pyramid
BRIC	Brazil, Russia, India and China
BRAC	Bangladesh Rural Advancement Committee
CDI	Center for Digital Inclusion
CE Solutions	Community Enterprise Solutions
CFWshops	Child and Family Wellness shops
CIA	Central Intelligence Agency
DDD	Digital Divide Data
DFID	UK Department for International Development
FINCA	Foundation for International Community Assistance
FMCG	fast-moving consumer goods
FSC	field service consultant
GDP	gross domestic product
GTZ	Deutsche Gesellschaft für Technische Zusammenarbeit (German Society for Technical Cooperation)
HLL	Hindustan Lever Limited
HSEA	HealthStore East Africa
HSF	HealthStore Foundation
ICT	information and communication technology
IFA	International Franchising Association
ILO	International Labour Organisation
Ksh	Kenyan shillings
LED	light-emitting diode
lm-hr	lumen hour
LP	liquefied petroleum
M&E	monitoring and evaluation
MAMN	Malawi Microfinance Network
MAP	Mobile Access Point 4
MDG	Millennium Development Goal
MLF	MicroLoan Foundation
MNC	multinational company
MSA	Michael H Seid & Associates
NGO	non-governmental organisation
PRI	programme-related investment
SIDA	Swedish International Development Cooperation Agency
SME	small or medium-sized enterprise
UNAIDS	Joint United Nations Programme on HIV and AIDS
UNDP	United Nations Development Programme
USAID	United States Agency for International Development
WHO	World Health Organisation
WISER	Women's Institute for Secondary Education

Acknowledgements

I would like to thank all the contributors to this book for their hard work: Harry Andrews, Lisa Jones Christensen, Jason Fairbourne, Nate Heller, Kurt Illetschko, Ryan Swee Ann Lee, David Lehr, Miguel D. Ramirez, Melissa Richer, P. Clint Rogers, Peter Ryan, Michael Seid and Robert C. Wolcott. It's been wonderful to work with such a group of inspirational academics and practitioners. I'm very grateful to my editor at Greenleaf, John Stuart, for agreeing so enthusiastically to this publishing project and for his assistance and advice throughout. I would also like to thank all those at SolarAid without whom this journey into microfranchising would never have been possible, particularly John Keane for his unwavering dedication to the cause and Jeremy Leggett for his inspiring vision, as well as everyone else on the SolarAid team and board. Finally, my thanks go out to my family for supporting me throughout this endeavour.

As a sign of their commitment, the contributors are donating their share of the royalties of this book to microfranchise programmes run by SolarAid's Sunny Money, Barefoot Power and the MicroLoan Foundation.

1

Introduction

Nicolas Sireau
SolarAid, UK

I first came across the concept of microfranchising in early 2007, when we were just starting SolarAid, the UK's first non-profit organisation to focus exclusively on solar power for developing countries. For the previous few months, we had been struggling with finding a model of micro-enterprise that could realistically be replicated on a large scale in order to wipe out the use of kerosene in Africa through the sustainable distribution of solar lamps. John Keane, SolarAid's new head of programmes, had extensive experience of setting up solar micro-enterprises with community groups across Africa—something he had been doing for years. But his experience, and that of SolarAid's first projects, was that reaching scale was difficult without a clear business model and a well-defined way of identifying, training and supporting entrepreneurs.

Our first project in late 2006 and early 2007, in Malawi, involved training a small group of young people affected by HIV/AIDS to convert kerosene lamps into solar lamps using light-emitting diodes (LEDs), rechargeable batteries, thin-film solar glass, handmade wooden frames, a few locally sourced wires and some crocodile clips. We then trained them in business skills—market research, business planning, cash-flow forecasting—so that they could sell these solar products, generate an income and set up a self-sustaining business. As the project developed, we realised this was going to be difficult. First, there was a free-rider problem: the young people constituted themselves as a community group, but many of them made hardly any effort while benefiting from the hard work of the few dedicated ones, which eventually brought the group to a standstill. Then there was the problem of product quality: the converted kerosene lamps and handmade solar panels were poorly put together and broke quickly. There were problems with products being over-priced by entrepreneurs wanting to make a quick buck; logistical challenges with components running out and sourcing proving difficult; credit issues with consumers not being able to afford the products; problems with products going missing; and tax barriers with a 47.5% import tax into Malawi on our solar components. The list of challenges we faced seemed huge—yet we soon realised that these were the same cultural, logistical, financial, infrastructural, legal, human resource and other barriers facing any enterprise working in Africa.

Furthermore, the aid industry has made the situation much worse. Non-governmental organisations (NGOs) proliferate across Africa and have muddied the context to such a degree with their failed hand-out projects that a culture of dependency has settled in. SolarAid comes across this every day. In Zambia, for instance, we visited a community to find out whether they would be interested in setting up a solar business to sell solar lamps to villagers and create jobs. The reply was disappointing: community leaders explained to us that the day before our visit a German NGO had come by to distribute free products to the community, while the next day a French NGO was coming over to give cash for free for schooling. 'We don't need to set up a business,' the community leaders said. 'We can just wait for more NGOs to come over and give things out for free.' Although well intentioned, the NGOs were having a detrimental effect. They were killing enterprise, killing the market and killing any hope of pulling these communities out of poverty. Indeed, the only way Africa will ever develop is if it can build healthy market economies and create sustainable employment for a large part of its population. Unfortunately, most NGO programmes do the very opposite.

That's why we were so excited when we first read the World Resources Institute's report (Clemminck and Kadakia 2007) on VisionSpring (then called the Scojo Foundation)'s microfranchise programme. The origins of SolarAid lay deeply in the commercial sector—having been set up with a grant from Solarcentury, the UK's largest solar company—and the concept of microfranchising struck a chord. VisionSpring, with its vision entrepreneurs, its 'business-in-a-box' and its sustainable supply chain, was pioneering a new way of scaling up micro-enterprise that seemed adaptable to SolarAid's vision. Microfranchising provided a solution to many of the problems we faced, particularly the need to offer our entrepreneurs a standardised business model with access to a supply chain, marketing, financing, training and ongoing management. We immediately began finding out more and looking at how to implement this.

We began by looking at the history of franchising, which became during the 1990s the most popular method of expanding commercial retail stores rapidly with limited risk (Bradach 1998; Montagu 2002). The World Franchise Council and the International Franchise Association estimate that there are approximately 16,000 franchised systems operating in 140 countries, with more than 1.6 million franchised outlets generating total sales of $1 trillion (Duckett and Monaghan 2007). Franchising works across all sectors where businesses operate through branches: hotels, restaurants, real estate, car hire, coffee shops, cleaning, teaching to drive and more. Franchises such as McDonald's, Snappy Snaps or The Body Shop are everywhere, providing locally owned stores that deliver services from a standardised model. There are several reasons for this: it is particularly easier to scale up a franchise than a company-owned store because the capital investment and many of the management decisions are made by the franchisee; fixed costs are spread out over many outlets, providing significant economies of scale for marketing and advertising; and the franchisees have more incentives to work hard and make their franchise succeed because of their personal financial investment in the business. This means that franchisors do not have to provide the same level of supervision of franchisees as they would if they were running a network of company-owned businesses. Some franchisors are large brands, some are just regional networks, and many are somewhere in between (Duckett and Monaghan 2007). All of them are based on having a proven business system that others can be easily taught to operate at a profit.

The most widely accepted definition of a franchise is that of 'a contractual relationship between a franchisee (usually taking the form of a small business) and a franchisor (usually a larger business) in which the former agrees to produce or market a product or service in accordance with an overall "blueprint" devised by the franchisor' (Stanworth *et al.* 1995 cited in Montagu 2002). As will be explained in further detail in subsequent chapters, franchises exist in two broad types: traditional and business format. Traditional franchises grant the right to sell a product or service in a geographical area, such as for a car dealership or a gas station. The business format provides advertising, service methods and delivery models to a franchisee, while strictly regulating the activities of the franchisee. Montagu (2002) also draws a distinction between stand-alone franchises and fractional franchises. Stand-alone franchises are the norm in the West: they exclusively promote the goods and services of the franchisor, such as in the case of McDonald's, which does not allow franchisees to sell Burger King burgers or any others. A fractional franchise, which is more the norm for microfranchises in developing countries, adds a franchised product or service to an existing business, creating additional income for the franchisee and using existing business assets such as shop space.

The beauty of microfranchising—which some people also call social franchising—is that it uses franchising methods to achieve social as well as financial goals. According to Montagu (2002):

> The goal of social franchising programmes is to use the commercial relationship of a franchise network to benefit provider members, and then to leverage those benefits into socially beneficial services; socially beneficial either because they are of higher quality than services previously available, or because they are less expensive, or because greater availability and awareness of availability leads to greater use of a good service (Montagu 2002: 123).

The attraction of microfranchising for development is that it offers clear and well-practised business systems to minimise risk and maximise returns within a particularly difficult context. While traditional micro-enterprise techniques deliver moderate results at best within the context of the developing world, according to our experience, microfranchising, with its set format, clear-cut rules and franchisee-focused incentives system, can offer a faster and more effective way to reach scale. As mentioned, all the factors that businesses take for granted in the developed world are lacking, making business in poor countries risky: infrastructure is crumbling, creating serious problems for maintaining an effective supply chain; communication systems, despite the growth in mobile telephone networks, are unreliable; the banking system, particularly for providing working capital to the poor, is limited; the legal system, which should provide protection from corruption and business malpractice, is too weak; and the primary, secondary and tertiary education systems, which should train people for working life, are under severe strain.

Entrepreneurs in the informal economy—who form the majority of entrepreneurs in developing countries—suffer the most: they do not have the working capital, the business training, the backup or the support needed to grow their businesses. So any change in their circumstances—such as a drought for a farmer or an illness for a hairdresser—can ruin them rapidly. Most, therefore, choose to run a variety of small business enterprises, never investing much in any of them, and moving quickly from job to job or business idea to business idea. Hence microfranchising provides a less risky venture for such entrepreneurs. They can roll out a tried-and-tested business system, supported by a larger organisation's training, marketing and human resources, with access to a more reliable supply chain.

Microfranchising has had some significant achievements—as the case studies in this book will show. Nevertheless, it is not a formula for inevitable success, as the barriers to scale remain huge. While the SolarAid team embarked enthusiastically on developing and implementing a microfranchise model, we soon realised that it was not the magic bullet we were hoping it would be. Indeed, there is no magic bullet for solving global poverty: just much hard, painstaking work and a firm commitment to market-based solutions. Still, our experience and that of others shows that microfranchising, if implemented carefully and correctly, can go a long way towards resolving many of the replication and scale-up problems that social entrepreneurs face, as this book will demonstrate.

Following this introduction, Chapter 2 goes over the theory of microfranchising. Written by Kurt Illetschko, one of the founders of the South African franchise movement and a global expert on microfranchising, it explains the history of franchising, the emergence of business-format franchising, the legal and financial implications and the different theoretical models of franchising. The chapter is important as it places microfranchising squarely within the framework of the traditional franchising that emerged in the West over the past century or so. Nevertheless, as Chapter 3, also by Kurt, shows, microfranchising then adapts the franchising concept to the particularities of the developing world, which is so different from the Western world for which franchising was originally developed. Kurt provides an oversight of a few of the key microfranchise enterprises that will then be discussed in subsequent chapters. Indeed, the reader will notice that some examples—particularly microfranchise pioneers such as VisionSpring, HealthStore Foundation and Drishtee—are referred to throughout the book and analysed from a variety of angles. On the one hand, this is testimony to their central status in the development of microfranchising over the past decade. On the other hand, it shows that the microfranchise sector remains young, with still just a handful of organisations adopting its techniques.

Chapter 4 is by P. Clint Rogers, Jason Fairbourne and Robert Wolcott, researchers who are leaders in the field of microfranchising. They focus on the key principle of replicating success to scale through three enabling characteristics: organic nature, modularity and microscalability. They discuss how microfranchising can solve many of the problems of traditional approaches to introducing innovations in emerging economies. They describe as case studies two microfranchise organisations offering information and communication technology services: Drishtee and OneRoof.

Chapter 5 is by Harry Andrews, a social entrepreneur for whom I have huge admiration. Harry's Barefoot Power business has been leading the way in the solar-lighting industry for half a decade and has been a major source of inspiration for SolarAid. His chapter is a case study of Barefoot Power's microfranchise pilot programme in Uganda. It shows promising results and learnings and was only halted because of lack of financing to scale it up—which is a problem facing many social enterprises in developing countries.

Chapter 6, by David Lehr and Lisa Jones Christensen, two authors with years of relevant experience, deals with this issue of how to finance a microfranchise. This is an area many social entrepreneurs struggle with, as access to capital is difficult at the best of times. Many still rely on an unpredictable variety of grants that come with all kinds of strings attached and are not suitable for their scale-up needs. As David and Lisa explain, a range of social investment opportunities are starting to become available that may go some way towards addressing this problem.

Chapter 7, by Peter Ryan, tells the story of the creation and growth of the Micro-Loan Foundation, a microfinance organisation set up by Peter that works in Malawi and is now expanding to neighbouring countries. As well as giving insights into how microfinance and microfranchising can work together, Peter describes his experience of starting at a micro level and then slowly building the systems, teams and processes needed to scale up effectively. Indeed, a challenge for all social enterprises is to get it right from the start—otherwise, they may end up replicating a faulty model that will ultimately collapse.

Chapter 8 looks at how microfranchises have to create the market from scratch in order to generate demand for their products: rural communities have generally never heard of the products on offer and hence need to be educated about them before they can develop a desire to buy. The chapter also looks at the process for identifying and training franchisees, which is arguably the most important part of microfranchising. Without hard-working, skilled and honest franchisees, a microfranchise has no chance of reaching scale. The author, Miguel Ramirez, has been working for SolarAid for a number of years and has extensive field experience from which he draws to make his case, adding to this some examples from other successful microfranchises.

Chapter 9 looks at social-sector franchising, particularly applied to the healthcare sector. The author, Michael Seid, is a franchising expert who goes through all the key elements of setting up and running a franchise focusing on social outcomes. His argument that most aid fails because it focuses too much on funding levels and not enough on the method of execution is a sound one and reflects the experience of others in this field. Michael emphasises the need to build a strong brand for the social-sector franchise and to implement processes that allow the franchisor to stick to the brand's promises in order to provide consistent delivery of high-quality products and services—something that is often missing from NGO programmes and business services in developing countries.

Chapter 10 offers valuable insights into the challenges facing microfranchises trying to replicate and scale up their operations in the developing world. The author, Ryan Swee Ann Lee, starts by debunking some of the myths around franchising's success in the Western world, showing that a significant number of franchises fail over time. Although it is a proven and tested model for scaling up certain types of business, Ryan argues that franchising is not the unbeatable success formula that many of its proponents claim it is. Ryan then looks at the role of microfranchising within the context of the base of the pyramid (BoP). He shows how the BoP presents specific challenges—such as lack of infrastructure and lack of education— that many microfranchises struggle to overcome. He also argues that social entrepreneurs need to think carefully before adopting a microfranchise model in order to be sure that their particular business proposition is indeed franchisable—otherwise, it will not be replicable or scalable via a microfranchise system. He provides a few pointers from the BoP Protocol developed by Cornell University to help social entrepreneurs set up their pilot microfranchise businesses.

Chapter 11, by Melissa Richer and Nate Heller from Ayllu, is a solid piece of research looking at why social enterprises often cannot scale in the developing-world context. So many of us social entrepreneurs spend our time discussing business models and scaling strategies, yet without understanding the contextual factors that limit growth. These challenges include financing problems, difficult access to information, lack of learning from others, inadequate partnerships, corruption, and lack of skilled personnel. As Richer and Heller show, there is an urgent need to research how we can create a more enabling context that will allow social enterprises and microfranchises to flourish at the base of the pyramid.

I have structured the book to alternate between more theoretical chapters and case studies in order to emphasise how theory and practice are closely linked. As the reader will realise, there is still much to be learnt about the potential of microfranchising for tackling poverty and how the model can be improved. The context in which microfranchises operate is particularly difficult; yet it is clear that only through constant experimentation, learning and sharing can we hope to overcome the hurdles to scaling up and reducing poverty on a global basis. As the aid industry continues to implement a failed model of development that tends to promote dependency and corruption, there is an urgent need for socially guided, market-based solutions that can create employment and economic development on a sustainable basis. My belief, and that of the authors who contributed to this book, is that microfranchising is one of these solutions.

2
Microfranchising
The theory

Kurt Illetschko
Franchise consultant, South Africa

An introduction to franchising

Modern-day franchising originates from the USA but is now practised in all corners of the globe. This is because the underlying concept is compelling in its simplicity and highly efficient. If developed properly and implemented ethically, a franchise is a blueprint for business success. The granting of a franchise implies that if the franchisee follows the network's guidelines to the letter, the business should be successful. The odd franchise failure does occur, but on balance, franchising has established itself as the most successful business expansion mechanism known.

The support offered by the franchisor will enhance the franchisee's chances for building a successful business. This does not mean, however, that business success is guaranteed. The success or failure of a franchised outlet depends on the abilities, dedication and hard work of the franchisee as well as on his or her willingness to follow the system. Compelling evidence exists that franchising has helped many individuals to make the difficult transition from employee or unemployed to successful entrepreneur. Unfortunately, this is not widely publicised. The media appear to be convinced that articles reporting on franchise failures attract a wider readership, so this is what they generally focus on. As a result, franchising's potential, including its potential to be adapted to various needs, continues to be underestimated.

Given the concept's advantages and the pressing need that exists for the cost-effective delivery of goods and services to people living in remote areas of South America, Africa and Asia, it is surprising that franchising has not been used in these regions to a far greater extent. Experience has shown that franchise schemes can address not just one but two or three pressing needs that exist in these areas: namely, access to basic services, the promotion of a viable small business sector and the creation of employment opportunities. Franchising can take care of all these needs in a cost-effective and sustainable manner.

This chapter explains how franchising has evolved and includes some theory in order to facilitate an in-depth understanding of the concept's vast potential. The next chapter will focus on the special problems linked to the implementation of microfranchise schemes and how they can be overcome. The inclusion of several case studies of direct relevance to the microfranchising environment will bring the material to life.

A history of franchising

The first record of a franchise, albeit in its most rudimentary form, dates back to 200 BC. A trader called Los Kas created a franchised chain-store concept for the distribution of branded food items throughout China. What led to the eventual collapse of this operation is not known. All we know is that, after promising beginnings, franchising vanished from the record books for a long time. It only surfaced again in medieval England. Historians tell us that British royalty rewarded deserving soldiers and politicians by granting them a franchise. These early franchisees were entitled to collect taxes within a defined territory, on condition that they would pay a percentage of the monies collected to the royal treasury. This gave rise to the term 'royalty payment', which some solicitors continue to use to this day when drafting franchise agreements. I will explain later why this is no longer appropriate.

The mid-1850s saw the emergence of 'tied houses', English pubs that were owned by breweries but operated by licensees under franchise agreements of sorts. Although some such arrangements continue today, they had one major flaw. Because the breweries retained full ownership of the pubs, their licensees were little more than glorified managers. They had long-term contracts and benefited from profit-sharing schemes, but ownership was beyond their reach. It has long since been shown that ownership is the ultimate motivator, and today's franchise arrangements take account of this.

Modern-day franchising evolved during the 1850s when the Singer Sewing Machine Company established a network of franchised dealers that soon serviced the entire USA. The rationale for this was compelling. Newly developed mass-production techniques made it possible for Singer to produce more sewing machines than its local market could absorb. To move stock, it needed to create a national distribution network as a matter of priority. This need created two closely related problems. First, Singer's management knew that to ship sewing machines to all parts of the country without offering user training and local technical support would damage their brand. Second, the establishment of such a vast network of company-owned outlets exceeded Singer's capacity, both in terms of funding and in depth of management.

It was at this point that Singer's management decided to appoint franchisees. To qualify, interested entrepreneurs had to meet certain basic requirements. They were obliged to set up a dedicated operation, their staff had to undergo specialised training and they had to be prepared to keep a full range of models and spares in stock. The arrangement suited both parties. The franchisees became part of a dynamic network with guaranteed access to preferential buying, ongoing training and some marketing support. Singer could roll out a national network of distribution points in record time without having to invest in the necessary infrastructure. Because the franchisees had invested their own capital, they were highly motivated to drive the business. This removed the need for Singer to build a substantial management structure.

The advantages of the arrangement weren't limited to the franchisor and its franchisees alone. Users of Singer sewing machines benefited from the arrangement as well. No matter where in the country they lived, they always had access to the owner of the business that had sold them the machine. In most instances, this resulted in much better service levels than a manager-operated factory outlet would have offered. Probably without realising it, Singer's management had single-handedly created the first product franchise. This turned out to be a pioneering move that would be copied for many years into the future. Over time, a growing number of companies, many of them involved with the sale and servicing of motor vehicles and the distribution of petrol, adopted the same modus operandi. They rolled out their distribution and service networks under product franchise arrangements and never looked back.

The emergence of business-format franchising

During the late 1940s, the market was ready for a new business format. The need originated from fast-food restaurants. These were a new concept at the time and the American public loved them. They were so successful that their owners were unable to keep up with the demand for new locations. In keeping with the entrepreneurial spirit, where there is a need someone finds a solution and offers it for sale. In this instance, the solution was the development of a more intricate franchise concept that later became known as business-format franchising. Typically, the fast-food pioneers' background was not in the restaurant sector but in commerce. They were business people who used fast food as a means to make money. These fast-food entrepreneurs soon realised that to wait for trained chefs to take up their franchises would slow down expansion. Besides, they themselves were living proof that it wasn't really necessary to be a trained chef to operate a hamburger joint. Individuals with a passion for customer service who were prepared to follow a proven blueprint would be much more likely to succeed.

This new approach proved to be an overnight success. With the buying public becoming increasingly demanding and brand-conscious, the success of a brand could only be assured by offering utmost uniformity plus excellent service. Business-format franchising was the way to go because it placed franchisees under a contractual obligation to follow the network's tried-and-tested blueprint to the letter. As a result, it did not really matter whether an outlet was company-owned (owned and operated by the original founder) or owned and operated by a franchisee. The mere fact that the outlet operated under a specific brand assured customers that the product range and quality as well as customer service standards would be identical no matter where in the country the outlet was located. The network's operating blueprint, recorded in one or more operations manuals, and the ongoing support and supervision from the network's support staff made sure of that.

Early business-format franchises emerged primarily in the fast-food sector because these restaurants, with their limited menu, standardised operating systems and mass-market appeal, were ideally suited to large-scale replication. However, other industry sectors were quick to adopt the new concept. Today, franchise opportunities can be found in many different business sectors.

Entrepreneurs the world over have recognised that almost every activity that can be standardised can be successfully brought to market through a network of franchised outlets. In the USA, for example, franchised chains account for over 50% of all consumer sales activity. This translates into sales exceeding $880 billion, channelled through over 900,000 franchised outlets, which provide employment for more than 21 million individuals. Franchising's market share is slightly lower in other countries, but nevertheless strong. Currently, the European Union countries and Australia are leading the way.

Franchising's worldwide victory march was no coincidence. Although business tourists (entrepreneurs who travelled to the USA) came across franchising and brought the concept back to their home countries, worldwide expansion was driven by USA-based franchisors. Having established strong footholds in their home market, they were looking for opportunities elsewhere. To move into foreign markets successfully, they either set up subsidiaries in target countries or appointed master licensees, companies that assumed the mantle of franchisor. While some local entrepreneurs were content to enter into master licence agreements, others developed their own home-grown concepts. Fortunately for the development of franchising, the same basic principles that made franchising successful in the USA were kept intact. This was in no small measure due to the efforts of national franchise associations that were established early on. Their guidelines for ethical franchising were largely modelled on material published by the International Franchise Association, the world's longest established franchise body, with its seat in Washington, DC, USA.

Legal aspects

Although franchising has been with us for a long time, few countries have franchise-specific legislation. This does not mean that franchising operates outside the legislative framework. In most countries, franchise agreements are treated like normal commercial agreements. This has turned out to be a mixed blessing. On the one hand, complex legislative requirements tend to increase the amount of red tape entrepreneurs have to contend with, which they would rather do without. On the other hand, franchise arrangements differ from normal commercial arrangements in several respects, and while franchise agreements should reflect that, standard contract law does not provide for it. This keeps the door open for unscrupulous entrepreneurs to exploit the good name of franchising for their own ends.

In practice, for a franchise arrangement to be sustainable, the underlying contract must reflect the spirit of franchising. This means, among other things, that the interests of both parties are taken into account. It also means that a franchise agreement is usually not negotiable: every franchisee in the network will enjoy the same set of rights and obligations. If this were not the case, the administration of the network would create administrative nightmares. It would also give rise to petty jealousies because franchisees would be convinced that the other guy received a more favourable agreement.

Self-regulation of the sector administered by national franchise associations has gone a long way towards ensuring that franchise agreements have become workable and fair to both parties. The only problem is that these associations generally lack the legal powers to enforce their codes of ethics outside their membership. As a result, non-members are not bound by these requirements and often offer their franchisees a raw deal. This has prompted a growing number of countries to introduce franchise-specific legislation. In the absence of specific legislation, forward-looking legal practitioners will draft franchise agreements to conform to the code of ethics published by their country's franchise association. Subject to goodwill on both sides, this generally works well enough.

Some essential clauses

Validity

Franchise agreements are usually valid for a period of five to seven years. In some countries, this period can be as long as 20 years. It is customary to grant the franchisee an option to renew the agreement for a similar period. The franchisee's right to exercise the option to renew will usually be conditional. The relevant clause may stipulate, for example, that renewal will only be granted subject to the franchisee upgrading the unit to reflect the network's corporate identity at that time. The franchisee may also be compelled to sign the then current version of the franchise agreement.

Rights and obligations

A good franchise agreement will define the grant of the franchise and stipulate the rights and obligations of both parties. It is important to explain the circumstances under which one or other party has the right to terminate the agreement prematurely, and how such termination will be dealt with. The initial and ongoing financial obligations of the franchisee must also be set out in full. Should the franchisee be obliged to purchase goods from the franchisor or from a source stipulated by the franchisor then this must be recorded in this section of the franchise agreement, together with an escape clause if one is granted.

Operations

As the guardian of the brand, the franchisor will insist on controlling the way franchised units operate. As it would be unwieldy to include detailed guidelines in the franchise agreement, this is done by reference to the network's operations manual. Essentially, the operations manual tells the franchisee how the business must be operated. Provided that the franchise agreement records the franchisor's right to control specific activities, operational details can be addressed in the operations manual. In the interest of fairness, a similar clause cannot be used to make material changes to the conditions under which the franchise agreement was entered into in the first place. For example, should it become necessary for the franchisor to increase fee percentages, this would have to be negotiated with affected franchisees. Implementation would be subject to franchisees signing an amendment to the franchise agreement.

Change in management or ownership

The question of change in ownership must be addressed. In a legal sense, the franchisee may be an incorporated body. In practice, however, a franchise is granted to an individual who conforms to the network's franchisee profile. It follows that the franchisor has a legitimate interest to ensure that no unsuitable individuals enter the network, either as managers or as new owners. With this in mind, the franchisor will reserve the right to approve managers or buyers. Some franchisors will insert a clause into the franchise agreement that gives them the right of first refusal. This means that if and when a franchisee wants to sell the business, he or she is obliged to offer it to the franchisor. Applicable terms will be set out in the franchise agreement.

Disclosure document

The disclosure document provides qualified prospects with the information they require before they can make an informed investment decision. Guidelines for the compilation of disclosure documents are published by many national franchise associations and most forward-looking franchisors provide such a document.

Given that the disclosure document contains sensitive information, franchisors will ask recipients to sign a confidentiality undertaking.

Financial implications

Rolling out a franchise has financial implications for the franchisor and the franchisees of the network.

Financial implications for the franchisor

Inexperienced entrepreneurs often turn to franchising expecting to make a quick profit. If so, they will be sorely disappointed. Seen from the franchisor's viewpoint, franchising can be highly profitable, but only if the network is built for the long term. At the outset, prospective franchisors need to fund the cost of creating the franchise package and the franchisee support infrastructure. These costs, which include the costs of obtaining competent professional advice, tend to be substantial. On the income side, franchisors can look forward to receiving initial fees and ongoing fees and may even act as suppliers to their franchisees. This notwithstanding, experience has shown that it will typically take three to five years before a new franchisor reaches profitability.

Initial franchise fee

Most franchisors accept that the initial fee should be kept low. This is because the new franchisee sees a great deal of money going out at a time when no money is coming in. This could scare off otherwise sound prospects because, having paid out a large sum of money in exchange for the rights, they would no longer possess the funds they need to get the business off the ground. With this in mind, the upfront fee is usually calculated to cover the cost of setting up the franchise, spread over a reasonable number of new franchisees, plus the cost of easing each new franchisee into business. Franchisors know that their profitability should come from ongoing fees.

Ongoing franchise fee

At the outset, all franchisees in the network are new and require considerable support. At the same time, their businesses are building up and sales will be relatively low. Because the franchisor's income accrues as a percentage of franchisees' turnovers, it will be low as well.

Mark-ups on product supplies

In some sectors, franchisors act as their franchisees' main or even sole suppliers. Alternatively, they may prescribe sources of supply. In the spirit of franchising, franchisees should be allowed to participate in the resulting bulk purchasing benefits. Should this not be the case, dissatisfaction will ensue. Moreover, a growing number of countries have competition legislation in place or are about to introduce it. At the very least, such legislation will limit franchisors' right to insist on compulsory purchasing arrangements.

Financial implications for franchisees

Prospective franchisees are often shocked to find that to set up a business under franchise will cost them more than if they were to set up a business independently. In addition to paying an initial fee, they will receive strict guidelines for the setting up of the business. No short cuts are permitted. In the long term, this approach will benefit the franchisee because it will result in the establishment of a more professional operation. This in turn is likely to instil confidence in customers and should reduce the time it takes to reach breakeven.

In most instances, franchisees can expect to come across the following financial obligations:

Initial franchise fee

Mentioned above, this fee is also known as an upfront fee. It pays for the right to trade under the network's brand and receive initial training and support. This includes help with site selection, purchasing advice, introduction to preferential sources of supply and a host of other issues a newcomer would otherwise struggle with. In this context, it is important to note that a franchise is granted, never sold. While the franchisee has the right to use the network's intellectual property, this right is conditional on compliance with the terms and conditions of the franchise agreement. Should the franchise agreement be terminated because the franchisee is in breach, or the agreement comes to an end for any other reason, the right to use the intellectual property ceases.

Capital investment

The franchisee is responsible for payments arising from the setting up of the business, including acquisition of furnishings, fittings, equipment and motor vehicles.

Working capital

The franchisee will incur expenses long before the business is ready to start trading. For a good few months after the grand opening, expenses are likely to be higher than income from sales. In the meantime, the franchisee has to pay salaries, rentals, creditors' accounts and a host of other expenses that are part of running a growing business. The franchisee's living expenses must also be covered. This is why provision must be made for working capital.

Ongoing franchise fees

There are also ongoing franchise fees that affect both franchisor and franchisees:

Management services fee

This fee is usually calculated as a percentage of sales. A fixed franchise fee is not recommended because it would remove the all-important aspect of risk-sharing between franchisor and franchisee. Percentage figures vary from one industry sector to the next. They even vary from one franchisor to the other within the same sector. Factors to be taken into account are the amount of support the network offers, whether the franchisee can afford the payment and whether the franchisor can make a profit.

Marketing contribution

In most franchised networks, franchisees are compelled to contribute to a national marketing fund. Moneys accrued in this fund are used for product advertising. The franchisor's company-owned stores should contribute to this fund to the same extent.

Other fees

Some franchisors charge other fees: for example, in exchange for keeping franchisees' business books up to date and assisting with the fulfilment of statutory obligations. Franchisors are entitled to charge for such services but on condition that they create a genuine benefit for franchisees.

Franchising is a method of doing business, nothing more and nothing less. As such, it must make commercial sense. Unless both parties benefit from the arrangement, the franchised network is unlikely to endure.

Franchise models

The difference between product franchising and business-format franchising goes beyond mere semantics, which is why this section goes into more theoretical detail. Several other business models exist that are often confused with franchise opportunities but are nothing of the sort. To ensure the success of any social-franchise venture, it is critical that its promoters are aware of the advantages and disadvantages of each format. Observation over the past five decades suggests that the only format that will deliver on expectations is business-format franchising, or a legitimate adaptation of it.

Product franchise. A product franchise, also known as a trademark franchise, focuses on access to the product itself. In addition to granting the franchisee the right to the product and preferential pricing, the promoter of a product franchise permits the franchisee to trade under the common trademark and use the network's corporate identity. Some training may form part of the deal but operational assistance will be limited at best. The franchisor's main interest lies in shifting product. Apart from certain basics such as customer service delivery and the fulfilment of warranty obligations, the way in which the franchisee operates the business will not be prescribed to any great extent. Profitable operation of the franchise remains the sole responsibility of the franchisee, with no assistance from the franchisor.

Business-format franchise. As mentioned above, this is franchising at its best. In addition to granting the franchisee access to a product or service, the network's corporate identity and the right to trade under a common brand, he or she will also receive a comprehensive operating system. This will cover every aspect of operating the business to best effect and will help the franchisee maximise profitability.

Although the core principles of franchising have stood the test of time, the sector continues to develop. The impetus for this is the need to address the requirements of niche markets as they emerge. This has led to the emergence of conversion franchising, area franchising, master franchising, tandem franchising, social franchising and microfranchising. All these formats have one thing in common: they are legitimate adaptations of the original business-format franchise model and conform to its basic requirements.

Conversion franchise. A conversion franchise operates under a standard franchise agreement. The only difference is that instead of establishing a new franchisee in a new outlet, the franchise is offered to the owner of an established business who is trading within the same sector. If implemented properly, such an arrangement can benefit both parties. By joining a franchise, the owner of an existing business will be able to trade under a national brand and benefit from the network's bulk-purchasing and advertising arrangements. Access to its research and development facilities and IT infrastructure are added attractions. The franchisor benefits as well because it acquires an experienced operator, gets access to a site that may otherwise not be available and gains existing market share.

Area franchise. While most franchises are granted for the operation of one business unit, an area-franchise arrangement grants the franchisee the right to establish several outlets within a specified territory. These outlets can be operated by the same company, or the company may be given the right to sub-franchise to others. If the area franchise is granted for an entire region or country, it is described as a master franchise.

Tandem franchise. A tandem franchise is a standard franchise arrangement with a twist. While in most instances the franchisee owns the business outright from day one, this is not the case in a tandem franchise. A tandem franchise is a joint venture, usually set up by at least two parties: namely the franchisor and the future franchisee. Initially, the franchisor retains a large stake in the business and shares in its profits. In return, the franchisor provides management support and mentoring to the franchisee at a level that exceeds standard franchisee support. Over time, the franchisee will be able to purchase additional shares in the business, usually at a predetermined price, until he or she becomes the outright owner of the business. At this point, the arrangement changes to become a standard franchise. The tandem-franchise model makes it possible for a deserving candidate, such as a staff member of the franchisor who lacks the capital and the management experience, to operate a franchise successfully and become a franchisee. The model is eminently suited for the implementation of sustainable empowerment schemes.

Social franchise. This model lends itself to the delivery of products and services that are usually provided by government structures or NGOs to the poorer segment of a country's population. Examples are the provision of basic health services and the supply of contraceptives. It has been found that private enterprise can deliver such services more cost-effectively. Subject to the target population being able and willing to pay at least part of the cost, it makes sense for donors or government to subsidise the operation of a franchise. To ensure the long-term sustainability of such a project, it should be structured in such a manner that it will eventually become financially self-reliant.

Microfranchise. The promoters of a microfranchise use the proven principles of skills transfer in operations, marketing and customer-service excellence and the benefits of initial and ongoing support, all hallmarks of a standard franchise arrangement. In combination with the power of a brand, they are able to create business opportunities for the poorest of the poor that are viable in the short term and sustainable in the long term. The funding of such schemes is a thorny issue. While traditionally the raising of funds has been the franchisee's responsibility, this would not be feasible in this case. This is where the adaptability of franchising comes to the fore. For a microfranchise scheme to take off, it can be paired with a customised funding scheme, such as a microfinancing initiative. Funders of such schemes tend to derive great comfort from the fact that the borrower's business will operate under a recognised brand and within a formal business system. They know that this will enable them to track the flow of money through the business, usually a matter of grave concern within the small business environment.

Other business formats

Franchising's success notwithstanding, it is not the only way to expand an existing business or to put a newcomer into business. Not everyone wants to be a franchisee. For a franchise to operate successfully, its systems and procedures need to be quite rigid. Individuals who want to do things their own way will resent this and will be bitterly unhappy in a franchise environment. Fortunately for them, several other business formats exist. I am not advocating their use, but for the sake of completeness, I will list them below.

Business opportunity. A business opportunity is what its name suggests: an opportunity to carry on business. This format is mostly used in door-to-door and roadside selling. The investor purchases goods from the promoter of the business opportunity, usually a manufacturer, importer or wholesaler, and sells them for his or her own account. In some instances, the promoter will grant the investor some form of territorial protection. If so, this will be subject to reorder levels warranting that. Beyond that, neither party has any obligations *vis-à-vis* the other.

Multi-level marketing. This is a form of direct selling used in the marketing of consumer goods. Participants in such a scheme are entitled to purchase products from the promoter for on-sale to the public. They are also encouraged to set up a network of distributors that they supply with product. Because some money does change hands in exchange for the granting of territorial rights, such schemes may seem similar to pyramid schemes (discussed later in this section) but they are nothing of the sort. Multi-level marketing is a legitimate business format because the bulk of the income is derived from product sales.

Agency agreement. This is where an agent acts on behalf of one or more companies, known as principals. He or she will represent the company in sales negotiations with potential customers. Deals are struck in the name of the company; the company is responsible for delivery of the product or service, invoicing and collecting payment. The agent receives a commission.

Distributorship. This is where a manufacturer, importer or wholesaler appoints one or several distributors. These distributors are normally selected on the strength of their existing contacts in the target market. Distributors will be obliged to stock, sell and service the product within a defined area and usually operate for their own account.

Voluntary chain. Voluntary chains are usually established by a successful retailer, who creates a loose grouping of other independent retailers in the same field but active in other areas. The chief motivation for this is to create economies of scale, primarily in purchasing. On occasion, some branding is involved as well, which would then give rise to joint promotions. Other than that, the businesses remain independent.

Dealership. This format is widely used in the distribution of motor vehicles and capital equipment. Dealerships are contracted to stock, sell and service one manufacturer's products. They receive some branding and a limited amount of operational support, for example in the form of technical training. Beyond that, they operate independently.

As long as the formats listed above are presented as what they are, they offer perfectly legitimate opportunities for prospective entrepreneurs to gain a foothold in the world of business. Unfortunately, some less than honourable promoters of such schemes see fit to present them as franchise opportunities, which they are clearly not. This happens primarily in the field of business opportunities; it is highly unethical and may even border on fraud.

Pyramid schemes are another business model that is sometimes disguised as a franchise. Fortunately, there is no grey area here: pyramid schemes are unworkable and have been outlawed in most countries, with good reason. The promoter of a pyramid scheme pretends to want to sell a product that is either of poor quality, does not have a ready market or is over-priced; in some instances, a combination of these factors applies. Either way, the promoter does not care. His or her interest lies in the selling of area rights. Early entrants into the scheme are allocated large territories. They are permitted to sub-divide those and sell them on to other investors. These investors sub-divide their territories further and sell them on to the next level of investors. This activity continues until the territories become so small that they cannot be divided any further. At this point, the scheme collapses. Those who joined the pyramid at the bottom are left with stock they cannot sell and no way to recoup their investment.

Early entrants, including the initial promoter of the scheme, tend to do extremely well for themselves because they get to keep most of the money they receive from the direct sale of territories and receive a percentage from the sale of every territorial right downstream. As it is a mathematical impossibility for such a scheme to succeed in the long term, legislators in most countries have made their promotion a criminal offence. Although this has reduced the number of schemes that come on the market, they continue to pop up from time to time, usually disguised as franchises.

The status of franchising in developing economies

Although some sizable pockets of franchise activity are in evidence throughout the developing world, these tend to revolve around foreign fast-food outlets and other retail brands that appeal to the growing upper segment of the consumer market. Even in this segment, however, the concept falls short of realising its true potential. This is surprising because franchising has much to offer to developing economies. It holds true even for relatively sophisticated markets such as South Africa, where franchising activity has been in evidence since the mid-1960s. Franchise operations, most of them home-grown, are of world-class standard and the concept has become the preferred vehicle for expansion in over 30 industry sectors. This notwithstanding, however, franchising still holds a mere 12.5% share of the local retail market. Egypt, Morocco and Nigeria are other examples of African countries where franchising is reasonably well entrenched, but nowhere has franchising reached saturation point. In fact, throughout the bulk of the African continent, the concept has made little inroads so far. Social franchising has barely made any impact at all.

I firmly believe that the reason for the slow expansion of franchise concepts in developing countries is a lack of understanding of the concept's potential and cultural barriers. I will deal with this in more detail in the next chapter. Yet franchising offers vast opportunities for social entrepreneurs who want to use the power of franchising to achieve social objectives in a sustainable manner. Although a large percentage of Africa's population continues to live on less than $4 a day, the continent's middle class is growing. A healthy combination of improved access to international media and growing interest in foreign travel has created growing demand for branded goods and services. While franchise concepts can be imported under master licence agreements, these will mainly address the needs of the middle class, not the target population described in this book. The greatest promise lies in the further development of social franchising, especially in combination with microfranchise concepts and microfinance initiatives. Such programmes leverage the strengths of a capitalist approach to doing business with social objectives. Seen from donors' point of view, this should create an unbeatable combination of social acceptability and commercial sustainability.

In this context, it is reassuring to learn that African entrepreneurs are more than capable of developing winning concepts. Some of these are eminently suited to addressing social needs in a cost-effective manner, although they may require donor assistance during the roll-out phase. This should not be seen as an indictment of African entrepreneurs, but a result of a combination of circumstances. On the one hand, it may take several years before programmes of this nature are accepted by their target markets. On the other hand, certain members of the target population may never be able to pay market-related prices.

When assessing the commercial viability of social-franchise programmes, we need to remember that governments have an obligation to make certain basic services available to every citizen, even those who cannot afford to pay for them. I am referring to basic healthcare and access to clean water, sanitation and electricity, services that are taken for granted in the Western world but are not available to everyone in developing economies. There can be no disputing the fact that, subject to proper control being exercised, service providers drawn from the private sector can deliver these services more cost-effectively than government-controlled institutions. If franchisees of well-structured social-franchise schemes can make a profit in their businesses and create employment opportunities in the process, then we have a winner on our hands. In the next chapter, I will deal with some of the special problems the roll-out of social-franchise schemes in developing countries is likely to pose. I will also provide some practical examples of successful implementation of appropriate franchise concepts.

3

Microfranchising in practice

Kurt Illetschko

Franchise consultant, South Africa

Agreement exists that business-format franchising is a sophisticated business tool that functions well in developed economies. This has prompted a growing number of companies to expand their footprint through franchising. It has had the unintended side-effect of creating a shortage of prospective franchisees who match a network's franchisee profile and could support the required investment. To attract to the network suitable individuals who cannot come up with the necessary funding, financially strong franchisors have developed a model that includes a joint-venture component. As mentioned in the previous chapter, this model works as follows: the franchisor registers a company that is granted a franchise for a specific territory. Shareholding is initially split between the franchisor and the new franchisee. The franchisor puts up most if not all of the required capital, while the franchisee accepts responsibility for profitable day-to-day operations. The franchisee works for a relatively low salary to begin with, but is entitled to a disproportionate share of profits from day one. Such an arrangement is also known as 'sweat equity' because the franchisee's main contribution to the venture is his or her labour. The franchisee uses his or her share of profits to purchase additional shares in the business at a pre-arranged price. In most instances, and assuming that everything goes according to plan, the franchisee should own the business outright within three to five years. At this point, the arrangement between the joint-venture partners changes to a standard franchise agreement.

In some countries, for example in South Africa where a change in political dispensation during the early 1990s gave rise to black economic empowerment schemes, a new problem arose. Having freed themselves of the political and economic shackles of the apartheid era, enterprising individuals were keen to join the economic mainstream. Having been disadvantaged in the past, they qualified for 100% loans, but it soon emerged that in the absence of equity capital contributed by its owners, businesses struggled to succeed. In response, the joint-venture scheme was further refined to address the needs of deserving individuals who lacked not only the necessary capital, but also the experience needed to make the transition to franchisee unaided. Such arrangements became known as tandem franchising, a model described in the previous chapter.

In addition to its suitability for the creation of empowerment schemes, tandem franchising is ideally suited for the conversion of under-performing branches into franchised units. The 'owner-behind-the-counter' syndrome is usually sufficiently powerful to turn an ailing branch into a profitable business within a relatively short space of time. Seen from a large corporation's viewpoint, this is a far more attractive option than closing the branch, with attendant loss of employment opportunities and footprint. It is also an ideal mechanism for rewarding deserving employees.

Crossing the next hurdle

In traditional franchise arrangements, the combination of large company resources provided by the franchisor with the capital, skills and dedication of franchisees forms an unbeatable combination. It does not, however, address the needs of poor and uneducated individuals. This has left a vast number of people living in developing countries out in the cold. Over the past few decades, it has become abundantly clear that developing economies are not progressing at the desired rate. This, in combination with the population explosion they experience, points towards a looming disaster. The rich Western countries have tried to help by making various aid programmes available, but this has not achieved the desired results either. It is clear that hand-outs are not the way to go. Programmes are needed that can help the poor of this world to help themselves. This has prompted well-meaning donors to make small loans available to aspiring grass-roots entrepreneurs. However, they soon found to their dismay that this was not always the answer either. Not every poor person is a born entrepreneur and the free enterprise system can be a cruel taskmaster. The failure rate encountered by grass-roots entrepreneurs is unacceptably high and it has become apparent that what is really needed is a programme that can provide aspiring entrepreneurs with more than just money.

Franchising, with its strong components of skills transfer, brand recognition, initial and ongoing support and supervision, is an obvious solution. Unfortunately, franchise practitioners do not consider small franchises to be viable. They reason, firstly, that because the establishment and ongoing operation of a franchise is expensive, neither the franchisor nor the franchisees in the network can make any money in a grassroots environment. Secondly, they hold that franchising is a marketing concept. To achieve its potential, it needs to operate in an environment where brand awareness is strong, competition is fierce and success depends on slick marketing ploys. The ability to deliver basic goods and services cheaply is not seen as a prerequisite for success in franchising. I subscribed to this line of thought for far too long but have since recognised that we were wrong. My transformation was triggered by sheer necessity. I was invited to become part of a project team that was hired to develop what turned out to be a microfranchise. To ensure that I could do the job I was hired to do, I undertook some research and soon found that the traditional approach to franchising is, to put it mildly, short-sighted.

A strong influence was the work of Kirk Magleby, who is well known for his work in this field. I was especially impressed by his paper *MicroFranchises as a Solution to Global Poverty* (2005) in which he analysed the problems faced by the poorest of the poor. Key points in this paper are as follows: In the developing world, formal jobs are so scarce that the vast majority of people are forced into self-employment in the informal sector. These micro entrepreneurs operate hundreds of millions of tiny, low-productivity, copy-cat businesses that seldom generate profits, build little wealth and create few jobs. Our planet needs millions of successful, locally owned SMEs (small and medium-sized enterprises) helping to develop low-income communities. The franchise business model is the most effective tool currently available to create large numbers of successful SMEs. The emergent social movement called microfranchising is quickly learning how to adapt the powerful franchise business model to the stark reality on the ground in developing countries.

The potential of microfranchising

Magleby's paper made me realise that franchising is sufficiently adaptable to serve the needs of this vast but badly under-resourced market. Subject to correct structuring and implementation, microfranchising schemes can be used to satisfy universal needs that prevail throughout developing countries in a sustainable and cost-effective manner. At present, these needs are not met at all or are met badly. Delivery is usually accomplished through government-controlled welfare channels, with varying success and always at great cost to the taxpayer. On occasion, NGOs lend a helping hand; their efforts are laudable, but in the absence of a profit motive, long-term sustainability is not always guaranteed. The introduction of microfranchising networks has the potential to improve the quality of service delivery while enhancing efficiencies and reducing dependency on government grants or donor funding. Examples of services that lend themselves to this approach are:

- The delivery of basic health services to the poorer segments of the population, especially if they live in remote areas: for instance, tuberculosis screening, AIDS testing and the provision of basic dental and optical care

- The provision of services related to sexual and reproductive health, including the distribution of AIDS information and support of those already infected

- Caring for the health needs of expecting and new mothers

- The provision of trustworthy and affordable childcare facilities for children of working parents

- The delivery of education and edutainment (extramural classes, sports, music, games) to older children and young adults

- Caring for the health and social needs of the elderly, including feeding schemes

- The delivery and maintenance of affordable energy solutions and sanitary facilities

These are just some of the most obvious applications that come to mind. In reality, there is virtually no limit to the range of needs that can be addressed effectively through microfranchising. As I live in South Africa and take a strong interest in the affairs of the entire African continent, my focus is on Africa. Western nations see Africa as a charity case, a bottomless pit even, where vast amounts of donor funding disappear, often without achieving its stated objectives. Perhaps the problem is not Africa itself but the approach taken by donors? It puzzles me that instead of attempting to build sustainable upliftment programmes in Africa as they have done in South America and certain parts of Asia, donors continue to provide money, food and medical supplies. Hand-outs of this nature provide short-term relief but do not offer sustainable long-term solutions. Donations are sorely needed, but charitable initiatives, no matter how well intended, will not bring Africa's population any closer towards achieving the widely proclaimed Millennium Development Goals, certainly not by 2015, and probably not ever. To change this gloomy picture once and for all, a different approach will be needed.

To understand the magnitude of the existing need as well as the enormous potential Africa offers, we need to remember that this continent is populated by more than 900 million consumers. Despite the AIDS epidemic, their numbers are growing at a faster rate than ever before. Granted, many of those people are extremely poor, but this is hardly the issue here. Even the poverty-stricken need to eat; they also need access to clean water, acceptable standards of sanitation, basic healthcare and affordable energy solutions. And just like people in other parts of the world, Africa's poor have aspirations to build a better life, if not for themselves then at least for their children. To achieve this, they need access to high-quality education. All these needs can be met in a sustainable manner through microfranchising. While close cooperation between governments, donor organisations and the private sector will be required to set up such initiatives, they should ultimately become self-sustaining.

There is widespread agreement among franchise experts that microfranchising can do more to save the world than anything else invented by humans. We need to accept that true upliftment cannot be achieved by means of handing out care parcels but by empowering people so that they can take care of themselves. Microfranchising's ability to meet this challenge is embedded in the following definition:

Microfranchising is a development tool that adapts the proven operational principles of traditional franchising to the needs of very small businesses located in the developing world. The primary feature of microfranchising is its suitability for replication. Although microfranchising is relatively little known and even less well understood, about 200 concepts have already been put in place. Many of them have become outstanding success stories as shown by the following examples—some of which will be discussed in more detail in other chapters of this book.

Muhammad Yunus promotes microfranchising

Muhammad Yunus, founder of Grameen Bank in Bangladesh won the Nobel Peace Prize in recognition of his work in the microfinance sector. Not being content to rest on his laurels, he soon realised that, while granting small loans to poor people without asking them for collateral can be useful, it does not lift every poor person out of poverty. He said:

> Poverty is unnecessary. People are capable of getting out of poverty. They are not waiting for charity or handouts. Charity is good, but it is not enough. If you turn it into a business proposition then it is very powerful because it can run on its own steam (Moharana *et al.* 2009).

A large portion of the loans granted by Grameen Bank are intended to help poor people start grass-roots businesses. Unfortunately, while some recipients use their loans to build viable businesses, others fail. Research among the bank's customers revealed that not everyone is a born entrepreneur and a small loan cannot change that. Granting small loans was not enough; what was needed was a simple yet effective business package underpinned by initial and ongoing training, motivation and support. Yunus recognised that a simplified franchise model would best fit the bill, so he created not one but several.

Village Phone is a joint venture between Grameen Bank and Telenor, an Oslo-based giant in the field of mobile phone technology. Grameen Bank members with a good record of repaying loans were trained and financed to acquire businesses that provide access to telephones for villagers who would otherwise remain cut off from the world. The programme was extremely successful, with Village Phone operating through more than 260,000, mostly women, phone operators in Bangladesh alone. Based on this success, the project was extended to Uganda and Rwanda. More recently, the programme has lost steam, not because there is something inherently wrong with it but because a growing number of villagers now buy their own mobile phones. The women continue to operate; in addition to public access telephone services, they offer air time and even handsets, but there can be no doubt that the business has lost some of its glitter. (Village Phone is discussed further in Chapter 6.)

Muhammad Yunus's next venture into microfranchising involved the establishment of a yoghurt business, also in Bangladesh, under the name Danone Foods. He knew nothing about making yoghurt and is far too impatient to reinvent the wheel, so he formed a joint venture with a giant in this field, Danone. The factory produces a yoghurt called Shakti-da (which means 'yoghurt with strength') because it is fortified with vitamins to address one of Bangladesh's most pressing problems: malnourishment among small children. It also provides a business opportunity for women who purchase the yoghurts from the factory in bulk and resell them door-to-door. The joint venture is structured as a for-profit social enterprise, with Danone having contributed $500,000 of seed capital. After Danone has recouped its initial investment, the joint-venture partners plan to reinvest all profits into expanding the venture, first throughout Bangladesh, later to other parts of the developing world. The factory buys milk from micro-vendors who are clients of Grameen Bank, having received loans to buy cows. Each factory will employ 15–20 women directly and up to 1,600 people in an area as sales people. The enterprise is designed to be environmentally friendly: it uses cups made from cornstarch that are biodegradable and solar panels to create electricity, and rainwater is collected to reduce pressure on water reticulation.

Giving the gift of sight

VisionSpring, formerly known as the Scojo Foundation, is a non-profit social enterprise based in the USA. It provides reading glasses to the poor at affordable prices. When it started in 2001, it targeted areas in rural parts of India where it trained entrepreneurs to deal with minor eyesight problems. In suitable circumstances, the patient is supplied with good-quality reading glasses. Those with more serious eye ailments are referred to contracted specialists. Today, VisionSpring operates in 12 countries throughout Asia, Latin America and Africa. During 2008, its network of microfranchisees sold 71,000 pairs of glasses. It expects to sell another 600,000 or more pairs over the next five years. This creates economies of scale that make it possible to reduce prices to end-users while allowing its distribution partners fair mark-ups. (Further discussion of VisionSpring can be found in Chapter 8.)

Solar-powered mobile phone kiosks in Uganda

Mobile phones don't work without electricity. This hampered the development of the mobile phone market in Uganda where access to electricity is relatively scarce. To address this, Motorola developed a solar-powered kiosk that is powered by a 55-watt solar panel and can charge up to 20 mobile phones at any given time. Following extensive testing, Motorola launched the Motopower project. Under this scheme, Motorola made an initial quantity of 55 of these kiosks available to previously unemployed entrepreneurs, mostly women. The scheme operates as a microfranchise. As part of the start-up package, each microfranchisee receives several Motorola handsets and a business-skills training course. The training course equips these microfranchisees to sell handsets and air time, offer a recharging service and undertake minor repairs. This is a typical example of a win–win situation because it provides viable entrepreneurial opportunities for individuals who would otherwise be consigned to live below the poverty line. It also helps Ugandans to stay connected and secures a growing market share for Motorola.

Healthcare in Kenya

Worldwide, Malaria affects 300 million people each year; many of them live in remote rural areas of Africa where proper medical care is difficult to find. To address this problem, the HealthStore Foundation has set up a programme designed to get drugs to sick people when and where they need them. The USA-based foundation gives healthcare workers microloans to open their own for-profit Child and Family Wellness shops (CFWshops). Knowing full well that the granting of loans, while essential, is not enough to ensure the success of the programme, founder Scott Hillstrom developed a microfranchise package. This package provides microfranchisees with training in proven basic healthcare procedures and business operation, helps them with the selection of a suitable site and conducts regular inspections to ensure adherence to the network's tried-and-tested systems and procedures.

Founded in 1997, CFWshops provide good healthcare at affordable cost, clearly with great success. Currently operating through 85 stores, they have treated over 2 million patients. The shops' distinctive black and red signage is recognised throughout Kenya as a beacon of hope for poor sick people. Economies of scale resulting from the ongoing expansion of the programme make it possible to keep prices affordable while providing a good living for its microfranchisees. The HealthStore Foundation's turnkey model gives entrepreneurs and healthcare workers much-needed opportunities to operate viable businesses. At the same time, the shops help Kenyans, including children, gain access to good-quality medicines and basic healthcare. This, once more, presents a win–win scenario. (Further discussion of Healthcare Foundation can be found in subsequent chapters; see especially Chapter 6, pages 81ff. for more on CFWshops.)

Keeping the plumbing intact

A large plumbing repair company in South Africa with a national network of traditional franchisees developed a concept that operates as a microfranchise. Often with the help of local municipalities that made strategically placed facilities available, hubs were established in low-income areas with a high population density. After receiving training in carrying out basic plumbing repairs, successful applicants are contracted as microfranchisees. They are equipped with a specially designed bicycle that can carry a set of tools and basic spares and are allocated areas based on the number of homes. Residents who need a leaking tap or toilet fixed call the hub and purchase a repair voucher. Their details are recorded and passed on to the microfranchisee responsible for the particular area. Every morning, franchisees collect repair vouchers for their allocated areas and carry out the necessary repairs. If satisfied with the work, the resident signs the microfranchisee's worksheet. Payments to the microfranchisees are made weekly, based on the number of signed repair vouchers they present at the hub.

Should the resident have understated the extent of the problem and the microfranchisee finds on arrival at the premises that the work required falls outside the parameters of the system of repair vouchers, he or she notifies the hub. The hub sends out a trained technician who will assess the work and issue the resident with a quotation. Subject to acceptance of the quotation, the hub will arrange for a fully equipped plumbing team to carry out the work. The amount paid for the repair voucher is deducted from the total.

Lighting up villages

While the examples I have given up to now originate from extensive reading and Internet searches, the following project is based on my own personal experience. Franchising Plus, South Africa's leading franchise consultancy, was retained to assist with the implementation of a programme that would provide affordable energy solutions to rural dwellers in remote areas and protect the environment. I was recruited as part of this team and have dedicated hundreds of hours to the project. Unfortunately, client confidentiality prevents me from identifying the parties involved but I am convinced that the lessons we have learned will be useful to anyone who wants to roll out a similar project anywhere in the developing world.

The project is being implemented in a small country on the southern tip of Africa. Its aim is to meet the energy needs of individuals living in remote rural areas where no fixed-grid electricity supply exists. Implementation of the project will create a cleaner environment and will provide local residents with an opportunity to build viable businesses under a microfranchise arrangement. Over time, the project may even create some jobs. Although the initiative enjoys the backing of a large USA-based donor organisation and the country's government, it is not charitable in its nature. While the sponsors are carrying the (not unsubstantial) development costs and subsidise the roll-out of the required infrastructure, end-users are expected to pay ongoing usage and maintenance costs.

The target country enjoys sunshine all year round. This means that solar energy is available in abundance. It is also more affordable, healthier, cleaner and safer than traditional energy sources, these being candles or paraffin lamps for lighting and open wood fires for cooking. Liquefied petroleum (LP) gas is also used for cooking but is accessible to only a small but relatively wealthy segment of the population. Market research carried out before the programme was set in motion confirmed that the target population wants the service and will be able to pay for it. The researchers found, for example, that the average target household spends more money on candles, paraffin and LP gas combined than they are expected to pay in ongoing fees for a small solar-panel installation. In addition to the social and environmental objectives set out above, this initiative will over time create about 120 highly attractive microfranchise opportunities. Franchisees will be drawn from the local rural population and will receive the necessary training, financial assistance, mentoring and supervision to build sustainable businesses.

Although in a contractual sense, the stakeholders are the donor organisation and the parastatal body, we soon realised that several other organisations would have an important role to play. The reasons for participation of all these partners are wide-ranging and definitely worth exploring. First, the government has a keen interest to provide all its citizens with energy solutions that are affordable, healthy and kind on the environment. In this instance, the target population is rural dwellers who live in small villages located in remote parts of the country. Second, a company that is owned outright by government is responsible for national power distribution. Given the enormous distances involved in supplying rural dwellers with electricity and the low population density, the energy supplier is reluctant to extend the national grid to supply these areas. Initial construction costs and ongoing maintenance costs would be prohibitive and experience has shown that uptake would be low. The reason for this is that most members of the target population cannot afford the connection fee, which, although heavily subsidised, remains relatively high. For all these reasons, the energy supplier was searching for an energy solution that did not require extensive fixed infrastructure and was affordable to the target population. After reviewing several options, a decision was taken to provide energy in the form of solar power, brought to the target market through a network of franchisees.

Third, the donor organisation is keen to improve the quality of life enjoyed by the country's rural population in a manner that is affordable and leads to a reduction of harmful emissions resulting from the use of fossil fuels.

Fourth, several other government-appointed bodies are involved in the project to varying degrees. The country's business development agency is tasked with the promotion of entrepreneurship, especially in the SME (small and medium-sized enterprise) sector, and the creation of jobs. The project on hand qualifies on both counts. As is the case in most countries the world over, the target country's competition legislation has the potential to impact on the implementation of activities that are vital to the successful execution of the project. To create certainty, the competition authority was consulted early on and indicated that it did not foresee any problems. Access to grants intended to enhance skills levels are subject to the training being certified by the local training authority. It follows that this body's involvement in the project from the outset is vital to its ultimate success.

Fifth, the donor organisation appointed Franchising Plus, a franchise consultancy based in Johannesburg, South Africa, as the lead consultants. In addition to bringing its own expertise and infrastructure to bear, Franchising Plus sub-contracted with experts in the fields of training, law and manual writing to assemble the strongest-possible project team.

The product range includes:

- High-quality lanterns equipped with LED globes and having a life expectancy of two to three years. These lanterns have an operating (recharge) cycle of 25–30 hours if used at full strength; double that if the torch setting is selected

- Rechargeable batteries of various sizes, which are intended to power radios and CD players

- Recharge service for rechargeable batteries and mobile phones

- The promotion of the electrification of dwellings through solar-panel installations. Although these installations are designed to supply the energy needs of an average family, they are not sufficiently powerful to feed an electric cooking stove

- Energy-efficient wood stoves and cooking bags. Because large solar installations are still expensive, the use of firewood for cooking remains unavoidable. The energy-efficient stoves can be produced cheaply yet are of such a revolutionary design that the quantity of firewood needed will be reduced by up to 80%. Inclusion of these stoves into the range helps to achieve overall programme objectives while at the same time enhancing the commercial viability of the microfranchise

A separate company has been formed that will operate as the franchisor from dedicated premises located in the country's capital. Field service consultants (FSCs) will be employed by the franchisor but will be permanently stationed at strategic locations throughout the target area. Each FSC will eventually support the activities of between 12 and 15 microfranchisees. The FSCs will maintain a small stock of products and spares. They will also enter into contracts with independent installers who will undergo training at the franchisor's facilities but will operate as independent businesses. Microfranchisees will operate within their villages. In addition to extensive training and support, they will receive a kiosk or container shop from where they will sell lanterns, batteries and related products and offer a recharge service. Orders for complete solar panel installations will be accepted by the microfranchisees but will be passed on to the local FSC. The FSC will arrange installation of the system by the local installer.

Nevertheless, the introduction of microfranchise concepts in remote rural areas has its pitfalls. Cultural norms and a lack of understanding of the franchise concept create resistance from those who stand to benefit the most. Lack of existing infrastructure, lack of necessary skills and an ingrained reluctance to pay taxes are other stumbling blocks. To address them requires patience and the ability to demonstrate to the various target groups how they will benefit.

Unlike normal franchises, microfranchises are typically created from scratch. The franchisor is most likely a parastatal body, an NGO or the social responsibility arm of a large corporation. It follows that implementation will, of necessity, be the responsibility of people who may not have operated a small business before. This can be problematic because it is an accepted credo of franchising that the franchisor needs to have a solid track record in the business to be franchised. We had to accept that, in this instance, a slightly unorthodox approach would be needed, so we fast-tracked the process by designing the concept on paper. Many hours of brainstorming later, we were ready to create written guidelines for the franchisor, which will be used in the field to roll out the franchise. The franchisor recruited and employed a small number of suitable individuals who will operate the pilot outlets for a period of three to six months. These individuals receive intensive initial and ongoing training as well as ongoing operational support. To ensure a high level of motivation, they were told that subject to performance, they would have an opportunity to become microfranchisees. Throughout this period, we will observe operations, record what works and modify what doesn't work. The operations manual will be based on the resulting findings.

We also learned that you can't just waltz into a remote rural village and tell the local population that you are going to improve their lives and this is how you are going to do it. In these parts of the world, new concepts are generally received with distrust. To overcome this requires the creation of strong trust relationships with tribal chiefs and other respected members of the target communities. Tribal and family affiliations can become additional stumbling blocks. For example, unless franchisees are recruited from among the local community, they may find it extremely difficult to gain acceptance. Furthermore, many rural dwellers are born entrepreneurs. In the franchise environment, this is not necessarily a good thing. For franchising to deliver on its promise, franchisees need to follow the network's operating procedures to the letter. Some grass-roots entrepreneurs resent the rigidity this imposes. They are used to taking short cuts and tend to get upset if told that in a branded business this approach is unacceptable. Full initial disclosure followed by extensive initial training, ongoing support and careful monitoring of business performance should minimise the risk of this becoming an issue.

Conclusion: how to implement a successful microfranchise programme

Provided that the project is approached with sensitivity and patience, the obstacles I have listed above can be overcome. Adherence to the guidelines set out below should facilitate the success of any soundly structured microfranchise programme:

- Identify a real need and develop a programme that can address this. Then approach the project with humility and caring. Expect to encounter barriers along the way. In many instances, these barriers will make no sense to representatives of Western donor organisations, but ignoring them would be a grave mistake. This is why it is advisable to involve local agents from the start

- For the project to be sustainable, it should be designed along principles of ethical franchising and commercial soundness. This requires the incorporation of clearly defined exit criteria for the donor organisation. Donors should be able to withdraw from the project within three to five years. At that point, the microfranchise should have become self-sufficient. Should this be unlikely to happen then the project may not be franchisable; but see the next point

- Should the onus be on government to deliver an essential product or service—for example, the delivery of healthcare to the poor—and it can be shown that a microfranchise can do that more cost-effectively than a government department, a commercial justification for the granting of a permanent subsidy exists. The continuity of the programme would have to be ensured because you cannot put people into businesses then drop them

- Agreement exists that a franchise needs to operate according to a firm set of guidelines for it to be successful. There is no reason to treat a microfranchise differently. At the outset, some adaptation to the requirements of a specific country may be unavoidable. Once this has been accomplished, every microfranchisee must be obliged to conduct business in the same way. Some franchisees may resent that, but if leeway is given, chaos will ensue

- Full disclosure covering all aspects of the project must be provided to prospective franchisees before they enter into a contract. Test instruments that have been modified to remove possible cultural bias need to be developed and applied to qualified prospects. The outcome of such tests should reveal whether prospects have internalised the material and have the necessary passion to succeed as franchisees

- In addition to cultural barriers such as tribal affiliations and paternalism, language barriers need to be considered. Although English is widely spoken throughout the world, this does not necessarily mean that in a remote rural village business can be conducted successfully in English. To achieve optimal results, information sessions for prospects and training for franchisees should generally be delivered in the local language

- Expect funding to be an issue and design the package accordingly. It is best to forgo the inclusion of bells and whistles: the less capital-intensive the establishment of each franchised unit is, the easier it will be to finance it. Cooperation with local funders to ensure access to funding for a realistic period and at a fair level of interest is vital. In the spirit of entrepreneurship, however, franchisees should be left in no doubt that they will be held responsible for the punctual repayment of the loan

- It is the franchisor's responsibility to provide extensive assistance and exercise ongoing control. It follows that initial training given to franchisees needs to be reinforced through extensive ongoing training and mentoring. Periodic site visits and regional get-togethers are proven techniques for ensuring that the franchise remains true to its founders' objectives

- Marketing support is especially important. In addition to brand building, consumer education should rank high on the list of needs the franchisor should cater for. Marketing materials and operating instructions for end-users must be designed to make sense to the target market and must be produced in the local language. End-users should be able to express their dissatisfaction with the product and local service levels in a non-confrontational manner

- It is important to set up a robust communications infrastructure for the seamless exchange of information between franchisor and franchisees. The widespread use of mobile phones notwithstanding, poor infrastructure and the vast distances to be covered often combine to present formidable challenges. These must be carefully considered and a sustainable solution put in place before the programme is rolled out

4

The diffusion of innovations through microfranchising[1]

P. Clint Rogers
University of Eastern Finland

Jason Fairbourne
Fairbourne and Sunesson Consulting Group and Brigham Young University, USA

Robert C. Wolcott
Kellogg Innovation Network (KIN), Kellogg School of Management, Northwestern University, USA

As the world's economic and political landscape changes, significantly more emphasis is being placed on understanding the unique opportunities and constraints of emerging markets. The number of multinational companies (MNCs) moving into these markets has sharply increased in many sectors, and the number of MNCs arising from them has nearly tripled in the last two decades (Chang, Wilkinson and Mellahi 2007). Unique approaches are necessary to understand and pursue the opportunities and challenges of these markets: responding to consumers and enabling nascent entrepreneurs who live at or near subsistence and who comprise a majority of the world's population. Today, three billion people live on less than two dollars a day. To survive, a large percentage of them, including those in the BRIC countries (Brazil, Russia, India and China), operate informal microbusinesses. A majority of them, however, do not have the tools needed to succeed beyond more than subsistence. Current management theory and practice, optimised for the

1 We would like to thank Amir Hasson, David Lehr and Dwight Wilson for their input on the topic and their willingness to contribute some of the information presented in the case studies.

developed world, often fails to provide governments, people and organisations with satisfactory guidance in the context of radical scarcity and traditional societies under rapid transformation (De Soto 2000; Yunus 2007).

Microfranchising represents one emerging management paradigm specifically designed to perform within such environments. The scale, structure and objectives of microfranchising initiatives enable local entrepreneurs to respond better to the needs of people in their local communities. Such a bottom-up focus differs in critical ways from the macro-level economic approaches or current educational paradigms and firm-level business strategy approaches, such as the base of the pyramid (BoP), that have characterised research on this topic (Khanna, Palepu and Sinha 2005; Prahalad 2006). Rather than employing significant amounts of capital and expertise for macro-scale initiatives, properly designed projects at the micro scale can produce dramatic results with the right mix of factors, as evidenced by the success of microlending and related phenomena (Yunus 2003).

This chapter offers a description of microfranchising and a discussion of the factors that characterise successful programmes through two case studies. By successfully supporting the activities of individual entrepreneurs (who are able to respond directly to the unique context of the local consumers), there is evidence that microfranchising can accelerate the diffusion of innovations and dramatically enhance the promise of BoP development.

Microfranchising and innovation

The concept of microfranchising has been described and discussed by Bracken *et al.* (2006), Fairbourne (2006, 2007b) and Magleby (2005). Although it is still a fairly new concept, it is quickly gaining momentum. Originally born from comparative observations on successful and unsuccessful entrepreneurial students in the Philippines, microfranchising can be broken into two components, according to Fairbourne (2006). The **micro** in microfranchising is borrowed from the concept of microcredit (also known as 'microfinance' or 'microloans'), referring to very small loans provided to impoverished people to enable self-employment. As Karnani (2007) suggested, however, simply providing the poor with money (through microcredit) does not necessarily result in thriving businesses. **Franchising** refers to structures that enable 'the systematisation and replication of [successful] enterprises' (Fairbourne 2006: 19). Figure 4.1 shows the relationship between the factors which, when combined, characterise microfranchising.

Figure 4.1 **Venn diagram defining microfranchising**

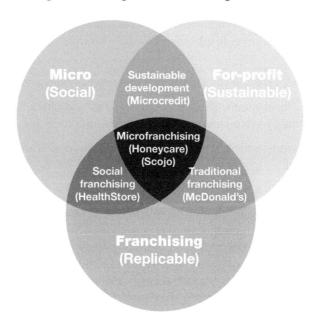

Source: Fairbourne 2007b

Easily recognised franchises such as McDonald's succeed largely owing to the systematisation of their operations to the point that it is easy to train franchisees to replicate and scale with a high degree of standardisation and consistency. Microfranchising includes this same replication process, but does so in a way that simultaneously leverages energy from and assists those living at the base of the pyramid. As Fairbourne (2006) summarised, 'The idea of microfranchising is to create successful business models and to provide those sound opportunities and services to the poor.' Microfranchise models are best when they are appropriate to local needs, are simple enough for people with little education to operate, involve some degree of mentoring between the franchisor and franchisees, and function under a detailed operating system developed and ensured by the franchisor. In this way, they can provide a sustainable vehicle for the diffusion of innovation within emerging economies.

For example, rural villagers throughout the developing world could make use of many of the same digital innovations available to wealthier consumers and businesses, but do not have the infrastructure or resources to allow access. The firm United Villages has implemented microfranchising to provide villagers with a digital identity and access to locally relevant products and services using low-cost, store-and-forward 'drive-by WiFi' technology. Mobile access points (MAPs) are installed on existing vehicles of nearly any type (such as buses and motorcycles) and automatically provide access for WiFi-enabled kiosks along the roads. Whenever a MAP is within range of a real-time wireless Internet connection, it transfers the appropriate data to and from those kiosks. United Villages (franchisor) sells prepaid cards to village kiosk operators (franchisees) and local sales agents who resell the cards to users at a profit and provide a human interface for their products and services, including:

- Sending and receiving voicemails, text messages, emails and faxes

- Purchasing locally unavailable products such as medicines, books and seeds, which are delivered to kiosks on the MAP-mounted vehicles

- Accessing value-added services such as job searches, travel bookings and matrimonial

- Browsing locally relevant websites and information caches

United Villages is working to improve further its approach to microfranchising through finding ways to recruit, train (technically and business-wise) and launch its service providers at a faster pace so that it can scale its network more rapidly while reducing expansion costs. Its goal is to provide 2 billion villagers with an email address, phone number and basic web access—and to do so profitably. United Villages provides an example of bridging the digital divide through sustainable microfranchising, contributing to the diffusion of innovation in India and other emerging economies.

Three characteristics and four challenges

Three characteristics seem to enable microfranchises such as United Villages. The microfranchises are (a) organic, (b) modular and (c) microscalable. Microfranchising models must be **organic** in that they must be executable at a grass-roots franchisee level with minimal involvement from the core franchiser organisation, while still maintaining a level of quality and consistency. In order to achieve quality and consistency with minimal involvement from the core organisation, microfranchising programmes are typically **modular** in that they consist of discrete, interconnected components that can be added or subtracted to enhance or simplify functionality or capabilities as the franchisees' businesses grow. And a microfranchise must be **microscalable**: achievable and repeatable with severely limited financial and professional resources. Although this third characteristic, microscalability, appears oxymoronic, it is an accurate description of successful microfranchises. Microfranchising assumes that one can provide a simple toolbox for individuals or small organisations with *very* limited resources (often enabled by microcredit) to build a new business. These new businesses must be scalable on a micro level. In other words, they must be replicable without the same amount of capital that a traditional franchise would require in the USA or Europe, and without much or any expertise. The notion of microscalability is that a business can scale by adding more and more nodes, but each node starts quite small, some possibly remaining small for their entire life-cycle, with the overall impact of the network of franchisees still being quite large. While many developed-world models are quite scalable, they are typically not microscalable. McDonald's franchises, for example, require from hundreds of thousands to millions of US dollars to found, and further capital for growth. Thus microscalability represents a critical component of microfranchising.

At the core, microfranchising addresses four primary challenges found in emerging economies: (1) the lack of jobs in many communities, (2) the lack of business skills among the poor needed to grow a successful business, (3) the lack of goods and services available to the poor (such as the lack of efficient technologies), and (4) the lack of MNCs' understanding or ability to operate successfully in this vastly different context. For the franchisor, microfranchising provides an effective method of delivery for its goods and services to the world's billions living at the base of the economic pyramid. For the local entrepreneur franchisee, it provides critical support in the ascent up the economic ladder. For consumers, it allows increased access to goods, services and a higher quality of life. And it offers everyone the ability to provide and consume these goods and services with reduced risk due to the proven business system, consistency, standards control and brand confidence.

We will next discuss the usefulness of microfranchising and the challenges it overcomes through two case studies. We then expand the discussion and illustrate how the enabling characteristics of microfranchising (organic nature, modularity and microscalability) are applicable more broadly to firms, governments and even education in developing and developed markets.

Drishtee

Drishtee is a for-profit organisation incorporated in 2000 to establish a sustainable, scalable platform of entrepreneurship (with the use of information and communications technology [ICT]) in rural economies and societies. By using a tiered franchise and partnership model, Drishtee has been able to facilitate the establishment of kiosk nodes (which provide access to information and other local services) to the rural community at nominal price. The business model (as seen in Fig. 4.2) is driven by the village entrepreneur, who owns the village node to operate a self-sustaining, profitable kiosk. These nodes provide an innovative distribution channel for a variety of products and services (including ICT) to the rural sector. The kiosk allows, among other things, enhanced access to web-based services such as e-education, health, insurance and a growing amount of e-governance.

There are currently up to 12 main services provided through the network, including the ICT services as well as the sale of products such as recharge vouchers, mobile phones, insurance, reading glasses and batteries. The entrepreneur earns by charging the community a fee for the services provided and products sold. The entrepreneur is charged a licence fee in order to cover some of the costs of expansion as well as give the entrepreneur a better sense of ownership and greater desire to succeed. Drishtee has a fixed sharing with the kiosk operator and a variable revenue-sharing plan with the service providers. Not all of the kiosks are profitable yet, but Drishtee overall is profitable. (Chapter 6 looks at how Drishtee is financed in more detail.)

Figure 4.2 **Drishtee's business model**

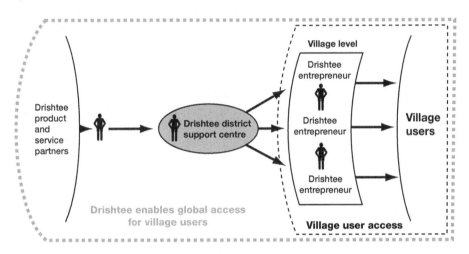

Source: www.drishteefoundation.org, accessed 28 March 2008

The Drishtee model has already made an impact (see Fig. 4.3). By 2008, Drishtee had successfully demonstrated this concept in about 4,000 kiosks in 12 states across India, with plans to keep adding thousands more. Each kiosk caters to approximately 1,200 households, the majority of which have an aggregated income of less than $2 a day. Over a longer period, Drishtee is geared up to try to become a type of electronic Wal-Mart for the rural world.

Each of the three enabling characteristics of microfranchising has played a role in Drishtee's overall success:

- **Organic.** The Drishtee model is driven by what is learned in the field and by the reports and needs identified by local staff, who are given significant autonomy. At the same time, the model depends on the core infrastructure, systems, training and purchasing power that result from aggregating at the centre. There is a high level of involvement from the core that is different from other models (such as VisionSpring). The more Drishtee can get all players to adopt its systems, the more profitable it can be

Figure 4.3 **Impact of the Drishtee model**

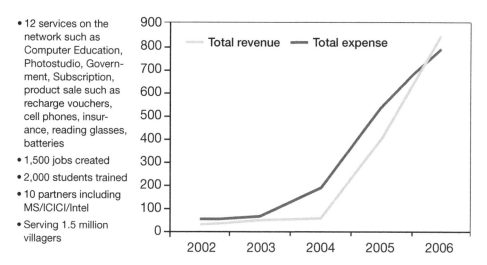

- 12 services on the network such as Computer Education, Photostudio, Government, Subscription, product sale such as recharge vouchers, cell phones, insurance, reading glasses, batteries
- 1,500 jobs created
- 2,000 students trained
- 10 partners including MS/ICICI/Intel
- Serving 1.5 million villagers

Source: www.drishteefoundation.org, accessed 28 March 2008

- **Modular.** Drishtee franchisees can sell as many or as few of the Drishtee products and services available as they want (although since 2008 this has been changing, with increasing segmentation of services). The ones successful in maintaining a strong business seem to choose to sell a broad range of services and products. The ones who are strong for a while and then get stuck are the ones that concentrate on only one or two products. The modularity piece is also applicable in the sense that different products require different competences, and licensees must adopt at least a few or they cannot be successful in long term. The business model enables Drishtee to be responsive to demand. Additionally, Drishtee entrepreneurs can carry non-Drishtee products and services including competing ones. Drishtee wants to offer the best service and price and this allows it to learn about and, if at all possible, beat the competition

- **Microscalable.** Each aspect of Drishtee must have a business model that is sustainable in the long term. The organisation is quick to change or drop an offering if it is not profitable or sustainable. Drishtee is microscalable, yet not as much as other microfranchises. In Drishtee's case, franchisees pay $250 to get started with the licence and maybe some investment in hardware or a physical space. This is still significantly lower than franchises in the USA or Europe, but still expensive for those in emerging economies. Entrepreneurs also need some time to build a reputation, to understand how things work and to learn how to sell before they become profitable. This is not a great option for the poorest of the poor, though working with microfinance institutions opens the opportunity to more people

Drishtee also provides an opportunity for us to examine the impact of microfranchising on the four challenges mentioned above.

1. **Lack of jobs.** Unlike a number of projects financed by microcredit, many microfranchises are able to begin to employ people directly and can have a big impact in terms of bringing in new services and jobs instead of copying what already exists in an area. In the case of Drishtee, each kiosk provides employment for an average of two to three people

2. **Lack of skills to grow a business.** Drishtee's model is meeting this challenge by providing training in most aspects of business. Most people usually have neither the skills nor the exposure to new ideas that might spur entrepreneurship. Drishtee recognises that its model allows motivated people who may not be entrepreneurial to create their own jobs. Therefore, the return on these models only has to be as high (or perhaps slightly higher) as the return from working in agriculture

3. **Lack of goods and services available to poor.** This is one of the main reasons why the Drishtee model has so much impact—because it is able to deliver products and services to areas that do not yet have them. Sometimes they are new, and at other times they are just cheaper (also decreasing the need for customers to travel to the city for some products and services)

4. **Lack of outsiders' understanding and ability to operate in this new context.** Drishtee has grown in a way that has not yet happened anywhere in the world where its services and products are needed. This provides clues as to how operating in this context is different from what most MNCs are used to. Effective distribution and logistics are key to Drishtee's survival, which are problems that other larger companies looking at rural India are scrambling to solve. Drishtee carries close to 25 products and services, which still is not enough to serve all needs. It is hard to imagine any one MNC (apart from a Wal-Mart, Reliance or pure distribution company) having so many products and being able to serve so many needs. Furthermore, Drishtee's target market is rural areas with very poor people and low population density, which means that the return on investment is still probably lower than other businesses are interested in. Most businesses, even if they could operate in the same market, would probably go after different markets where returns are higher. Even Nokia does not yet invest in sales in the areas that Drishtee serves. In these areas, few people need to use a mobile phone every day, but when a few need one every month then Drishtee can serve them. Drishtee, as with many other microfranchise models, is driven by the desire of the founder to promote social change

and progress. Therefore, it often chooses to take a lower profit margin and approach situations in different ways than a commercial entrepreneur might.

The following are some other valuable lessons from the first years of operation:

- It is hard to predict which nodes will be successful, but having a licence fee gives all participants more ownership and makes them more likely to succeed

- Drishtee carries a broad variety of products to meet demand, but these products do not always get sold on a large enough basis to reach economies of scale. In small amounts, the costs of distribution have been high

- The limited banking and lack of credit card system is a fundamental structural problem of the Indian economy, and this influences business processes. Drishtee offers little or no credit for purchases of inventory. Kiosks rarely have inventory and so they often sell products from a catalogue. They must collect money from the customer and pay Drishtee before the product gets shipped to them

- Internet access is still expensive and not always available, making some products much harder to sell

- The sales and servicing model is hard to manage when so geographically diverse

- Once an idea seems good and some basic strategy and calculations have been made, one should try to implement it. It is better not to spend too much time trying to nail down every detail, as there are many contextual factors that cannot be predicted before beginning

- Strong partner relationships are important

- One must always treat licensees fairly and be as transparent as possible

- Social benefits to the model match or exceed the financial benefits. For example, successful licensees develop a pride in their success and begin developing a new confidence that reverberates throughout the village

- Entrepreneurs must be local and trusted. The goal is to strengthen, not replace, the local ecosystem

- Microfranchising works, and it can be a powerful way to bring new ideas, opportunities and services into emerging markets

OneRoof

OneRoof is a for-profit business operating in the developing world that is driven by dual social and financial missions: to change the way that essential services are delivered to the world's rural poor; and to ensure that franchisees, subsidiaries, and headquarters make a profit in the process. The OneRoof business platform provides a strategic way of doing business that aims to be more sustainable for providing jobs and simultaneously delivering needed innovations in rural areas at a profit. OneRoof's intellectual property is not a new service or product. It is a new way of doing business and international development. The successes of its initial centrally owned stores located in India and Mexico are now allowing it to scale up through franchising. In 2009, OneRoof opened its first 12 franchise stores.

In the company-owned stores and in the franchise stores, OneRoof is testing a new delivery platform that provides citizens of rural communities with access to nine essential services: ICT, education, financial services, health, energy, sanitation, clean water, employment generation (partially through 'BPO at the BoP': business process outsourcing at the base of the pyramid) and agricultural technologies. Coming from 20 years in the NGO world, the founders realised that the best development projects always had a strong sense of local ownership. They started with the idea of turning an NGO into a for-profit enterprise in order to make it more replicable and sustainable; franchising then arose as the best way to obtain local ownership in the communities.

So how do the three characteristics of microfranchises play a role in the overall success of OneRoof?

- **Organic.** OneRoof recognises the need to be organic as there is only a certain amount of field support it can give. It helps franchisees as much as possible through the franchise business model. However, because it is not always available at a moment's notice (as this kind of support is expensive), it encourages franchisees to be innovative. This can present a challenge in getting franchisees to adhere to quality standards. But the need to be flexible is important enough for OneRoof to count on the 85–95% getting through and hoping that the other 5–15% do not reflect negatively on the brand. The bottom line has always been about local ownership. OneRoof is still refining its model, recognising that this boosts the potential to increase scalability at a faster pace. As the OneRoof model becomes more established and people catch on, the organic nature of microfranchising makes it easier for it to expand virally than it would through centrally owned and operated stores

- **Modular.** Modularity is also important for OneRoof. It wants to have a continually growing range of services that can be interchanged at a local level depending on need and demand. It sees the need to capture input and suggestions from customers or franchisees so that additional goods and services can be developed. The ability to add or subtract things effectively and easily makes a huge difference for each franchisee. OneRoof has also developed a management system that helps franchisees see revenue sources each day. Each franchisee, the Chennai and San Francisco offices can see which modular units are being the most productive and can form an accurate idea of what is happening. This makes franchisees easily able to monitor, for example, what the utilisation rate has been for each machine so they know when to add or subtract a computer. It allows them to understand their business and customers much better

- **Microscalable.** While OneRoof sees the importance of microscalability, its model is still more expensive than the poorest franchisees can afford. It struggles to find the right price point for franchisees to buy in and the return on investment to promise. OneRoof is more expensive than a mom-and-pop browser service, but it also offers more services. Its goal is to make an impact through giving tools and opportunities to franchisees that they have never had before, and make it profitable for all stockholders, including the Indian employees who have ownership in the big company

OneRoof also provides an opportunity for us to examine the impact of microfranchising on the four challenges mentioned above:

1. **Lack of jobs.** OneRoof wants to provide good jobs locally so that people can stay in rural areas and not be forced to migrate to cities

2. **Lack of skills to grow a business.** Training and support is provided so that people who are not born entrepreneurs can have a chance to succeed. One difficulty is that OneRoof's concept is not as easy to understand or explain as a cybercafé

3. **Lack of goods and services available to the poor.** OneRoof recognises this as a big reason for its existence and believes that microfranchising can answer this in a sustainable way. Although it is always monitoring which goods and services are the most profitable, it focuses also on improving educational opportunities, financial services and so on

4. **Lack of outsiders' understanding or ability to operate in this new context.** Addressing this challenge has been part of the OneRoof mind-set from the beginning. The organisation sees itself as a bridge-builder for those who might know urban India but not necessarily rural India

The following are other valuable lessons from the first years of operation:

- The more ownership franchisees have, the better things go, which leads to a more profitable and scalable enterprise

- The first two franchisees were well respected, older individuals in their communities. This helped establish the OneRoof name, added instant credibility and drew people in

- OneRoof is still small and new and looking for the right sort of franchisees in order to maximise the chance for a sustainable market to support the stores, requiring fairly strict requirements for location, space needed and so on

- OneRoof lost some franchisees because of the high capital expenditure needed for a store. Having a smaller initial expense makes it easier to recruit franchisees

- It takes time to develop when you are new, particularly with a new concept, especially in a country where 'new' is not always embraced

- There is a need to think long-term and consider the social impact of the business. OneRoof is doing this by trying to attract more women and children by creating a safe environment. For example, it aims to minimise use of violent games and pornography, so that everyone can feel safe and welcome. It configures the equipment so that every screen is visible to everyone else in the store. It is consciously making decisions that might go against some of the bottom-line decisions that franchisees would otherwise make

- Some things are specific to India. For example, one of the challenges when working in rural areas—where traditions are stronger and there is a greater sense of hierarchy—is that 20- to 25-year-olds tend to be more risk-averse and not think as creatively. They are not particularly entrepreneurial, especially when compared to a college graduate in the USA who usually has more feedback and creative ideas

- The best franchisees are those that take the initiative, provide good leadership and try new things

- The cost and complexity of the franchise is an issue in the ease of its scalability[2]

2 OneRoof adopted a new business model in 2010 when they acquired CyberCafe Pro. Some of the franchised stores were sold to their operators and still operate independently. However, OneRoof now provides business solutions software customised to the needs of telecentres worldwide. (Information as at 10 January 2011.)

Discussion

The Drishtee and OneRoof cases illustrate the under-developed potential of microfranchising to create jobs, provide goods and services, scale up in order to increase impact and ultimately become financially viable. Rural BoP markets are under-served. Not only do residents lack access to basic necessities, the products and services that are available in these areas are often over-priced even relative to developed-world benchmarks. Our research confirms that the rural poor do indeed suffer from this 'poverty penalty'. This primarily arises from distribution challenges. These cases clearly indicate that the microfranchise model provides one possible solution for overcoming the distribution dilemma. Indeed, rural markets are not centralised communities; they are dispersed and agricultural societies often centred on farms. Thus, centralised superstores that most large organisations are good at creating are not an option.

At the same time, certain factors could minimise and even negate the impact and sustainability of microfranchises. Best (2008) described a microfranchise telecentre effort that struggled with sustainability. Infrastructure costs, vandalism, theft and inadequately skilled staff contributed to the failure of many of the centres. Ratan and Gogineni (2008) provided one explanation for why technology-intensive efforts can fail, even when based on microfranchising principles. In their study of the financial sector of the market in India, they found that the relationship between an intervention and its ability to benefit a local economic environment is dependent on costs (fixed and variable, which are often not totally taken into consideration) and the relative per-transaction gain produced. They state that 'in certain contexts, the per-transaction gains from using capital-intensive technologies are overwhelmed by the fixed and operating resources required to generate and sustain these gains' (Ratan and Gogineni 2008: 2). For reasons like this, one microfranchising institution strongly recommended piloting with each channel partner (such as a soft launch where adaptations can be made until reliably successful), and only then replicating and scaling the microfranchise businesses (DeWitt 2008).

Key similarities between Drishtee and OneRoof contribute to their success. First, both organisations have created a microfranchise model able to provide affordable services and products. Second, they both create additional jobs. Third, they provide the necessary training needed to operate the business, though their models require a modest level of training. In both cases, training is essential as they introduce services otherwise unavailable. Moreover, without the training and microfranchise platform, the ITC services these small businesses offer might not be available at all in the local community for an accessible price. Fourth, they have a social mission that creates impact for the microfranchisee and the consumer. Fifth, they are microscalable, imperative to making a broad impact. Sixth, they are profitable models, both at the franchisor and franchisee levels—although as noted in the Drishtee case, each individual microfranchisee is not necessarily profitable, but when the losses are spread across all of the microfranchises, the microfranchisor can remain profitable. In both cases, the microfranchising model provides an effective decentralised distribution solution scalable through the addition of franchisees and sustainable by its own surpluses from ongoing operations.

Market forces in developing countries challenge traditional approaches to business foundation and growth. The principles that enable microfranchising provide one way to address these challenges. By examining the organic nature of microfranchising, modularity and what we have coined microscalability, we note the applicability of these enabling characteristics for more established companies, governments and non-profit entities. For example, car manufacturer Tata employs modularity in the business model for its recently announced Nano, a $2,500 car. It has built a modular system that can be shipped and assembled anywhere, in this case by local entrepreneurs.

As an example of organic and modular necessity, education has scalability challenges when it comes to taking educational programmes that have been proven in a few isolated instances and rolling them out on a larger scale. Part of one solution is to design such programmes to be microscalable, having modular features and creating a franchise model for local schools and districts from which they could opt in (providing the organic feeling of ownership), rather than attempting a top-down mandate.

On a different level, microscalability is evident in direct-selling company Amway's huge success in China. When entering the Chinese market, the company created a slightly different business model and found huge success. While Amway has suffered from negative reputational issues in the USA and Europe, the company enjoys a superb reputation in China, where it generates a substantial portion of its overall annual revenues. Amway distributors are required to provide a limited amount of capital to get started and then act as independent businesses enabled by the core. Though Amway distributorships in China are not microfranchises strictly speaking, in that they do not generally serve the very lowest income brackets, the organic, microscalable nature of the Amway model has worked quite well in this emerging market. As a major (nearly $7 billion) global corporation, Amway illustrates that the insights of microfranchising pertain to enterprises well beyond the BoP context.

Chuck Slaughter, the founder of Living Goods, a microfranchise organisation set up to deliver health services in developing countries, noted the applicability of the Avon model (founded in the USA in 1886) to the developing world today. The population Avon focused on in 1886 was mostly rural and agricultural, the standard of living was substantially lower than today, access to good-quality products in rural areas was poor, there were strong village social connections, and the business model targeted rural women needing extra income. The replicability of this model is proven as today Avon sells more than $8 billion, thriving in 140 diverse cultures around the world (Slaughter 2008).

Exploring the diffusion of innovation through microfranchising can clearly have impact for large as well as small corporations in developing and developed markets, because management and development teams must become adroit at doing more with less for competitive, economic, social and environmental reasons.

Conclusion

Microfranchising provides a breakthrough strategy for meeting the unique challenges presented by emerging markets, but we acknowledge that is not a stand-alone solution. It is best served in the context of support situations as identified in the case studies. By providing well-developed turnkey enterprises to the poor, microfranchising provides added capability for the diffusion of innovation in a way that meets the needs of those in emerging economies. In addition, the principles derived from microfranchising have applicability on a wider scale to large and small corporations operating in the developing and developed world.

5

Barefoot Power
A case study in Uganda[1]

Harry Andrews
Barefoot Power Pty Ltd, Kenya

It was at the Microcredit Summit in Halifax, Nova Scotia, in 2006 that the concept of microfranchising first started to gain some traction in my mind. I attended the conference representing Barefoot Power, a new solar energy enterprise, as an exhibitor. I happened to be in the USA for a wedding of a close friend, and the marginal cost of attending the conference in Canada was seen as tolerable for our cash-strapped start-up. I arrived, along with my brother Sam, equipped with overflowing suitcases of lamps, batteries and solar panels, determined to show off our pro-poor solar lighting products to the world. Looking back on the event, I think of how our product range was far from developed. In fact, it looked like a mismatch of products, more appropriately referred to as prototypes that had been assembled in a garden shed. Our little display took on a shade of shabby when compared to the glistening booths of the big boys, such as Grameen Technology Centre and ACCION.

Three things struck me about the event. First, Barefoot Power was the only product supplier in a 2,000-delegate summit. These delegates represented microfinance institutions that form the world's only significant infrastructure designed specifically to reach the poor. Second, we were absolutely overwhelmed with the interest in the low price points that we were advertising for our prototype lighting systems.

1 I would like to thank Becca Schwartz, Boldwejin Sloet and James Wire Lunghabo for their integral role in implementing the pilot; Stewart Craine and Sam Andrews for their tireless work in product development and technical support; Paul Rippey for his networking and philosophical support; and Ana Klinčić Andrews for her support, insight and patience.

Our exhibit had a constant flow of people and we collated a database with more than 150 microfinance institutions that were interested in exploring collaboration. Third, I attended a session where Jason Fairbourne was presenting on the Scojo Foundation's microfranchising experience with vision entrepreneurs. Stimulating a network of mobile entrepreneurs who would sell low-cost ($13) solar lighting systems had been a topic of discussion since Barefoot Power's inception. The term microfranchising suddenly provided a conceptual framework for what we were trying to achieve. This forced me to focus my efforts over the following two years to develop and pilot a solar energy microfranchise programme in Uganda. This pilot, its difficulties and successes, provides the main content of this chapter.

Energy poverty

The poor burn $36 billions-worth of kerosene each year in lanterns to light their homes. The light cast from a kerosene lamp is poorly distributed, has a low intensity and is expensive. The poor lighting level from kerosene lamps makes it difficult for children to study, affecting literacy and education, and minimises the effective working hours for home-based businesses. The open flame, smoke and soot from kerosene lamps endanger lives by reducing indoor air quality and increasing the likelihood of fire. The lighting service the poor receive from a kerosene lamp is up to 350 times less than the same service per dollar delivered by the electricity grid in developed countries.[2] It is this huge market inefficiency that Barefoot Power aims to help correct by redirecting expenditure away from fuel-based lighting to more efficient and safer modern alternatives, starting with small solar lamps. The negative impacts of energy poverty are sobering. The World Health Organisation (WHO) reports that there are over 300,000 deaths every year from burns, the vast majority occurring in low- and middle-income countries (WHO 2008). Nearly 4 million women suffer from severe burns from open fires and kerosene lighting each year: similar to the number who are diagnosed with AIDS each year. More children die from fire-related injuries than from tuberculosis or malaria (Interplast n.d.).

However, burns are only part of the debilitating impact of energy poverty. The poor, mostly women and children, consume the equivalent of two packs of cigarettes per day from smoke from indoor cooking, resulting in chronic respiratory and eye diseases (UNDP and WHO 2004). The United Nations Development Programme and the WHO report that 1.6 million deaths per year in developing countries are

2 Light is measured in lumens (lm); lighting service is measured in lumen hours (lm-hr). A kerosene lamp produces 35 lm and can be run for four hours per night (140 lm-hr). This costs $1/week, resulting in a service efficiency of 1,000 lm-hr/$. A 40W fluorescent lamp running from the grid produces about 2,000 lm, so at $0.15/kWh, a week of lighting costs about $0.15 and produces 56,000 lm-hr of lighting service. This lighting service is delivered with an efficiency of 350,000 lm-hr/$.

caused by the indoor air pollution attributed to traditional fuels—that's one life lost every 20 seconds (UNDP and WHO 2004).

Energy poverty must be reduced.

Organisational history

Barefoot Power is a social enterprise established in early 2005 by Stewart Craine and me. We were previously working as engineering and environmental consultants in Australia's largest renewable energy utility. Tired of serving the wealthy with more and more electricity, and animated by a six-month consultancy project we had just completed in Papua New Guinea, we somewhat naively left our cushy jobs and established Barefoot Power. Our vision when establishing the company was to disrupt the multi-billion-dollar kerosene lighting market in developing countries with 21st-century solar-lighting technologies designed specifically for the poor.

Financing is always a huge hurdle for social enterprises to overcome, and Barefoot Power is by no means an exception. In setting up Barefoot Power, we quickly exhausted financing opportunities from so-called 'family, friends and fools'. Making the transition from individual investors to institutional investors was a difficult task. Instrumental in this transition has been Oikocredit, one of the world's largest funds for microfinance institutions. The first connection with Oikocredit was made when Barefoot Power won a major prize at the Business in Development Challenge run by the Dutch government in 2006. Oikocredit has assisted Barefoot Power's liquidity and governance by providing equity investments and a board director. Oikocredit has also worked with Barefoot Power to create a Barefoot Angels Fund, which allows Barefoot Power to provide favourable supply conditions to its distribution partners. The key objective of the fund is to engage microfinance distribution partners, or partners with strong linkages to microfinance, to work with Barefoot Power to bring clean, affordable and modern lighting systems to the poor.

Barefoot Power is a multifaceted enterprise. The company combines pro-poor design and mass manufacturing to produce low-cost and appropriate energy equipment for use in developing countries. Barefoot Power's entry-level solar-lighting product retails for approximately $13 when sold by a micro-entrepreneur. It became apparent early on, however, that engineering the technological side of the puzzle was not our key barrier. Excluding the challenges in attracting sufficient financing for our business, the key barrier to success was developing and piloting appropriate distribution models to reach those people who have been left in the dark. We realised that we could have the best solar-lighting product on the planet, but if we didn't have a strong model to distribute the products we were little more than travelling salesmen peddling our widgets.

Barefoot Power established Base Technologies (Uganda) Ltd in 2008 as a company to experiment with different distribution models, starting with a pilot for a solar-energy microfranchising model. Base Technologies is expanding the model in collaboration with local distributors and microfinance institutions. Barefoot Power is replicating aspects of this pilot in Kenya, Ghana, Mali and India. I am now based in Kenya managing a joint venture company that Barefoot Power has established: one of the first to replicate the microfranchise pilot undertaken in Uganda and the first to use the Barefoot Angels Fund.

Microfinance and microfranchising

The opening section of this chapter highlights the fact that Barefoot Power has a particular interest in the synergies between microfinance and microfranchising. As mentioned, microfinance constitutes the world's largest infrastructure designed specifically to reach the poor. Microfinance institutions have created the distribution networks needed to reach into millions of villages and towns. John Hatch stated in a recent publication on microfranchising that 'no social movement or foreign aid programme in human history has impacted more of the world's most disadvantaged citizens, nor done so more quickly and less expensively, than microfinance' (Fairbourne 2007c). More than 10,000 microfinance programmes exist worldwide, serving as many as 5 million towns and villages. These programmes have reached more than 100 million clients with financial services and have created the infrastructure through which many more will be reached. Organisations that specialise in microfranchising, such as Barefoot Power, may have sufficient resources for a pilot using supply-side financial mechanisms such as consignment or supplier credit. However, we lack the financial capital and capacity to scale these financial mechanisms. That is why we seek to reach scale in multiple countries via partnerships with microfinance institutions.

The Ugandan target market

Uganda is a land-locked country located in East Africa, nestled between the peaceful shores of Lake Victoria in the south and the war-ravaged northern border with Sudan. More than 85% of the country's population of 24 million is rural-based (SIDA 1999). More than 80% of the population lack access to electricity and almost all of these households use light from an open-flame kerosene lamp called a *tabooda* to penetrate the darkness.[3] A typical Ugandan household burns between $0.50 and $1

---

3   Ministry of Health Uganda MoHU, 2007.

each week in its kerosene lamps. These tiny amounts from the pockets of the poor accumulate to more than $200 million in revenue each year for oil companies.[4]

The majority of families in Uganda generate their livelihoods from small-scale home-based agriculture. The greatest non-farm employer in Uganda, however, is the informal sector (UMI GDLC 2005). It is estimated that there are more than 800,000 micro-enterprises operating in Uganda, employing 90% of total non-farm-based workers (Ikoja-Odongo 2001). The informal sector contributes 20% of Uganda's gross domestic product. Trade makes up 72% of the activities of the informal sector, followed by 22% manufacturing and 6% services. The Ugandan informal sector, however, has one of the highest private business failure rates in the world. This is largely due to the lack of entrepreneurial skills, lack of access to high-quality and affordable business development services, limited access to finance, lack of adequate technical and management support services and limited access to information on market opportunities (Tushabomwe-Kazooba 2006; UNDP Uganda 2008).

In late 2007 and early 2008, Barefoot Power was debating where to establish its first office in East Africa. We thought at the time that we had a reliable and trustworthy partner in Tanzania. Kenya was reeling from the turmoil of the violence in the aftermath of the December 2007 elections. The choice was clear. We envisioned that the low electrification rate in Uganda and an active informal market would be an ideal starting point for our microfranchising concept. Our local partner, James Wire Lughabou, a young entrepreneur who had operated an ICT company in Uganda for over a decade, had undertaken extensive research into the solar products available on the Ugandan market. Conversations with James revealed that the solar system most heavily marketed in Uganda was targeted at the rural upper middle class and cost more than $150. We sent James some of Barefoot Power's solar lighting products for market testing. James let us know that there were no similar products on the market and that he was overwhelmed with requests to purchase his demonstration systems.

The market gap that Barefoot Power targets is between the poor who are spending approximately $1 per week on kerosene and the rural upper middle class who can afford the solar systems already available on the market. Barefoot Power has been able to reduce the cost of entry-level solar-lighting systems by using highly efficient technology: white light-emitting diodes (LEDs). The smallest solar LED lamps have targeted a price point equal to what a household spends on kerosene in four to six months. Barefoot Power has also been careful to design systems using plug-and-play wiring and easy-to-follow self-install instructions to avoid the need for specific technical skills for installation. The products Barefoot Power used in the pilot ranged from a 0.5 Wp solar lamp retailing for $13 to a 5 Wp[5] multiple lamp system retailing for $100.

---

4 Kerosene expenditure estimated from data collected in the field in Uganda by Barefoot Power and referenced to Lumina Project (light.lbl.gov).
5 Wp refers to the peak watts of the solar panel that accompany the lamps (Lumina Project, light.lbl.gov).

Developing the microfranchising model

I arrived in Uganda in early 2008 and quickly established a small team to plan and implement the pilot. I have structured my discussion of the pilot to follow the steps involved in developing the business. We called the microfranchise businesses 'Firefly microfranchises', named after our smallest solar Firefly lamps.

Step 1: Business plan

As with all enterprises, the first step was to put together a comprehensive business plan. I had drafted the majority of the plan in the months before arriving in Uganda, mainly concerned with forecasting costs and revenues. But the plan lacked brainstorming by a team on the operational details for the pilot. The operational model gathered substance as we worked through the next steps: process mapping, tool development and training development. The business plan allowed us to justify expenditure for the pilot, but more importantly it framed the objectives that we were all adamant we wanted to achieve: providing a better and cleaner alternative to kerosene lighting to the poor in Uganda, developing a financially sustainable business, and doing this by creating jobs via a microfranchising model.

Step 2: Process mapping

The mapping exercise was our method for problem identification, thereby allowing us to develop effective processes and tools. The map of our system provided the skeleton of how we thought the microfranchising model would work in practice. A basic map of the model is presented in Figure 5.1. The actual mapping exercise is far more organic and would be incomprehensible if reproduced. Our aim was to develop a network of mobile Firefly microfranchisees, who were trained, equipped with a business-in-a-bag and encouraged to directly market to customers. As we mapped out the model, it became apparent that the business would require an additional level in the supply chain: a regional distributor or master franchisor. This was to help with the management, monitoring and product distribution if undertaken from the central location of Kampala. While the pilot did not have sufficient scale to implement the master franchise level, it was important to acknowledge the need as it affected the tools we designed and, importantly, the product pricing structure for the pilot.

Step 3: Tool development

Developing systematic tools for all levels of the franchise model is fundamental for creating a replicable model. The tools represent the unique and proprietary operating model for the franchise and form the blueprint for replication. The tools and guides we developed for the microfranchise pilot in Uganda included:

- Cash receipt books
- Operations manual
- Daily, weekly and monthly checklists
- A daily date book/diary
- Basic book-keeping aids
- Marketing and customer service guides
- Promotional material
- Marketing flip booklets
- Franchise agreement
- Incentive scheme
- Franchise application form
- Franchise identification tags
- Branded uniforms
- A branded carry-bag

There are too many tools to go into the detail of each. Instead I have chosen two items to discuss in brief: the operations manual and the marketing flip booklet.

Figure 5.1 **Map of the franchise model**

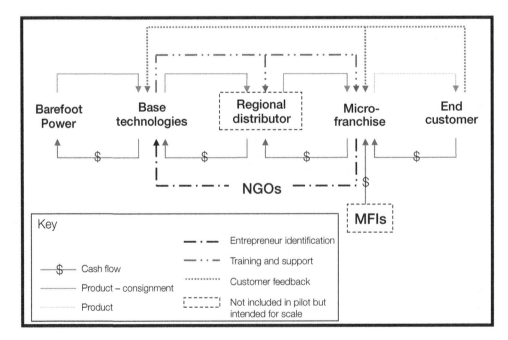

The operations manual is the heart of the microfranchise. It is a bound copy of the business systems and provides a step-by-step guide to operating on a daily, weekly and monthly basis. The manual connects all the tools and outlines relations between the franchisor and the franchisee including: policies, best practices, ordering and delivery, banking, record-keeping, faults and repairs, credit repayment, communications and customer relations. To provide detail on one procedure outlined in the operations manual, presented in Figure 5.2 is a diagram of the daily record-keeping process developed for the Firefly microfranchises. In the operations manual, this process is broken down into steps: recording costs, recording sales, developing payment plans for customers, entering data into the journal of transactions, inventory tracking and submitting record-keeping documents to Base Technologies. Practical examples were presented in the operations manual to help the entrepreneur to understand their use. Figure 5.3 provides an illustration of how the daily diary and date book were used to assist the microfranchise in maintaining daily records.

Figure 5.2 **Overview of microfranchise record-keeping as presented in the operations manual**

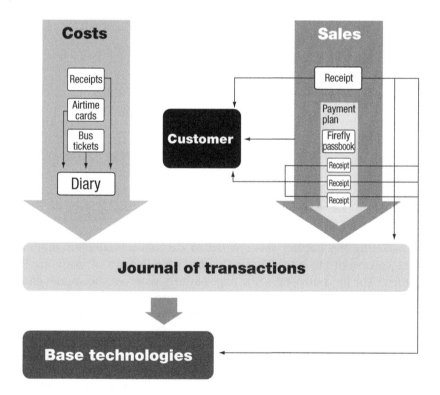

Figure 5.3 **Completed diary/date book for record-keeping as presented in the operations manual**

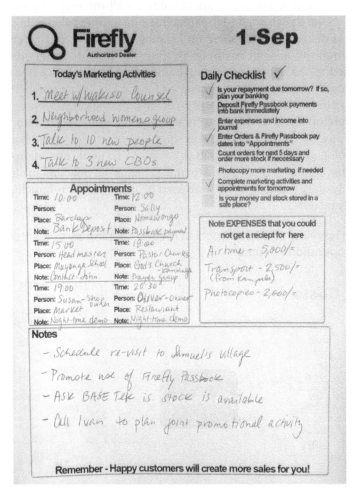

The marketing flip booklet was created to develop a systematic method for achieving consistent marketing messages about the benefits of using the Firefly solar lamps.[6] The flip sides of the first page of the booklet are shown in Figures 5.4 and 5.5.[7] A potential customer would view the picture in Figure 5.4, while the entrepreneur would use the prompts on the back side (Fig. 5.5) to market the product.

6 Paul Rippey, who had spent five years in Uganda with the UK Department for International Development (DFID) Financial Sector Deepening Project, had returned to Uganda as the manager of ACCION's Energy Links project. ACCION kindly paid for, and provided valued input to, the development of the flip booklet.
7 The flip booklet in Figures 5.4 and 5.5 is presented in English, but the material was translated into Uganda's five major language groups for the pilot.

Figure 5.4 **Flip booklet page viewed by the customer**

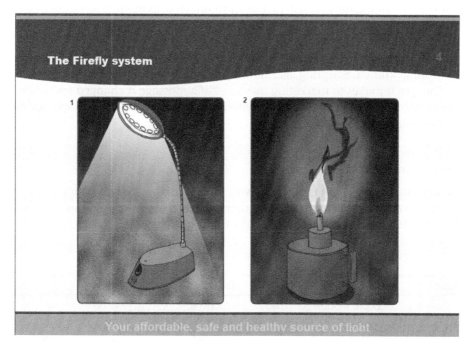

Figure 5.5 **Flip booklet page viewed by the microfranchisee**

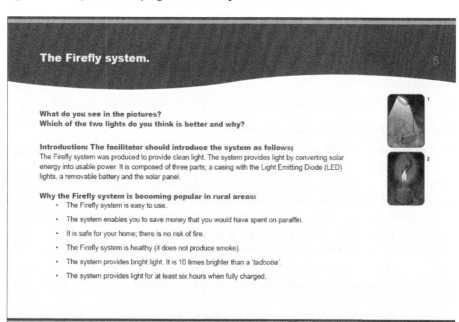

The scripted marketing messages were particularly important when the entrepreneur was describing the performance of a product. If the entrepreneur understates performance, a customer is likely to be discouraged from purchasing the product. On the other hand, if the entrepreneur overstates performance, a customer may be disappointed with the product and spread negative sentiment about the underperforming product. Scripting also allows Barefoot Power to monitor the effects of any changes it makes to marketing messages. If a message is changed and implemented across the whole network, the effect of the change can be analysed against revenue to identify correlations.

Step 4: Training development

The next step in developing the pilot was to construct training materials. These included a training facilitator's guide, training exercises, role plays, and training aids. The list of modules developed for the training is presented in Table 5.1.

Table 5.1 **Firefly microfranchise training modules**

Day 1	Day 2	Day 3	Day 4
Module 1: Introduction	Module 5: Detailed fundraising and entrepreneurship	Module 8: Incentive scheme	Module 12: Branding
Module 2: Introduction to technical skills and marketing	Module 6: Detailed technical training	Module 9: Cost, revenue and profit calculations	Module 13: Verbal examination
Module 3: Business proposition	Module 7: Marketing	Module 10: Financial management	
Module 4: Introduction to fundraising and entrepreneurship		Module 11: Communications	

Step 5: Entrepreneur identification

The key methods for identifying potential microfranchise candidates in the pilot were via walk-in interest and personal contacts from existing networks. Of the 16 candidates who made it to the final training, 11 were identified via NGO partners such as BRAC Uganda, CARE Uganda, Ugandan Effort to Save Orphans, Uganda Microfinance Ltd and the Communication Development Foundation of Uganda. Those who had a history with an existing organisation were seen to be excellent candidates. They were often part-time community-based trainers who saw the Firefly microfranchise as a great way to supplement their income. Not only did these candidates have links into existing networks, but there was also a direct reference to their employment performance available via the NGO.

Step 6: Entrepreneur screening

The first part of the candidate screening was via a one-day introductory training session. For the pilot we undertook two introductory sessions: one in Masaka, two hours south-west of Kampala, with six candidates; and one in Kampala with ten candidates. The aim of the introductory day was to introduce the candidates to the business vision and the products, to present the business proposition and to challenge them to raise funds to start a microfranchise. The day involved brainstorming, hands-on exercises and role playing to identify their own goals and ambitions for business and life; understand the technical aspects of the products; explore their potential markets; and practise their sales and marketing pitch. These exercises were used by the training facilitator as inputs into simple individual business plans. The candidates did not know that these business plans were being developed and were surprised at the end of the day when presented with them. An example of a business plan is presented in Box 5.1. At the close of the introductory training, we put a challenge to the candidates to raise capital and advance orders for products before the in-depth training to be held 14 days later. Before leaving to take up their challenge, the candidates were provided with a Firefly solar system for demonstration, their business plan, a laminated trainee card and an application form to become a Firefly microfranchisee.

Box 5.1 **Example of Firefly business plan for Joseph Kato**

Business plan summary for Firefly entrepreneurs

1. General information

Name:	Joseph	Surname:	Kato
Address:	Katwe Butego	Phone number:	12345678
Community/parish:	Katwe Butego	Sub-county/ District:	Masaka

2. Description of experience

I am a social worker by profession. I offer social services to self-help groups in various activities, including training in income-generating activities such as brick-making communal projects. I also offer counselling and guidance to HIV-infected people as well as psychological support services. I am a small-scale farmer and trader dealing in agricultural products such as maize beans, etc.

3. Description of motivation and goals

Goals: To become a sole agent in three districts (Masaka, Rakai, Sembab-ule) for Firefly. To become a technical support adviser in other countries where the product has not yet been introduced.

Plans to achieve my goals: I have to be smart and transparent in the initial process of marketing the product. I have to get training in technical areas. I have to handle my clients and my bosses with integrity, love, and compassion.

4. Products

The Firefly system was pro-duced to provide clean light. The system provides light by converting solar energy into usable power. It is composed of three parts: a casing with

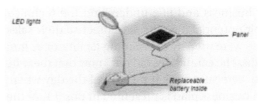

the Light Emitting Diodes (LED), a replaceable battery and the solar panel. The Firefly lamp has a warranty of three months and the panel has a war-ranty of one year.

5. Markets

List the areas where you will market your business:

- Market places
- Road-side vendors
- Women and youth groups
- Pedestrians
- Community officers
- Parish chiefs
- Lay councillors
- Community health workers
- NGOs
- Security officers

6. Business proposition

If Joseph maintains good records, provides good customer service, and repays any money owing to Base Technologies in a timely manner, he will receive significant sales bonuses. Joseph aims to meet sales targets, with a medium-term goal of selling 80 lamps per month. This is equal to selling two to three lamps per day. If Joseph achieves this sales target and receives bonuses, he will earn more than 300,000 Ugandan Shillings per month profit.

Signature Harry Andrews
General Manager
Base Technologies

Signature Joseph Kato
Firefly Trainee

Note: Information given in the business plan is strictly confidential and is used for Base Technologies' purposes only.

Step 7: Training and franchise agreement

Two weeks after the introductory session, those who took up the challenge came to Kampala for an intense training programme. Eleven candidates came to attend the two and a half days training. The aim was to provide detailed information and extensive exercises so that the candidates understood the systems and processes necessary to operate a Firefly microfranchise. After the training, we held a group oral exam. After this, we interviewed all candidates to assess their franchise application forms and the level of capital and advance orders they had been able to raise. The aim of the interview process was to identify the level of supplier credit and consignment the candidate would receive in his or her franchise probation period. In our planning phase, we had designed a system to allocate supplier credit levels via a grading that was weighted on training results, advance orders for products and capital raised. It was clear that the candidates had developed as a team during the training and that some candidates had greater social capital and were thus able to raise money more easily than others. I decided that we would start all the candidates off at the same level of credit: the product value that candidates would receive was double their capital raised.

Once the interviews were over, each candidate signed a franchise agreement and was allocated a business-in-a-bag, which contained the franchise kit. The cost value of this kit was deducted from the initial capital the candidate had raised. Cartons of product were then provided to each candidate equal to twice the value of the capital raised.

Step 8: Sales and supplier credit repayment

Once the candidates finished their training, and signed the franchise agreement, they became owners of a Firefly microfranchise and began marketing and sales. The entrepreneurs communicated with Base Technologies predominately via SMS: informing the head office when credit repayments were deposited, requesting orders to be packed ready for pick-up and reporting any problems or queries.

Most of the entrepreneurs were returning to Base Technologies within one week to repay credit and collect more stock. The credit repayment dates and amounts were outlined in an account statement (see Fig. 5.6), which was given to entrepreneurs each time they collected additional stock. Credit was provided with three repayment dates spread over two weeks. An incentive scheme was developed for the microfranchises based on sales volume. Penalties were also employed to encourage on-time repayment, return of sales receipts to head office and good book-keeping. The account statement provided the entrepreneurs with a summary of their bonus account. Bonuses were redeemable as a reduction of credit owing or as part of a down payment on new product purchases. When the entrepreneurs came to the head office to restock we would discuss problems and challenges and review the diary/date book that contained daily, weekly and monthly checklists and the journal of transactions.

Figure 5.6 **Firefly franchise account statement**

ACCOUNT STATEMENT

Dealer Name: Becca Schwartz
Dealer Number: 012

Statement Number: 12345
Statement Date: 3/9/2008

PRODUCTS DELIVERED

		Date	Amount
Deposit Received		1/9/2008	248,000

Product Name	Units	Price/unit	Total Price
Firefly LED Lamp	15	11,350	170,250
Firefly 1W Solar Panel	15	13,450	201,750
Replacement LEDs	0	2,700	0
Replacement Batteries	0	2,700	0
Total Value of Order			**372,000**

BASE Technologies Bonus Account

Bonus Balance from Previous Month	0
Number of Units Sold in Statement Month	45
Total Value of Bonus	**18,000**

LESS	YES/NO	Penalty (max. 100%)	Penalty
Credit Paid in Full	YES	75%	0%
Repayments Made on Time	YES	25%	0%
Reciepts/Journal Delivered on Time	NO	12.50%	13%
Reciepts Completed Correctly	YES	12.50%	0%
Total Penalty			**13%**

Total Credit in Account	**15,750**

Supplier Credit Account

Balance from Previous Orders	0
Value of Product Ordered	372,000
Total Less Deposit	124,000
Total Less Bonus Credit	108,250
Value of Supplier Credit	**108,250**

Repayment Schedule

	Date	% of Total	Amount
Repayment 1	7/09/2008	20%	21650
Repayment 2	12/09/2008	40%	43300
Repayment 3	17/09/2008	40%	43300

Pilot results

Overall, Barefoot Power regards the pilot as a success. Base Technologies was in an enviable, but regrettable, situation: it sold out of stock within ten weeks of starting the sales within the microfranchise programme. The duration of the pilot was six months from the point of arriving in Uganda to the selling out of stock. The microfranchise programme accounted for approximately half of the stock sold during the pilot phase; the other stock was sold to wholesale partners and specific NGO projects. Of the 16 people who were trained, 11 graduated and signed franchise agreements. The total capital raised by the 11 candidates was $1,700, while $1,400 of product was provided on credit at the end of the training session, after deductions for the costs of the business kits. During the ten-week sales phase of the pilot, the microfranchises generated $20,000 of sales by selling 1,200 solar lamps. These lamps improved lighting conditions for approximately 6,000 people. More than $10,000 of supplier credit was provided to the microfranchises, with an average credit amount per two-week cycle of $570. Late repayment totalled $450, but by the end of the pilot all credit had been repaid in full.

One entrepreneur, Joseph Kato, was outstanding. He generated about half the total sales by selling more than 50 lamps per week ($930 per week), generating an income for himself of $200 per week. While Joseph Kato's sales have since stabilised at a lower level, he is our leading microfranchisee and his story can be found in the next section. If Joseph's sales are excluded, the microfranchises were selling on average six solar lamps per week, generating revenue of $90 per week. This created approximately $20 per week profit, or $3 per day additional income. Assuming that the solar lamps cut kerosene consumption in a household by two-thirds, and that prior to the intervention the households were spending $1 per week on kerosene, the pilot saved more than $40,000 per year on kerosene purchases by the households that now owned a solar lamp.

Joseph Kato's microfranchise success

One of the great success stories to come out of this pilot is Joseph. He was recruited for the original training through a local NGO called the Ugandan Women's Effort to Save Orphans, where he was working as a community-based trainer in the Masaka District of Uganda, south-west of Kampala. After training, Joseph used the NGO's networks and community groups that he had formed relationships with to sell nearly 600 solar lamps. Since the pilot phase, Joseph is now operating his Firefly microfranchise as a full-time occupation, paying himself a monthly salary of $120, well above the national average. In addition to this salary, Joseph has saved enough money to buy a plot of land and a motorcycle to help him with distribution. He has been able to pay his university tuition fee for a course in community development.

Joseph is now renting a storefront in Masaka town to help him distribute Barefoot Power's products. In the near future, Joseph is planning to recruit and implement training for 20 entrepreneurs in his region to operate microfranchises, in line with Base Technologies' scaling of the pilot. He is planning to join forces with another of the Firefly microfranchises in order to open a Firefly master franchise, from which he will supply and support a network of microfranchises. Joseph says he enjoys the business and being part of Barefoot Power's mission of bringing solar lighting to rural communities.

Challenges and improvement

Despite the pilot phase's success, we faced many challenges, as this section will explain.

Recruitment. Identification and recruitment of high-quality entrepreneurs is fundamental for creating a successful microfranchise programme. In our pilot we saw the best sales and business management results from people who had been involved in promoting behavioural change and had linkages with existing networks. The most successful entrepreneurs were those identified via NGO networks, often community-based trainers or popular opinion leaders. These people were already circulating in the communities and training people in how to better their lives. They had the skills to impart knowledge and experience to encourage behavioural change. Furthermore, these people had access to, and were trusted by, large networks of potential customers.

Attrition. The pilot revealed that most of the microfranchisees experienced a high level of sales at the beginning of the pilot that started to decline over time. We believe this occurred as the entrepreneurs met the needs of their immediate family, friends and associates but had difficultly pushing beyond these networks to create additional customers. This led to reduced interest from some entrepreneurs as their immediate market became saturated. Because we sold out of stock within 2.5 months of starting the pilot, it is difficult to assess the actual rate of attrition. We do believe, however, that given a steady supply of stock, many of the entrepreneurs would have trouble maintaining their sales at a level that would provide them with a reasonable income. This reinforces the need to recruit people with extensive networks, but it also highlights the need to provide more in-depth and tailored marketing support to the microfranchisees.

Decentralised support. The pilot encompassed four districts: Kampala, Wakiso, Jinja and Masaka. Jinja and Masaka, being further from our office in Kampala, were at a disadvantage compared to their peers because of the difficulty of providing adequate support for these areas. The pilot highlighted the need to decentralise support and re-supply of product in order to reduce transaction and opportunity costs for the microfranchises. The master franchise model we are developing should help resolve this. These master franchisors will distribute product at the wholesale level within the master franchise area; assist Base Technologies in recruiting and training suitable people within their franchise area to become Firefly microfranchises; and provide on-going marketing and business support to these microfranchises. Furthermore, a certain comradeship developed between the entrepreneurs during the pilot, where a natural exchange of ideas about marketing and sales took place. In moving to a master franchise model, a sense of community must be encouraged between the microfranchises within each master franchise area. In scaling, Base Technologies will endeavour to build a culture where the microfranchises are brought together by the master franchisor to facilitate exchange of ideas, build relationships and create identification with the franchise brand.

Simplification. During the pilot we found that some of the systems and processes that we developed were too complex and time consuming for the microfranchises and for Base Technologies. In particular, we found our credit-tracking, banking and incentive programme to be overly complex. We believe that simple concepts, training and operations will ease the path to replication and scale. For example, we are experimenting with batch processing of transactions with regards to credit payments and incentives. We are also developing a much more simple and easy-to-understand incentive (and penalty) programme for the microfranchises. The aids that we developed for marketing were also too complex. Our material mixed end-use instructions with the key benefit messages related to our products. We have redesigned our material to make a clear distinction between marketing and sales. Four simple benefit messages now form our marketing platform: better education, longer working hours, less money spent on kerosene and safer homes.

Capital for microfranchises via microfinance. Base Technologies implemented a successful supplier credit model during the pilot phase. There are two key reasons, however, why it is difficult for Base Technologies to expand this supplier credit model in Uganda: lack of sufficient capital and lack of capacity to collect debt at scale. Extending credit to microfranchises increases the financing required by Base Technologies, extends the time that capital is tied up in a sales cycle and reduces the return on investment. Microfinance institutions are designed, and have the capacity, to provide and collect small loans for enterprises. Microfinance institutions have also started to tap into the mainstream financial sector. Capital is therefore available for new small enterprise initiatives. There is no need to reinvent the wheel. The pilot proved that micro-energy franchisees were a success, and the franchises achieved 100% repayment rates. To effectively scale, Base Technologies will focus on its strength—creating and supporting the microfranchises—while encouraging linkages between the micro-entrepreneurs and several microfinance institutions in Uganda. Barefoot Power is partnering with BRAC in Uganda to add solar-lighting products to their health microfranchising model. We are also in discussions with other microfinance institutions to fund Base Technologies' Firefly microfranchises. Barefoot Power has formed a joint venture to replicate this model.

Supply gaps. One of the key challenges in the pilot was ensuring that a steady supply of products was available to the entrepreneurs. The supply gaps caused the entrepreneurs difficulties in maintaining income levels, as well as affecting their enthusiasm for remaining involved. Owing to financing issues for Base Technologies, it has taken over six months since the end of the pilot to achieve a steady supply of solar products to Uganda. While the supply gap between a pilot and scale-up is inevitable, adequate financial planning should be in place to ensure that this gap is kept to a minimum.

Conclusion

After completing what I believe is a successful pilot, Barefoot Power is expanding the microfranchise model in Uganda via Base Technologies. It aims to create a network of 150 Firefly microfranchises to bring modern lighting to 100,000 households, or 500,000 people, by the end of 2010. In Kenya, Barefoot Power, via its joint venture aims to set up 400 entrepreneurs who restock at the microfinance branches, using a variation on the franchise model. We also aim to reach 100,000 households in Kenya by the end of 2010. Barefoot Power will meet the goal we set in 2005, which was to reach 1 million people or 200,000 households by 2010. Barefoot Power is working hard to identify appropriate organisations with which we can collaborate to create access to modern lighting for millions more people. Beyond 2010, our impact is only limited by the finance that can be raised and the number of sound local organisations that are willing to partner with us in order to bring modern lighting to the poor. By 2020, we are confident that the kerosene lamp will be sitting on the shelf in the museum of poverty: a relic of the past.

6
Financing microfranchise start-up and growth

David Lehr
Consultant, International Economic Development, University of North Carolina, USA

Lisa Jones Christensen
Kenan-Flagler Business School, University of North Carolina, USA

Social businesses: constraints and opportunities

Accessing funds to start a business is always a challenge, but it can be even more difficult for social businesses that sell products or services to the very poor. Most of these enterprises focus on improving lives and serving low-income customers and rarely produce financial returns at the pace or scale that traditional investors require. Many lack the financial track record that a bank requires to extend a loan, and their founders and managers often have limited formal business education or prior business experience. These very real challenges, whether in isolation or in combination, inhibit these businesses' ability to secure the funds they need. Micro-franchising organisations face even greater challenges, as they usually require a substantial amount of time to develop and test their business models. It also takes additional time to recruit franchisees—and this must occur *before* the microfranchise can begin generating significant revenues. Furthermore, since there are few options for microfranchisees to secure financing, most microfranchising organisations need to assist with franchisee financing as part of recruitment or immediately thereafter.

Franchising and microfranchising basics: start-up expenses you can expect

This chapter provides readers with a guide to financing a microfranchise in the start-up phase as well as during different periods of growth. To accomplish this, we discuss elements that traditional franchising and microfranchising have in common and the areas in which they differ. In so doing, we highlight how the traditional franchising business model has been translated to a new context and how financing issues—particularly start-up financing issues—have been altered and adjusted in that transformation. We also include several case write-ups that illustrate how existing organisations approach and secure funding.

Franchising as practised in developed countries has historical precedent as far back as the Middle Ages when feudal lords would grant the rights for delivery of services, such as water wells, in exchange for a fee.[1] However, as mentioned in Chapter 2, most people credit Isaac Singer and the Singer Sewing Machine Company as establishing the first formal US franchise in the 1850s. Singer's first hurdle was a lack of finance to manufacture his sewing machines; his second was that he was introducing a new product that few people knew how to use and were reluctant to purchase without training. In response, Singer offered individuals the right to sell his machines in a particular sales territory in exchange for a licensing fee. He then used those fees to build the first sewing machines, selling them and training potential customers through this newly formed Singer network.

All forms of franchising distinguish between the entity that grants the right to sell goods or services in a certain territory (the franchisor) and the one that purchases that right and abides by its formal regulations (the franchisee). And, while most franchising literature focuses on the for-profit and developed-country examples of popular food franchises such as McDonald's or Burger King, the model applies to a much wider range of products and services. Whether invoking food products or a service offering as business examples, the for-profit franchise model has a long history and provides useful context for comparison to other types of franchising.

As many already know, microfranchising is a development tool that leverages the basic concepts of traditional franchising while also creating opportunities for the world's poorest people to own and manage their own businesses (Lehr 2008). Though its roots are in franchising, microfranchising differs from the practices of developed-country franchising in many important ways. In particular, it differs because the profit motive is secondary to social goals, and because the microfranchisor usually operates within a much more difficult working environment. Typical challenges for the microfranchisor include inadequate basic infrastructure (roads, water, power, human resources, etc.), coupled with hobbled supply chains and legal systems that do not enforce or respect contracts. In addition, the microfranchisee is often poorer and less educated than the typical developed-country franchisee

---

1 www.theukfranchisedirectory.net/page/history-of-franchising.php, accessed 12 August 2010.

Table 6.1 **Major franchising costs by business model**

	Developed-country franchisee	**Microfranchisee**
Franchise fees	• Buy-in fees are often a profit source for the franchisor • Covers cost of some training, support and site selection	• Buy-in fees designed specifically to be low and minimise barriers to entry • Covers costs and ensures franchisee has some 'skin in the game' • May be waived in some cases for philosophical reasons
Build out costs	• Pays for furniture, fixtures, signage and equipment • Usually must meet branding and image standards	• Pays for furniture, fixtures, signage and equipment; may be financed or subsidised by microfranchisor • Usually must meet branding and image standards
Inventory costs	• Initial stock typically paid for in advance	• Initial stock often available on consignment
Supply fees	• For purchase of other essential items for business operation, such as computers and machinery, for running day-to-day operations	• For purchase of other essential items for business operation, but generally very limited. If computers or machinery needed, usually financed by the microfranchisor
Working capital	• For day-to-day operations	• For day-to-day operations. Likely to be matched closely to businesses' actual cash flow
Legal fees	• Ensures compliance with local and national laws. Contract regulates and enforces overall business relationship	• Ensures compliance with local laws. Contract helps define business relationships but enforcement via formal legal system is uncommon
Travel and training	• Usually borne by the franchisee	• Usually borne by the microfranchisor

(Jones Christensen *et al.* 2010a). Despite these differences, there are critical commonalities between franchising and microfranchising: both rely on the creation and replication of a proven business model and both require following a consistent set of well-defined processes and procedures. They also require a symbiotic relationship between franchisor and franchisee and the need for financing. This need for financing is the main focus of this chapter.

When it comes to operating a for-profit developed-country franchise, there are typically six major start-up costs for the franchisee: (1) franchise fees that represent an upfront licensing or buy-in to join the network, which also covers costs of training and support;[2] (2) build-out costs, which typically cover furniture, fixtures, signage and equipment that usually must meet branding and image standards; (3) inventory fees to cover the cost of goods and which might have to meet required minimums; (4) supply fees to cover items not included in the build-out but essential to running the business to specifications; (5) working capital to cover day-to-day expenses;[3] and (6) legal fees to help navigate regulations and contracting issues. Clearly, all of these costs are not *directly* transferable to the microfranchising context, but most of them still occur at different levels of scale and scope. However, there can be additional costs that are unique to the microfranchising model. These additional costs include expenses or fees related to issues as simple as planning for travel and translation expenses (because most microfranchises operate in developing countries with founders or supporters still operating from developed countries) or for issues as complex as investigating international legal issues or building a supply chain and distribution system.

Certainly some of the fees are idiosyncratic to a particular business or country and there may be others apart from those described here. It is most critical to understand, however, that *both* microfranchisors and microfranchisees need start-up money and ongoing access to funds or else the entire business model implodes. The next sections clarify basic funding options currently available and include case studies to illustrate how different product or service microfranchises have successfully (or unsuccessfully) financed start-up and growth. For both the microfranchisor and the microfranchisee, different funding mechanisms play a smaller or larger role at different stages in the life-cycle of the business, influenced mainly by which of these two parties actually needs the money at the time.

Beyond the basics: options for financing microfranchise expenses

The funding paths below apply to both the microfranchisor and the microfranchisee. While the majority of these options are also available to traditional franchises, the descriptions are purposely tailored to the microfranchise context. We begin with actions that one individual can pursue (such as self-financing) and continue by identifying options (such as issuing equity or requesting consulting) that require the involvement of more people and institutions.

2 The more established a franchise is in terms of brand and reputation, the more valuable it is for a particular franchisee to participate. Franchisees with an established brand often have a competitive advantage over newcomers and can charge a premium for their brand. Microfranchisors, by contrast, are less focused on profiting from their brand via buy-in fees, but also rely on it as tool to recruit franchisees and garner community trust.

3 franchises.about.com/od/franchisebasics/tp/how-much-does-a-franchise-cost.htm, accessed 12 August 2010.

Self-financing

As the name implies, self-financing occurs when an individual uses his or her own funds to provide the initial monies for starting or running a business. Self-financing can also be done via a group lending model characterised by friends or family pooling money to allow for one member to use the accrued funds (Armendariz de Aghion and Morduch 2005: 57-83).[4] This form of funding is often referred to as 'bootstrap' financing.

Example (microfranchisee)

The Fan Milk franchise in Ghana sells ice cream and dairy products through individual microfranchisees who make sales using branded bicycles and coolers. Costs to become a franchisee are about $55, and reports are that most of the microfranchisees self-finance those upfront costs (Jones Christensen *et al.* 2010a). See the full-length Fan Milk case study in the following section for more information.[5]

Pay as you go/pay from profits (also called revenue-sharing or consignment system)

When microfranchisors allow microfranchisees to finance some or part of the cost of business using funds generated once the business is in operation, they are using the pay-as-you-go funding model. The microfranchisee continues to pay small sums to the microfranchisor until the original costs and fees (and potentially interest) have been paid in full. This category of funding also covers situations, sometimes referred to as consignment situations, where the microfranchisee is given *product* instead of cash and they are allowed to pay back the value of the product (and/or other microfranchising fees) using profits from sales of the product (see Van Kirk 2010). We consider this form of selling as synonymous with microfranchising. Consignments can be especially effective when introducing new products as they lower the risk for the microfranchisee and may increase their willingness to add offerings with which they are less familiar.

Example (microfranchisor and microfranchisee)

In the early days of operation, VisionSpring (formerly known as Scojo) provided women microfranchisees with an initial inventory of diagnostic kits and eyeglasses in a 'business in a bag' format. The women did not have to pay for the materials upfront and were able to set up their businesses selling eyeglasses (targeting the very poor with extremely blurred but correctable vision) and paying back the

---

4 See also Chapter 3.

5 Some authors use the term 'self-financing' for situations where the microfranchisee finances the costs of entering the business from profits accrued while running the business. We refer to this funding arrangement as 'pay as you go' and describe it next.

cost of the inventory from the profits they accrued from sales. This approach was highly successful in recruiting low-income women entrepreneurs and overcoming the resistance that they, or their family members, had to investing in a new business. Over time, VisionSpring discontinued this offering as they found it difficult to recoup the costs for managing and consigning the eyeglasses and the high turnover in sales associates. The early attempt to use this model remains an example of the pay-as-you-go scenario. Certainly, this scenario has merit in situations where managers can easily and inexpensively manage recovery costs, or where other microfranchisee options are not available.

Grants

These are transfers of money with no expectation of repayment. Governments, development agencies and foundations (see also 'Venture Philanthropy' below) are the most common sources of grants. Corporations and individuals can also directly provide grants or form non-profit foundations to advance their social—and sometimes business-related—agendas. For example, the William and Flora Hewlett Foundation is the grant-making extension of the Bill Hewlett monies related to the original Hewlett-Packard Corporation engineering. Most grants have significant screening processes and disbursement stipulations as well as follow-up reporting requirements to protect against fraud and to ensure that the use of funds accords with the grant-making institution's mission. Grants can provide funds that offset the cost of doing business either for the microfranchisor or the microfranchisee—or both. Because both parties may need significant time before either one can recoup investment costs, grants can provide a much-needed supply of funds in the early phases as the money doesn't have to recycle.

Example (microfranchisor and microfranchisee)

Nike Foundation gave Drishtee (see the following section) funds specifically to support female entrepreneurs. While these funds were disbursed via microfinance loans, the payment terms were subsidised via the grant from Nike. Training and ongoing support activities were also more comprehensive owing to the support from the Nike grant. In return, Drishtee management had to focus on recruiting women and report specific use of the funds relating to the support of women entrepreneurs.

Programme-related investments (PRIs)

Programme-related investments are investments made by foundations—usually loans at below-market rates or equity investments—that further the foundation's charitable goals and allow them to stretch their philanthropic dollars.[6] Foundations

---

6 Programme-related investments were established in the USA in the 1960s and are a specific tool used by USA-based foundations.

making PRIs expect a return on their investments through either repayment or return on equity, and they use a wide range of commercial vehicles including loans, loan guarantees, linked deposits and equity investments. PRIs have typically been used to fund capital projects, provide bridge loans or to offer liquidity to loan funds. Currently, there is a growing trend in making equity investments in charitable organisations or in commercial ventures for charitable purposes.[7]

Generally, PRIs supplement a foundation's existing grant programmes and are given to organisations that already have an established relationship as a grantee. When the organisation seeks additional funding—possibly for a project with income-generating potential—the foundation may suggest a PRI in place of a grant. For the funder, the repayment or the return of equity enables its funds to be recycled for other charitable purposes. For the recipient, the benefit is access to capital at lower rates than may be otherwise available. PRIs can be an intermediate step in fostering long-term sustainability and improving cash flow for the recipient.

Microloans

As elaborated in Chapter 7, a microloan is a very small loan to finance the start-up or extension of a small microbusiness. Microcredit or microloans can range in size from the equivalent of hundreds of dollars to the equivalent of thousands, but average loan sizes are less than US$1,000.[8] Microloans have expanded from a focus on the poor in developing countries to reaching the poor in developed countries, with the average loan size in the USA close to $6,000.[9] Thus, microloans are increasingly a financing option available in developed *and* developing country markets.

Microloans typically carry interest rates at or below in-country market rates and are often made by microfinance institutions. Because the loans require frequent partial repayment (loan repayments are usually spaced from one week to one month apart) the *effective* annual interest rates range from about 20% to 50%.[10] While these weekly or bimonthly repayment schedules and the meetings that surround them were originally created with the preferences of the working poor in mind, research indicates that some borrowers in more mature businesses find the meeting frequency to be an expensive distraction (Karlan *et al.* 2006). The use of microfinance loans to microfranchisees is still in the early stages because often the payment terms are not well suited to the cash-flow needs of most microfranchisees. Many microfinance institutions have responded by creating new loan products targeted to individuals. Such new products may make microloans a more widely used

---

7 See www.socialcapitalmarkets.net for more information on social investing or commercial investments in charitable and social-purpose organisations.

8 ACCIONUSA, 'Microfinance FAQs', www.accionusa.org/home/support-u.s.-microfinance/about-accion-usa/microfinance-faq.aspx#8, accessed 12 August 2010. Unless otherwise noted all currency amounts are in US$.

9 Ibid.

10 Ibid.

option for microfranchisees. In the case of microfranchisors, however, the micro-loans are generally too small to serve their needs.

Example (microfranchisor and microfranchisee)

Village Phone is a microfranchise opportunity intentionally tied to a microfinance organisation (discussed briefly in Chapter 3). It was started in Bangladesh under the direction of Grameen Bank and has been replicated and adapted in Uganda, Rwanda, the Philippines, Cambodia, Haiti and Indonesia.[11] The goal of the pro-gramme is to offer the world's rural poor access to reliable and affordable telecom-munications on a commercially sustainable basis. Via a microfinance loan, local entrepreneurs can purchase a Village Phone kit that includes a mobile phone, an external antenna (for better coverage) a discounted service plan and an opera-tions manual. These grass-roots entrepreneurs, Village Phone operators, then rent the use of the phone on a per-call basis providing affordable telecommunications access in their community while earning enough to repay their loan and raise their level of income. Once they have paid back the loan, the Village Phone kit is theirs to keep and to continue using. (*Note:* the fact that the microfranchisors can pay back their loans using profits from the business also makes Village Phone an example of pay-as-you-go financing.)

Loans

For the purposes of this chapter, 'loans' refer to funds obtained at commercial rates from banks, a commercial investors or individuals, as opposed to funds obtained from microfinance institutions or informally from friends, or the loan of a physical asset. Commercial banks are generally reluctant to offer long-term loans to small firms or to social-purpose firms—especially if they are not backed by collateral—and may be more eager to extend short-term demand loans, seasonal lines of credit, or single-purpose loans for machinery or equipment. This type of bias is part of the reason that microfranchisees typically seek microloans and partially explains why microfranchisors often seek grants and PRI monies before they pursue commer-cial loans. Loans, however, are appropriate for franchisors and franchisees or for established ventures in the developed world, and they may be a funding source for microfranchisors that are showing strong growth.

Equity

Equity investment generally refers to the buying and holding of shares of stock (fractional portions of ownership) by individuals and investment funds. The own-ers earn returns from dividends and capital gain as the value of the stock rises.

---

11 Grameen Foundation, villagephonedirect.org/contents/index.php?option=com_conten t&task=view&id=17&Itemid=37, accessed 12 August 2010.

Companies seeking to raise funds may use equity financing (stock sales) instead of, or in addition to, debt financing (loans). To raise equity finance, a company creates new shares and sells them for cash. The new share owners become part-owners of the company and share in the risks and rewards of the company's business. Selling equity to the public often requires the assistance of investment banking or legal firms that help to navigate the regulatory environment and to find potential investors. Due to the costs of this approach and the relative size of most microfranchising organisations, this is usually not a practical option. Private equity investors who operate essentially as venture capitalists may be more promising sources of funds, and they are described immediately below.

Venture capital

A venture capitalist is typically a high-risk investor who seeks an equity or ownership position in a start-up or early-stage company perceived as having the potential for high financial returns. In return for providing capital, contacts and management assistance, the venture capitalist (or the venture capital firm) typically asks for a significant percentage of ownership and/or a position in the company or on its board. Venture capitalists are usually very involved with the strategic management of the companies in which they invest and often use their networks to connect the company with potential partners and additional personnel or resources. One rule of thumb is that venture capitalists seek out small firms that have the potential to return ten times their original investment in five years or less (Harvard Business School 2005: Ch. 6: 13). Most venture capitalists intend to harvest their investment during a public offering of stock, sale to a larger firm or with follow-on sales of company shares. We mention venture capitalists because they can play a significant role in funding developed-country franchise opportunities at the idea stage and because they provide historical background with which to understand *social* investors (described below). However, venture capitalists currently play a very marginal role in the microfranchising field. Any role they do play is usually limited to supporting and funding the microfranchisor, not the microfranchisee.

Angel investors

These are a subset of venture capital investors who invest their own funds rather than the pooled funds of many investors. Angel capital tends to fill the funding gap between seed funding and venture capital, as it provides smaller amounts than venture capital but higher amounts than seed loans or gifts. Angel investors also tend to invest for reasons beyond pure monetary reward and thus can be a particularly strategic resource for microfranchisors attempting to obtain the equivalent of second-round financing. They are also a 'bridge' between pure venture capital and social investors. Most angels, but not all, expect repayment although they may offer generous terms and timetables.

Social investors and impact investing

Social investors, often also called impact investors, differ from a typical investor in that they seek to achieve both financial return *and* social impact while still relying on the same tools that a venture capitalist uses. Social investors take a double- (or in some cases triple-) bottom-line approach to their investment capital, and they typically attribute real value to the social or environmental return in their investment decision-making. They often, but not always, are willing to exchange a lower economic return for potential social or environmental impact. For the social investor, the key metric is not solely a company's valuation but also a social outcome, such as the litres of clean water delivered, the cases of malaria prevented, the tons of CO_2 emissions averted or the number of lives changed in a substantive and demonstrable way (Trelstad 2009: 2). Social investors can be high-net-worth individuals as well as mission-driven non-profits, for-profits, governments, foundations or corporations. Most social investors source their capital from philanthropic and commercial sources. Like traditional venture capitalists, they use debt and equity, but they tend to be much more flexible about repayment terms based on evaluations of what is best for the social-purpose recipient. Social investors also accept longer time-frames before they expect a financial or social return. Besides providing valuable capital, social investors often serve as consultants or marketers and can play a key role in addressing management challenges, in developing partnerships and in sharing what they learn with a broader audience. Social investors may be a particularly good source of financing for microfranchising organisations, and social venture organisations such as Acumen Fund and Bamboo Finance have made significant investments in this area already.

Micro-equity conversion (also called sliding scale of ownership or BOOT model)[12]

Micro-equity conversion refers to the gradual transfer of ownership of the microfranchise to an operator who has been selected and tutored by the microfranchisor. Conversion typically involves significant coaching and mentoring, which is the main feature that differentiates it from the pay-as-you-go model above. The ultimate goal of this arrangement is for the ownership of the microfranchise to transfer to the operator, thereby eventually making him or her a microfranchisee rather than simply an employee. The micro-equity method of financing is time-consuming, as precedent suggests the process can take from six months to one year or longer for this type of transfer to take place. In some applications of the model, the operator earns a regular salary during his or her time as an employee and also has the opportunity to earn profit-sharing money once the microfranchisor has recouped start-up costs. Over time, the model assumes that the operator uses funds from

12 See Gibson 2007.

salary and profit-sharing to purchase ownership and become more invested in the business.

BOOT stands for 'build, own, operate and transfer' of ownership and describes the process from the point of view of the microfranchisor (Gibson 2007). (*Note:* to provide context around the emergence and use of this model [and the BOOT acronym in particular] it is critical to note that the model has typically been used when NGOs sponsored and funded the creation of a microfranchise but wished to withdraw from full-time sponsorship and management. Using micro-equity or the BOOT model is one way to withdraw from sponsorship without closing the business or harming the franchisees and employees [Gibson 2007].)

Example (conversion or transfer of ownership of an NGO-established microfranchise)

In 2009 Mercy Corps began a health microfranchise (Tiendas de Salud) in Guatemala to increase access to basic medicines and health-related products in isolated rural communities. Incomes are extremely low in these communities and few businesses exist—and there is almost no data on the purchasing power within the community. Due to these facts, a foundation grant provided the initial funding for testing the market and for developing the microfranchise and a microloan programme for potential microfranchisees. Now that the model is proving viable, Mercy Corps is partnering with the main supplier—Guatemala's largest private-sector pharmacy chain—to incorporate the Tiendas de Salud into its business model. In this case, the NGO (Mercy Corps) took both the business and reputational risk of establishing a microfranchise in order to prove to a commercial entity that a viable market opportunity existed. Since developing local management capacity and local ownership is a key piece of Mercy Corp's development model, it will exit from the Tiendas de Salud over time and transfer management to the private sector chain.

In-kind and management support

In-kind support from a funder can have significant monetary value. Forms of support can range from supplying products or raw materials to a microfranchisee free or at a reduced price to active participation in the microfranchisor's board of directors. This kind of support from board members and investors is common and is appropriate for microfranchisees and microfranchisors to request and pursue.

Example (microfranchisor)

Accenture has a programme for promising mid-career managers, which helps them gain field experience with social-purpose organisations in the developing world. In 2007, an Accenture consultant spent six weeks in India working with Drishtee's senior management to develop a financing model for a community-owned and -managed biomass electricity plant. The Accenture manager's in-country costs (salary, housing and health insurance) were covered by Accenture, while Drishtee gained access to talent that would otherwise have been prohibitively expensive.

Each funding source above has different levels of difficulty, complexity and/or shared risk associated with its access. And, while each option can be pursued at any stage in the microfranchise business life-cycle, some funding options are more likely to be leveraged at start-up, with others more prominent during the growth or the maturity phases of an enterprise. See Figure 6.1 for a depiction of how funding needs and funding sources vary depending on the life-cycle stage of the business.

Figure 6.1 **The microfranchise funding life-cycle**

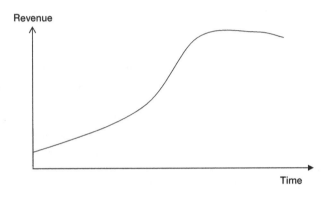

Start-up	Growth	Maturity
Personal savings	Internal cash flow	Internal cash flow
Loans from friends	Bank loans	Secondary infusions
Microloans	Microloans	(private or public)
Consumer credit	Asset-based loans/leases	Loan guarantees

Source: Adapted from Harvard Business School 2005: Ch. 6, Figure 6-1

Funding experiences of microfranchises: case studies

In our experience most microfranchisors and microfranchisees leverage multiple funding sources in the course of starting and growing their businesses (this finding is reflected in Fig. 6.1, where multiple sources of funds are listed in the same stage, while some sources repeat or carry through several stages). To illustrate the interplay between and among the various funding options, the next section provides in-depth descriptions of several microfranchise organisations. Each one is at a different stage in its business development, and they represent a mix of non-profit and for-profit organisations, with each using different combinations of funding sources for start-up and/or ongoing operations. The organisations profiled below are:

- HealthStore Foundation (Kenya and Rwanda)
- Drishtee (India)
- Fan Milk (Ghana)
- Coast Coconut Farms (Kenya)
- Living Goods (Uganda)

For each case study, we address the following:

- **Overview.** What does the organisation do? What social problem does it address using the franchise model?
- **Financial model.** What methods has the organisation used for financing its operations? What about for financing its microfranchisees? If applicable, how has funding changed over time?
- **Results.** A short mention of accomplishments to date is followed by discussion of linkages between results (or lack of results) and the funding situation

The HealthStore Foundation (HSF/CFWshops)

Overview

The HealthStore Foundation (HSF) was created in 1997 to improve access to high-quality essential drugs and basic healthcare and prevention services for children and families in the developing world. Using a particular franchising model, HSF has developed a network of 85 Child and Family Wellness (CFW) shops and clinics, primarily in Kenya, to provide marginalised populations with basic outpatient services and access to vital medicines. CFWshops address and target the most common diseases—those responsible for 70% of illness and death. CFWshops are purposely located in rural market centres or peri-urban areas with populations of at least 5,000 people and are owned and run by trained health workers or nurses (a prerequisite for becoming a franchisee), who make a modest living selling hygiene products and competitively priced drugs.

Financial model

Most individual CFWshops become profitable around the sixth month, and they subsequently provide a living income to the nurses and community health workers who own them. Until 2009, however, HSF has operated the overall network as a humanitarian endeavour and has not made profitability at the franchisor or country level a goal. Thus, income from the franchisees recoups only a small fraction of costs (about 5%), with the remainder covered with funds raised through grants and private donations. In 2008, for example, the network required core support from the non-profit HSF of almost $850,000. HSF's overall revenues to date have comprised initial fees paid by franchisees and mark-ups on products sold to franchisees. In 2008, HSF provided care to over 500,000 people for an all-in cost to donors (covering all costs worldwide) of $2.40 per visit.[13]

The foundation is supported by a number of institutions including United States Agency for International Development (USAID), Acumen Fund, ExxonMobil Foundation and individual donors. However, given the costs of raising donor monies and the uncertainly of continued funding—coupled with management's belief that a grant-funded model cannot scale as well as a commercial franchise model— HSF is presently restructuring in Kenya as a for-profit company and plans to fuel the growth of the CFW network in Kenya using social venture-capital investments.

In the past, the typical franchisee invested $300 of his or her funds to go into business, matched by a below-market loan (1% interest, repaid over three years) from HSF of about $1,200 for initial inventory, coupled with donor support of approximately $3,500. This combination of funds covered the start-up costs including furnishings and equipment, outfitting of the clinic and training on the CFW system. Patients pay directly for the services that they obtain at an average cost per visit of $1.00 at clinics and $0.51 at shops. This includes both the fees for consultation and for the purchase of any required drugs. The patients pay on a per-visit basis, although in some instances a CFWshop will treat a patient without receiving the treatment fee upfront and will try to collect later. HSF intends to integrate insurance schemes into its model and also develop a programme that subsidises care for the lowest-income patients while still maintaining the integrity of the business model and extending its reach even further down the economic pyramid.

Historically, the CFWshops network has served as low-income a clientele as possible while continuing to have profitable franchisees. This has led to a wide spectrum of financial outcomes for franchisees: some have paid back their three-year loans in less than six months, while others have consumed most of their profits servicing their debt, threatening their ability to survive. Similarly, HSF discontinued charging franchisees sales-based royalties in 2004–05 because of fears franchisees were under-reporting sales to avoid paying royalties.

13 This may be someone walking into a CFW outlet and being diagnosed and treated, someone walking into a CFW outlet and buying a hygiene/prevention item, someone at a school receiving HIV education from a CFW franchisee or staff member, someone in a nearby community attending a CFW event promoting proper use of bed nets, etc. Of the more than 500,000 patients and customers served in 2008, approximately two-thirds were walk-in clients with the other one-third served through outreach events.

Restructuring

Despite successfully serving over 2 million patients and customers efficiently since 2000, HSF began dramatically changing course in 2008. The first phase involved management change in Kenya and a reduction of headcount there from 38 to 14 employees, coupled with the opening of an additional 15 CFW clinics in the autumn of 2008. The second phase is a formal restructuring designed to yield long-term financial sustainability. A new for-profit entity, HealthStore East Africa (HSEA), will open CFW outlets in different geographical areas striving to become a self-sustaining network of approximately 300 outlets. Meanwhile, the existing 82 CFW outlets in Kenya will continue under the umbrella of HSF's affiliate non-profit entity in Kenya, supported by donations, with the hope that many will be transferred to the for-profit as their performance improves. Administrative personnel and associated costs of approximately $200,000 per year will be borne by the non-profit entity.

Additional key changes include:

- **Site selection.** All new CFW clinics will be located in more densely populated urban slums and rural towns

- **Franchisee selection.** HSEA will select new franchisees not only based on their clinical qualifications and skills, but also according to their business acumen and entrepreneurial drive

- **Outsourcing.** HSF has outsourced procurement, storage and distribution functions to a high-quality drug distributor in Kenya. This has improved the quality of its drug procurement and distribution and helped to avoid staff costs not directly linked to its core business

- **Efficiency.** Aside from the addition of one full-time field representative per 20 new CFW outlets, HSEA plans to add only two more full-time employees while expanding to 300 outlets, modelling its efficiency after leading franchisors in the private industry

Results

Since its inception in 2000, the network has provided for approximately 2,000,000 patient visits, mainly in Kenya and primarily for lower- or middle-income women and children subsisting on agriculture-based products and income. In May 2008, HSF launched its first CFW clinic in Rwanda and, over the next five years, pending funding, HSF plans to create up to 12 more CFW franchise networks in sub-Saharan Africa while continuing to grow the networks in Kenya and Rwanda. Much of this projected growth depends on the success of the transition to the use of a for-profit operating company in Kenya as well as HSF's ability to raise the necessary funds to launch networks in new countries.

Sources of funds

Sources of funds include franchise fees, grants, donations, product margins and below-market loans.

Drishtee

Overview

Drishtee is a for-profit social enterprise in India that has created a network of microentrepreneurs in India's rural villages that sell products and services that benefit local residents, improve information access and generate employment opportunities. Through over 4,000 microfranchised kiosks or small shops in 12 states of India, Drishtee and its microfranchisees deliver fee-based services, including education courses, microfinance and healthcare. Running parallel to its franchising network, Drishtee also supplies rural village retailers in the same areas with fast-moving consumer goods (FMCGs) such as soaps, hygiene products and biscuits. Drishtee was established in 2000, and has been operating on a near break-even basis since 2005. Drishtee's approach has always centred on rapid prototyping to incubate new ideas around efficient rural–urban market linkages, and its model has shifted over time. In the past, each kiosk offered a mix of services and products from Drishtee and usually coupled these offerings with local services such as printing and digital photography and sales of non-Drishtee items such as stationery or batteries that generate both revenue and customer traffic. More recently, in 2008, Drishtee began to segment its services and require each kiosk to focus on a particular offering of health, microfinance or education. FMCG products are now sold exclusively through the parallel FMCG network. Even though the services and FMCG businesses are run separately, the FMCG network helps Drishtee lower per-unit service costs by achieving economies of scale in distribution, site visits and back-office record-keeping.

Financial model

Drishtee's funding came originally from revenues the founders were generating from conducting computer classes and designing websites as well as from friends and family. To date, Drishtee has raised over $6 million from funders such as Acumen Fund and Nike Foundation to meet its ongoing needs for expansion capital and has received grants, loans and equity investment, as well as loan capital to sponsor low-interest loans to entrepreneurs. The investment outlay for an individual microfranchisee is approximately $200 for a health entrepreneur, while it ranges between $650 and $1,000 for entrepreneurs offering services in education and microfinance.[14] While some of these monies come from savings or family

---

14 Fees for education and microfinance services are variable as they are aided by technology, and its purchase—whether through computers or point-of-sales machines.

members, many Drishtee entrepreneurs need additional financing in the range of $250 to $1,250 to establish and scale their operations. In the past, Drishtee provided financing directly, but since this is not one of its key strengths, today it works with financing partners wherever possible.

Drishtee's franchising revenues come from the following sources, with the first two being most significant. Drishtee also licenses some of its services to competing networks, though this is not yet a significant source of earnings.

- **A one-time licence fee.** This fee has decreased over time from almost $1,000 when Drishtee first began, to approximately $150 today. It has been lowered to reduce the barriers and risk of becoming a franchisee and to allow franchisees more flexibility in determining their equipment purchases (many choose to purchase a computer, camera and printer), while still covering Drishtee's training and logistics costs for adding a franchisee

- **Transaction revenue based on sales.** Drishtee has a revenue-share agreement based on profit margins or a negotiated vendor arrangement. Roughly 80% of the profit goes to the franchisee and 20% goes to Drishtee

- **Microloan processing fees and annual interest on loans** accessed via kiosks

- **Health partnerships with revenue-sharing** on services offered through partner medical facilities in semi-urban areas

Outside the microfranchise network, Drishtee also earns money from sales of FMCG products bought by the rural retailers it supplies. It also operates a number of initiatives that vary in revenue structure. These include business-process outsourcing services, government-supported research projects related to livelihood generation, and web-based access to government records (EPK) at semi-urban centres.

Results

By May 2009, had established over 4,000 microfranchised kiosks. Each Drishtee kiosk caters to approximately 1,000 to 1,250 households (at an average of five persons per household), the majority of which have an aggregated income of less than $2 a day. With a vision to reach out to every village in India and beyond, Drishtee has set an ambitious target of creating 10,000 microfranchisees by the end of 2012.

Motivating and retaining microfranchisees has been a constant challenge that relies on a combination of proper training, good service and an appropriate earnings opportunity. To increase focus, Drishtee has required its microfranchisees to concentrate on a specific set of services: health, microfinance or education. Interestingly, Drishtee charges for essentially everything: a membership card in its health programme, or an application to sign up for computer classes. Even the application form for becoming a franchisee is charged for as part of the licence fee. In rural India, many non-profit and government agencies have provided services for free, though these have generally been low quality and unsustainable. By establishing a fee-for-service mind-set, Drishtee is trying to break this welfare mentality while also ensuring that it covers its costs for things like printing and distribution.

Sources of funds

Drishtee's sources of funds include profits from operations, fee for service, social investors, grants, donations, loans, in-kind support, self-financing and pay as you go.

Fan Milk

Overview

The Fan Milk Limited Company was incorporated in Ghana in 1962 and sells ice cream, yoghurt, ice lollies and juices. Fan Milk distributes its products in two ways: through existing retailers such as shops, supermarkets, hotels and schools, or through its network of 8,000 bicycle vendors who operate as individual micro-franchisees. The microfranchisee sells the products from a bicycle outfitted with a branded cooler purchased directly from Fan Milk. The Fan Milk Company (the microfranchisor) supplies the mobile vendors primarily through company depots. Each morning the microfranchisees retrieve their inventory from a depot or agent's store and they return unsold products from the previous day. Fan Milk operates 11 regional depots around the country where microfranchisees can purchase their inventory. In addition, Fan Milk has a network of 'agents' who run independent smaller depots. Entrepreneurs can become agents if they have a minimum of two new freezers, their own coolers and bicycles and their own network of bicycle vendors. The company's major shareholders are the Danish investor Fan Milk International Denmark, the Danish Industrialisation Fund for Developing Countries and the Ghanaian company Enterprise Insurance.

Financial model

On average, vendors buy daily inventory worth $33 and make a daily profit of $5.50. Vendors make a fixed profit and also receive a monthly commission from Fan Milk. While some sell from boxes balanced on their heads or from carts, the majority have bicycles. Fan Milk microfranchisees have start-up costs of approximately 20 Ghanaian cedis (approximately $14) to cover the bicycle equipped with a cooler that prominently displays the Fan Milk logo. Fan Milk provides free bicycle repair, training on product handling and prizes to top sellers. Fan Milk also requires all microfranchisees to save 10% of their profits, deposited into a bank and returned to the microfranchisees when they leave the company. Most vendors stay with Fan Milk for about eight years and the majority indicate they are saving their money to start their own businesses or to continue their education (Fairbourne *et al.* 2007).

Results

Fan Milk Limited in Ghana has 350 employees and over 8,000 franchisee distributors and earns approximately $10 million in profits annually. Its franchised distribution network has also expanded into Togo, Benin and Burkina Faso. The model is fully vetted. One sign of its success is that while some vendors ultimately save enough capital to become agents, typically vendors use their savings to start other businesses or to further their education. This type of outcome invites one to question the measure of success: is it a long-term and profitable relationship with the microfranchisor or the graduation to new business development?

Sources of funds

Fan Milk's sources of funds include profits from operations, self-financing and equity.

Coast Coconut Farms

Overview

Coast Coconut Farms was started in 2006 by the Pope Foundation as a social business and economic development project designed to lift the rural poor out of poverty. Coast Coconut Farms' mission is to provide sustainable employment, management and ownership opportunities for the rural people of Kenya and, eventually, other countries. This is done by offering access to capital, equipment and training to create organic coconut oil harvested from wild coconuts. Coast Coconut Farms' vision is to create thousands of sustainable livelihoods for the rural poor, particularly women, using Fair Trade Principles. Coast Coconut Farms believes in being earth-friendly and uses a fully sustainable production process with no waste. The coconut water is used by local residents, while the coconut husks and shells become fuel to dry the coconut meat and are converted to charcoal for cooking (also helping decrease the environmental impact from firewood collection). The lye created by this process is used to make soap with the residual—called seed cake—becoming feed for the local livestock. The company operates on two levels: first, it runs a small-scale coconut-oil processing facility, and second, it is launching a single-family processing unit that individuals can purchase and operate as a microfranchise opportunity.

The processing facility employs approximately 25 rural Kenyan women and is supplied by a local farm cooperative comprising 60 farmers who grow and harvest coconuts. With two shifts the factory processes 1,800 coconuts each day to produce 120 litres per day. Owing to increases in demand for the oil, Coast Coconut Farms is incorporating cutting-edge manufacturing techniques to increase productivity and build management skills among its workers. To increase sales, the company is creating a network of microfranchises suitable for a rural family living in Kenya. The model will consist of a kit to be purchased by a microfranchisee that would enable her to produce coconut oil to sell to neighbours for local consumption and also back to Coast Coconut Farms for use in skin-care products such as soap and lotions. The kit will include tools to crack, grate, dry and press the coconut to produce oil. To enable this microfranchise, the company contracted with a US university to develop an inexpensive hydraulic oil press and drying oven, two essential elements in the kit. The oven design is three times more efficient in its use of fuel than the three-stone open fire most commonly used in Kenya for cooking. Ovens may also be built of local bricks to further reduce the cost. The coconut-oil hand-press would be located just outside on the porch and an area to collect the nuts could be outside as well.

Financial model

The coconut-press microfranchise will allow rural women to work from home at a wage several times greater than the average. For example, in six hours, a group of five rural women who own a microfranchise could press 12 litres of fresh oil. Each litre could be produced for $1.00 and sold back to the company for $3.00. This would provide the group with a daily income of $36 (over $7 per person) as compared to the $1 per day typical of other rural Kenyan families. To purchase the press, microfranchisees will acquire a microcredit loan from Yehu Microfinance Trust (a rural Kenyan microcredit organisation also run by the Pope Foundation.) The initial loan will be for around $350 and should require approximately six months to repay. Even during the repayment period, microfranchisees will be making more take-home pay than the majority of their rural neighbours. Once the loan is repaid, microfranchisees can experience a standard of living perhaps unimagined prior to working with Coast Coconut Farms.

Results

Currently, Coast Coconut Farms has created employment for over 100 Kenyan families, including the farmers' cooperatives that harvest the coconuts. The 25 Kenyan factory workers (including three managers) make around Ksh250 per day (about $3), while the average income for the area is around Ksh60 per day (around 75¢). The organisation anticipates having 36 employees by the end of 2009. Also, at 2008 levels of demand, Coast Coconut Farms will purchase nearly 550,000 coconuts from local farmers during the year. Virtually all of the wages the Coast Coconut workers earn, along with the money coconut farmers earn by selling to an established customer such as Coast Coconut Farms, get flushed into the local economy. This has a multiplier effect, providing even more jobs and opportunities for community residents. At the current wage and price for coconut purchases, nearly $100,000 will permeate annually into an impoverished region from a simple coconut plant.

Results are still pending for the microfranchise portion of the business. However, the organisation has received initial funding to start up the microfranchise from Bamboo Finance. It also has significant contracts with US distributors to ensure an end-market for the individual suppliers. In contrast to Drishtee and the

HealthStore Foundation, Coast Coconut Farms has incorporated a microfinance entity directly within its model and is thus able to offer microcredit loans on terms that best match the microfranchisees' needs.

Sources of funds

Coast Coconut Farms' sources of funds include self-financing, microloans, social investors, programme-related investments, grants and in-kind support.

Living Goods

Overview

Living Goods (LG) operates Avon-like networks of door-to-door health promoters who make a modest income selling essential health products at prices affordable to the poor. The model is designed to significantly improve access to simple, proven health interventions focusing on the short list of diseases (malaria, diarrhoeal disease, worms and TB) that account for over two-thirds of mortality and can be prevented and/or treated at very low cost. LG also improves livelihoods by providing rural women with a reliable source of income as health promoters, by keeping wage earners healthy and productive and by averting costly medical treatments through prevention. Living Goods targets primarily rural and peri-urban communities whose residents live on $0.50 to $2 a day. Their residents generally suffer from inadequate access to essential health products, are under-served by the existing public and private health infrastructure and have relatively high disease burdens. Central to Living Goods' strategy is to partner with local NGOs, community groups and microfinance organisations to exploit these organisations' existing infrastructure for recruiting and possibly financing and supporting health promoters. Its first partnership began with microfinance institution BRAC in Uganda in early 2007.

Funding

Living Goods' initial funding came from smaller family foundations—almost all based in the San Francisco area—that were looking to support business-based interventions and willing to fund an innovative, though unproven, approach. As Living Goods has grown, both its credibility and funding needs have increased, and it has turned to larger foundations that are able to make larger grants. Living Goods expects to achieve sustainability within the next five to seven years and to secure non-grant sources of funds during this period. Living Goods earns money solely from a small margin on products that its microfranchisees sell and does not currently charge a separate microfranchising fee.[15] Microfranchisees each stock

15 Living Goods is dedicated to improving supply-chain efficiencies and decreasing the number of players between the manufacturer and the consumer. Its microfranchisees sell products at roughly 20% above wholesale pricing.

roughly $50 of product, which they receive from LG on starting their business. The $50 is financed by Living Goods,[16] and is repaid over a 48-week period via a microfinance loan (15% APR; just over $1 per payment) administered by BRAC. In addition, Living Goods provides training and lends each of the microfranchisees a 'business-in-a-box' that includes an LG uniform, signage, a branded delivery bag, a storage locker, sales and health messaging tools and a product and operational guide. Each microfranchisee has specific sales and performance targets and sells a broad range of products that includes everyday items such as sanitary pads and soap, as well as items used to treat specific illnesses. LG endeavours to set prices at or below relevant competitors and may also distribute donated products free or below market to help drive traffic and generate sales. Ongoing monitoring and field visits to ensure high product quality and agent performance are critical to the model.

Results

Living Goods operates only in Uganda today. Since implementing its partnership with BRAC in 2008, it has established 550 microfranchisees (as of November 2009) with many already operating on a sustainable basis. The next step in its model is to ensure that each branch or distribution point is also sustainable and covering its own costs. In the longer term, within the next 5–7 years, LG is striving to achieve country-level sustainability and also to cover the costs of a very small headquarters staff. Management also envisions Living Goods becoming a platform not just for health, but also for related products in the water, energy and agricultural sectors. Living Goods' core vision is to replicate its system across the developing world, prioritising Tanzania, Mozambique, Rwanda, Kenya, Ghana and India. Given the focus on partnerships, the operational and partnership model will vary from country to country. That said, some of the basic precepts are still being tested in Uganda. Living Goods was established to achieve very specific health impacts, and management considers this the most critical part of its mission. To measure the primary objectives of reducing mortality rates for children and lowering fertility rates for women, Living Goods is implementing randomised control-based research in collaboration with the MIT Poverty Action Lab.

Sources of funds

Living Goods' sources of funds include profits from operations, social investors, grants, donations, loans, in-kind support and pay as you go.

---

16 Initial inventory levels were set at $100. This was lowered to find the optimal balance between having stock on hand and minimising the costs of carrying a larger inventory.

Closing comments: social capital, blended value propositions, and the future of development financing

This chapter opened by contrasting traditional franchising and microfranchising to highlight their different foci on profit and social benefit and where the costs of doing business differ between the two models. The first section illustrated that while the *categories* of expenses are similar, the scale and scope of the expenses within those categories differ significantly. The section also illustrates that micro-franchises are typically smaller and less expensive to enter (in absolute terms) than their traditional franchise counterparts. Microfranchises tend to operate in developing countries whereas typical franchises operate in developed *and* developing markets. Despite these and other differences, the two business models share the need for franchisors and franchisees to cooperate in order to replicate successfully. Both models are also similar in that franchisors and franchisees of all types need funds at different stages in the business life-cycle. Thus, the second and third sections of this chapter clarify how funding options familiar in the world of traditional franchising become altered and adjusted when applied to the microfranchise context.

One way to make sense of how funding differs in these contexts is to think about the role of time and how it changes between the two types of franchise. Our experience and research consistently show that, in contrast to traditional franchises, microfranchises need more time to develop their business approach before they can become profitable (Jones Christensen *et al.* 2010a, 2010b; Lehr 2008). The need for more time means that every element of traditional financing needs to adapt accordingly in order to apply to the microfranchising field. The implications of the longer time-frames for profitability have spillover effects: both microfranchisors and microfranchisees may need a longer period to repay loans, both parties may need different terms on their grants or loans, and investors of all types may need to adjust their metrics and expectations accordingly. Making adjustments for time-to-profitability or true-to-break-even effects is one way to smooth the transition from a traditional franchise perspective to a microfranchise-appropriate perspective. However, even making adjustments for time to profitability or time to cost-recovery does not alter the reality that franchises *and* microfranchises need different amounts and types of funding depending on their stage in the business life-cycle. Some of the most cited new trends in finance—such as the move to blended value investing, social investing, social-capital investments and sustainable investing— all include provisions and support for development issues. By extension, these trends also support microfranchising. As the line between traditional and social investing becomes increasingly blurred, more investors and firms than ever before are considering approaches that blend elements of the traditional model with elements of development and social change. Microfranchising fits this description.

We predict that the number of firms and individuals with social-purpose investment goals will increase, and that increase will come with a concomitant rise in the amount of money available to the microfranchise sector. Soon, the bottleneck for the industry will not be financial resources. Instead, the human resource and infrastructure constraints will become the next area of focus. Until that time comes, however, financing will continue to be one of the major constraints to the success of the microfranchise field. Ideally, the ideas and concepts explained in this chapter will help both individuals and organisations as they seek to work around this challenge to build and grow effective and profitable microfranchises.

7

MicroLoan Foundation
A case study in Malawi

Peter Ryan
MicroLoan Foundation, UK

My first experience of franchising dates from the late 1960s. My father was working for Singer, the US company, to pioneer the use of franchisees as a way to service the large number of sewing machines that they had been selling successfully since the mid-1850s. He had been working as managing director of its household appliance division to launch this entirely new venture in the UK. It was a highly competitive market, which meant that the project was in reality doomed to failure before it had begun. And so at the early age of 50, like many before and since, he was forced to ask himself the question 'what next'?

Franchising had been already predicted as the next way forward in the USA, and there were many articles forecasting that it would be the same in the UK. My father subsequently decided to set up a company, European Franchise Marketing, to sell franchises to would-be entrepreneurs. It sounded brilliant, but the market in the UK was simply not ready and in retrospect the franchising industry in the UK would take another ten years before it took off. He abandoned the idea and went on to buy up the rights from one of his franchisors for specialist roofing products that he successfully branded and sold under his own name. But this first experience taught me a crucial lesson about franchising. Just because the concept sounds world-beating does not necessarily mean that it will work.

My second experience was in the early 1970s with McDonald's, the US hamburger chain, which was planning its launch into Europe. At this stage it was not interested in franchisees, as it was far too early; it just wanted to learn the lessons to get the base model right so that the future was built on solid foundations. This meant that it had to be company-owned and the location had to be sufficiently challenging to meet all the required test results. McDonald's chose Woolwich in south-east London as its first launch pad, a perfect choice for me because I happened to be living there and also studying marketing. Woolwich was also the perfect choice for McDonald's. It was a poor area of London, had a large percentage of unemployment with all the ensuing social and poverty issues, and boasted every sort of traditional take-away that could possibly be viewed as a competitor: fish and chips, Chinese, Indian, kebabs, the traditional working man's café and of course the Wimpy Bar. All were run in an amateurish fashion but were traditionally British and appreciated by all.

Into this time warp arrived McDonald's, the manager and his team leading from the front, dressed in smart, clean uniforms, smiling and serving a totally different type of food, with clients sitting in a highly stimulating yellow environment on chairs that tilted slightly forwards so they would not want to stay too long. To cap it, Ronald McDonald stared down from the children's play area, all designed to keep out the troublesome youth of the day. It was very clever, and clearly going to be a big success, but what struck me most was the cunning choice of location for the test launch. This taught me another two essential franchise lessons.

First, it is always important to start small—micro—to learn the key lessons in a focused low-risk environment. Second, choose a tough location to challenge the model. The tougher the challenge, the easier it will be to answer tough questions from potential franchisees, motivate others to become involved and replicate on a larger scale. The franchising or rolling-out is in many respects the easier end of the mission. More complicated is the micro part. Micro is seriously misunderstood in a society that has grown so used to the importance of macro and growth. If only our bankers had made sure they were more connected to the realities of the final borrowers for their subprime mortgages, maybe the macro growth they aspired to might have been achievable. Even the following definitions of micro, taken from a random Google search online, tend to undermine its importance:

'Small, very small, or on a small scale.'

'Very small in comparison with others of its kind.'

'Too small to be seen by the unaided eye.'

'Localised, restricted in scope or area.'

And yet every entrepreneur knows that approaching a topic differently is the key to the success of any new venture and that the first small step is essential to taking the second. It is not the size of the step that will generate the impact, but more the quality of it and the shrewd vision for the future. The principle is the same for the educated people reading this book as it is for the poor we are trying to help.

My own journey into microfinance and then microfranchising came as a result of one step. My family and I decided to give a small sum of money to support a friend, Richard Foster, who I had met in Woolwich. He too had studied marketing and ended up running two international sports clubs in Brussels. Aged 30, feeling it was time for a change, he resigned and set off on a world trip looking for some meaning in his life. He passed though the Philippines in the late 1970s at a time of great poverty and famine and decided to make a loan to a poor family. Richard had never heard of Muhammad Yunus, the acknowledged pioneer of microfinance. It was purely an instinctive reaction. A year later, having settled into teaching in Japan, he returned to the Philippines to pick up the repayment and then decided to make some more loans. And so was born a small charity called the Philippine Self Help Foundation, a highly focused organisation that makes around 1,500 loans a year while also giving loans for education and grants for health.

I was keen to understand more about this work and also wanted to take a break from running a business and taking the traditional type of holiday. So I took a small step, and in the late 1990s I flew to the Philippines to see what Richard was up to. The life-changing power of seeing the impact of small loans to the poor so impressed me that I made the commitment to get involved with the work. On the long flight home, I developed the idea of registering a UK charity to support him. I had no real idea of how to run a microfinance operation and certainly would not have all the skills, but I was keen to start and the vision was large. And that, I guess, is another lesson: you don't need to be a specialist to get involved with helping the poor; there is real value to bringing fresh perspectives to the tried-and-tested methods.

So I roped in my friends from my local community in Chiswick, west London, enlisted the support of Bob Geldof and the then bishop of Kensington as patrons, and registered the MicroLoan Foundation. Initially the idea was simple: raise money for the Philippines, make sure it was wisely spent and then set up new operations in East Asia. But of course it was not long before fate took a twist. Through a chance meeting, I was encouraged to go to Malawi to see whether we could set something up locally. At the time we had a mere £10,000 in the account. But why should that matter? So in November 2001, accompanied by one of the founding trustees, Nick Ridge, an accountant, I flew to Malawi.

Arriving at Lilongwe, the capital, I was immediately demotivated. I could see no centre of commercialism in which our proposed microcredit projects could integrate and develop. As I headed up country to Nkhotakota, a small rural town that was once a key centre of slavery, this sentiment grew stronger. How could we possibly make this work? And yet, scratching the surface, we could see that even in the rural villages there was a genuine need, that basic trading was of course taking place and that the women were intelligent and quick to learn. At the start of day four, supported by the briefest of market research, we decided to give it a try. I returned to the UK to see if I could seek some experience from others in the sector on processes and controls, software and other areas to help us get going more quickly. We certainly did receive some words of advice, but on matters of substance, such as policies, procedures and the all essential software, it was clear that we were going to have to steer our own course. Being independent has benefited us on the whole, but even then it struck me how much easier it would have been had we been able to obtain a microfinance franchise. Surely if we want to help others, we should be able to help one another to assist the change?

In August 2002, I returned to Malawi, recruited a programme director and installed him in a garage in Nkhotakota with a basic PC and a bicycle. It was deliberately a tough location to prove the concept. Being rural, it was an area that was ignored by most of the other microfinance NGOs, which normally start in the towns, where the logistics and levels of commercialisation make it easier to operate. My choice for the programme director was based on a number of key factors. Did the candidate have some related experience? Was he or she sufficiently numerate? Emotionally intelligent? Could he or she teach? Was the candidate a self-starter that would relish the challenge? And could we afford him or her? Our recruit from 12 shortlisted candidates was Kenson Chiphaka, a trained teacher with three years' experience as a loan manager. We equipped him with some procedures and processes that we had formulated in the UK through a combination of lessons from the Philippines, lessons we had now read from Yunus's book, *Banker for the Poor* (2003), and common sense. It wasn't perfect, but it was enough to get started. Above all, Kenson was emotionally intelligent, had a good, instinctive sense of direction and was hence fully equipped to build the operation from the ground up.

And so with little expertise and against the advice of various experts who said we would fail, we started by making loans to a group of 15 women so they could start basic businesses such as buying and selling rice, tomatoes or fish so they could look after their families from the profits. This initial group taught us that for each loan we made we were helping on average five dependents and one orphan, a figure that remains true to this day. As important was the fact that we received 100% of the money back after four months, which meant that we could lend to two further groups until the next step.

From this small beginning we have built an organisation that currently has 20 branches in Malawi, working with more than 1,200 groups of women, has lent to more than 26,000 women, impacting the lives of 140,000 dependents, achieves a 99% repayment rate and annually loans more than £3 million in Africa. We have also set up specialist projects aimed at developing skills around agricultural training and irrigation, knitting and sewing, and renewable energy, which are kick-started and supported by our loan programme. A new purpose-built training centre is under construction at our local head office. In addition, we have opened operations in Zambia (where Kenson Chiphaka is now CEO) and Namibia, are projecting to enter Mozambique in 2010 and have start-up fundraising offices in Australia and America. So how has this been achieved and what, if any, are the lessons for microfranchising?

The strength, I believe, has come from the small or micro. We were forced to do everything slowly, which has allowed us to build from the bottom up and continually refine our base model so that it is strong enough to be replicated. In many ways we were in the same position as the poor we were trying to help. First, we had insufficient money. This meant that we were forced to develop on a step-by-step basis from the outset to ensure that the maximum amount of cash went into our loan programme and that not a penny was wasted. Spending time assessing what had gone well or badly with those first groups was important and is a process that still underpins our whole programme.

Second, while we had a good level of management experience from a business environment (in my case marketing and setting up new business ventures in Europe, Africa and beyond) we had no experience of microfinance. We did not have the funds to buy in outside knowledge and we could only obtain general advice rather than specifics from the specialists we approached for assistance. We were probably too small for them to help. This meant that we had to think through the best way of upgrading the programme ourselves. The only people who could help us do this were the poor we were helping and the small embryonic local Malawi management team that we were building.

Third, and linked to my second point, was the ability to listen and, most importantly, listen well. This is considerably more difficult than it sounds, as Africans will tend to tell you what you want to hear rather than what you need to be hearing. This is partly cultural, but it is also a response to the fear that the MicroLoan Foundation might not make those all-essential loans if they should say something negative.

There is a widespread view among some critics and in particular the younger generation that a fundamental reason why aid is often wasted is that the solutions are often prepared by experts who prepare well-written proposals that are not properly discussed with the local community they are meant to help. While the predicted macro step change looks enticing to donors, outcomes often fail to live up to expectations: a catastrophe for donors and for the poor. As former fund manager Wesley McCoy, from Standard Life and now on secondment in Malawi, told us: 'Malawi is littered with projects that have been started and then wound up after three years, but the MicroLoan Foundation, due to its close contact with Malawian people, will be here for years to come.' So one of our core values is to be 'attentive: respect and listen to others, especially the individuals we are helping. They probably know best what they need.' This value has helped us develop and refine our loan and micro-venture programme. In addition, it has taught us how to integrate better into the local communities.

How do we work?

Women only

We only offer loans to poor, unsalaried women (normally those earning around $1 to $2 a day) living in rural or latterly peri-urban areas, and only women who want to start a business. Women make up two-thirds of the world's 1.3 billion people living in poverty, yet they own just 1% of the world's resources and earn 10% of the world's income. Women are not only poorer than men, they also face social, economic, political and cultural discrimination because of their gender. Nonetheless, women are the powerhouse of developing countries. They produce 60% of all food, run 70% of small-scale businesses and make up one-third of the official labour force, in addition to caring for families and homes.[1] Yet their status rarely reflects this contribution.

Muhammad Yunus said:

> When we started, we looked at all the other banks in Bangladesh and found that only 1% of their membership was women. We aimed for 50/50 in the beginning. The main challenge for a poor woman was overcoming the fear in her which was holding her up (Tharoor 2006).

The Grameen Bank set up by Yunus now has 97% women members—that is, 97% of its borrowers are women. According to the Consultative Group to Assist the Poor (CGAP), a consortium of organisations housed at the World Bank: 'Access to financial services can empower women to become more confident, more assertive, more likely to participate in family and community decisions, and better able to confront systemic gender inequities' (Littlefield *et al.* 2003).

Since the MicroLoan Foundation's remit is to help the poor work their way out of poverty, it is unsurprising that our services are focused on women. There is also a wide range of social and practical reasons for concentrating our lending activities with them. These include their role in running small businesses and their position within the household. As a charity we are often challenged on this point and have repeatedly gone back to the communities and local employees to listen to their views, which have always reinforced the women-only policy. We should not forget that it was only comparatively recently within the developed countries that women, the guardians of their families, ceased their weekly wait outside the factory gates to pick up the wage envelopes of their husbands, handing them a small amount of cash to go the pub.

Opening a branch

Our head office conducts a full feasibility service to ensure that it can match our objectives: 50 microcredit groups over two years to the right target market. The focus is to keep costs low to fit our mission to be the best value provider of microcredit in Africa. A branch manager is recruited from outside the selected region to ensure that the relationships that are subsequently built are not biased towards previous contacts. He or she is briefed to work from home until we have established the first 16 groups. The first priority is to build contact with local communities, villages, the traditional authority—chiefs and village headmen—and relevant organisations, such as women's groups (Mothers' Union), churches and schools. In so doing we learn about the community, raise awareness of the products we offer and signal that we will shortly be open for business.

The process culminates in the spontaneous formation of one group of 15–18 women. We ask them to select a group name to reflect their aspirations and

1   Source of data: MLF data confirmed by using the Grameen Progress out of Poverty Index (PPI) that MLF road-tested for the Grameen foundation.

ambitions. Names that translate as 'we will work together', 'let God protect us' and 'we will love one another' are common. As the group consolidates and they get to know one another they elect a chairman, treasurer and secretary. Once this has been completed, we open a bank account in the name of the group at the branch of the nearest bank. It is the women's money, but to protect both parties' interests the MicroLoan Foundation is a countersignatory. We then ask them to begin to save 10% of the value of their loans by way of a commitment. Commitment and dedication to the creation, induction and monitoring of this first group is a sacrosanct concept that we will never prejudice for the sake of rapid volume. If you go for the micro, the macro will follow.

Group quality and cohesion are key to success, so we examine the following areas:

- Is each individual capable of running a business?

- Is the business idea valid?

- Will they support other team members?

- Do they hit our poverty criteria?

- Can they read or write? (We provide assistance if not.)

- What is the residence address and type of house?

- How many dependents and orphans?

- What are their references?

We take references from their nominated referees and from the village headman. The latter is essential to safeguard the women and our work. The village headmen are also present at the election of the group's officials. They do not influence the programme, but it is their communities we are helping and getting them on board means they can assist with any issues that we as an external charity might find difficult and potentially mismanage.

Training

We then start the formal process of eight group training sessions to help them understand how we work as an organisation and to explain the essential issues for running a good business. These training sessions are highly detailed and critical to the success of working with poor communities. Like many of us, they need discipline and support to be successful. This is the beauty of microfinance and the MicroLoan Foundation's model. It develops strong personal and business relationships and is therefore a wonderful tool that can be extended to other activities such as microfranchising. Our training specifically covers:

- Assessment and choice of a good business

- Feasibility study and development of a business plan

- Costing and pricing of products
- Sales and marketing
- Simple record-keeping and accounts
- Group formation and the election and role of officers
- Development of the group constitution
- Meeting procedures and record-keeping
- Credit and repayment procedures
- Savings and their importance
- How to work effectively as a group
- MicroLoan Foundation contact points for recommendations or complaints

At the end of the last training session there is a separate ceremony held by the loan managers when the cheque for the full amount to be borrowed is given to the group officers, along with the related paperwork for the bank. Individual passbooks are handed to each group member. The cheque is made payable to the group account and is paid into the bank by the officers, but the cash or part thereof is then distributed by the bank to each individual member according to the individual contracts. Each member is committed to repaying her loan over the agreed period. In the event of one member not repaying, the other members must make up the difference through the system of cross-guarantee. This helps underpin group commitment.

Loan types and rates

Our typical loan is at an interest rate of 20% over four months, a period that we have set as being a time-frame most poor people can handle with consistency. We also offer specialist loans for bridging groups—clients that are preparing to enter the mainstream banking process—fertiliser and irrigation loans and loans for knitting and sewing equipment and trading in solar panels, which we do as a partnership with SolarAid's microfranchise, Sunny Money. We offer lower rates to long-standing clients taking out larger loans, with the best rate offered being an annualised rate of 43.2%. Our rates either match or beat market rates for microfinance in Malawi. Our average loan size, at £55, is among the lowest in the country, meaning that the cost of servicing loans is likely to be higher in percentage terms. We are regulated under Malawi law, and are registered with the NGO Board and the Malawi Microfinance Network (MAMN), which oversees matters including the appropriate levels for interest rates. We never ask for security against a loan and we do not charge clients extra when repayments are delayed. However, clients who are more than six weeks late repaying may not be eligible for further loans, depending on the reasons for the default. The interest charged covers all associated costs, including training, mentoring and loan administration. We do not charge clients for their loan pass-books or to insure their loans against default, as is the case with some institutions.

We are committed to making our in-country operations sustainable in the long term through the interest we charge on loans, a position we should achieve in 2010. However, a core part of our social mission is that we do not wish to achieve this goal at the expense of universal access to our services. This creative tension is inevitable in an organisation that wishes to continually assist poorer people.

Mentoring and repayments

Ongoing training and support is an essential ingredient to pull the loan process together. Hence, every two weeks after issuing the loans we meet our clients to understand their key concerns, answer questions, provide support and, of course, provide additional, ongoing business training. These discussions are not always about their businesses directly, but often about how they need to manage their cash flow correctly while responding to challenges such as family members falling sick and needing medicines, the pressures of taking in orphans after the death of relatives and funeral expenses. These are issues that challenge us in developed countries but they become critical in communities that have no financial or state security to fall back on. You cannot work successfully with social enterprise or microfranchise programmes without a holistic approach that takes these core issues on board.

Good systems

A socially driven microfinance model is like running a consumer goods company: making a great number of transactions to a large consumer customer base. Retail is detail, and the detail required spans many different areas:

- Budgets built from the ground up, by branch, by loan manager, by loan type
- Loan manager training and management
- Documents: loan application forms, group passbooks and training manuals
- Expense manuals
- Financial control: portfolio, repayments, arrears, sustainability and audit
- Human resources: recruitment and rewards
- Feedback to management

These systems have progressively been installed and refined as the size of the operation has increased. The MicroLoan Foundation has frequently capped growth to ensure that management time and resources were available to refine the model for the longer term. Historical examples include the times when we developed and installed our management information system and set up an in-depth internal financial audit department. Audit management is important to keep control of the operation and to make sure that the procedures set are being rigorously followed. But a core factor is that you cannot judge the effectiveness of a social model by numbers alone. Anyone would be proud of our 99% levels of repayment, but key is what lies behind the numbers. Is the repayment coming from the success of the business or, for example, the forced sale of an asset? Selling a pig that could be used for breeding or chickens that might lay and feed the family—real sustainable wealth creation—cannot possibly be judged a success. Are clients exiting the programme because their business is successful, because they have decided to take a break to take care of their smallholding in the rainy season, because they found they were not entrepreneurs or for some other reason? And are the livelihoods of those who stay with us showing real signs of progress?

These questions are often hidden by businesses operating in the social space and yet they are crucial if a programme is to go forward, with demonstrable benefits. Social impact and social audit is a much neglected topic and needs to be firmly built into the audit process. If not, the tendency of many players is to adopt quick fixes to satisfy the demand of those external parties that perhaps unconsciously favour the top-down approach to development and need to tick the box of social outcomes. Since our start we have brought in a well-respected, external local Malawian auditor to appraise the work of the MicroLoan Foundation. In October 2009 a director of the children's charity Barnardo's, after an intensive four-month study of the Micro-Loan Foundation, issued an independent report, *Listening to the Voices of Women and Children in Malawi* (Stacey and Parker 2009). It is a powerful and convincing document and in order to build on these initial steps we have set up a two-year programme to establish the right procedural system to map the progress of our clients quantitatively and qualitatively and to ensure that the right management systems are in place to implement them.

How we developed in the UK

Sitting in my spare bedroom as I write this chapter, I am reminded that I sat in the same seat when the charity was established. Of course, like any small business, first came the idea and then the first steps, choosing a name and creating a letterhead. The name was decided while walking in Chiswick Park, west London. The name on the tin (MicroLoan) had to explain our mission and it needed to sound serious, hence the choice of 'Foundation'. The letterhead and the simple inkjet printer gave power to the word. We were away. The first task was to sell the concept to my immediate circle of friends in order to enlist their support as trustees and to register as a charity. We also established three fundamental guidelines:

- The founders and volunteers would cover all their own operating and travel expenses. This ensured that all the monies raised went towards the work. This facilitated the raising of money and was a principle we held for the first five years of operation

- We would encourage as many people as possible to get involved with the project as we judged it to be a win for the poor and a win for the volunteers

- We would be transparent in what we did on the ground and in our reporting

Then we had to raise money. It was small beginnings: 50 pence here, a pound there. My first talk raised £150 from two donors, one for £50 and another for £100. It all helped contribute to a first year's income of just under £2,000. I sometimes wonder if those two donors realised how important those cheques were to keeping the momentum going. In hindsight it was not the size of the donation but rather the quality of intention that lay behind them that empowered us. It is a lesson that stays with me and the charity to this day. Treasure the micro-donation because it will lead to the larger donations in the future. How often do political parties ignore this lesson and then wonder why their all-essential grass-roots support has stopped?

The micro-contribution applied to our volunteers as well. While in the early days I did the lion's share of the work, I acknowledged that while doing a full-time job running a different business, I had neither the bandwidth nor the skills to cover all the management expertise we needed. Gradually, more people became involved, the speed of which increased as we began our journey into Malawi. The gifts that people have and continue to provide are humbling. I can only mention a fraction:

- A trustee and accountant, delivering all our initial financial control and processes

- The retired PR director of Guinness developing a local micro PR campaign

- The chairman of a large insurance company managing the micro-venture segment of our activity and raising money from the UK National Lottery to fund it

- An IT expert spending six months in Malawi to understand our procedures and write a management information system

- A retired bank director carrying out grass-roots research and setting up the charity in Zambia

- A retired senior executive from an oil company assessing and setting up the operation in Namibia and another corporate bank director helping the set-up in Mozambique

- City directors helping our fundraising activity in the City of London (the banking and finance community)

- A large UK advertising agency that put together a team to support our fundraising

- Business people in the USA and Australia who are launching local MicroLoan Foundation fundraising operations

- Interns who have worked in the UK and many who have gone to Malawi to work on specific projects linked to training, social audit and helping improve our processes and controls

These gifts and the comments and recommendations that come back from our numerous visitors to Africa keep the charity moving forwards. Micro-contributions really do make a substantial difference and have led us to receiving larger donations towards our core operating costs, branch sponsorship and the construction of a new training centre. They have also helped open up good fortune, such as being featured in the *Daily Telegraph* in their charity Christmas appeal of 2006 and much more.

Working with a large formal team—we employ 130 in Africa—but also many diverse skilled and independent volunteers (60) can provoke challenges. So with the help of a volunteer chartered psychologist we interviewed donors, staff and volunteers to ascertain the values that attracted them to the charity, the outcome of which we summarised as our core values. This is nothing to do with the normal corporate language of 'mission' and 'strategy', but the basic human aspects that bind us together on our social mission. We spent days analysing and agonising over the results as a team and then took advice from one of the directors of the Innocent Food Group. His advice, crucial to the success of driving the values through the organisation, was to put them into language that 'your granny would understand'. We hence arrived at:

- **Attentive.** Respect and listen to others, especially the individuals we are helping. They probably know best what they need

- **Far-reaching.** Find people stuck in poverty who would otherwise struggle to support themselves and others and help them build a sustainable life

- **Small.** Discover the point of greatest leverage where your small intervention can make the biggest impact. You can take a chance with someone if it's small. Take a million chances. Don't stop at a million

- **Consistent.** Do what is right with conviction, sensitivity, enthusiasm and inventiveness

- **Open.** Always use funds and time in a way you can justify: efficiently, sustainably, effectively and with strong focus

How does all this link to microfranchising?

There is significant excitement around the concept of microfranchising. But is the time right? The moment for investment is now. At the same time there are significant amounts of money being accumulated in social-investment funds, many of which are choosing developing countries as a potential target market, and in particular are looking for macro-investments of say £1 million to £10 million. This is potentially good news for poor people, but I do think it throws up a number of major challenges.

Macro-investments by their nature tend to take a top-down approach. Farming is a typical example where a number of external investors are buying up land in developing countries and running much larger farms focusing primarily on growing crops for export. Of course it makes sense: they generate significant economies of scale, farming expertise is injected, new jobs are created and the investors reap an immediate financial return while also feeling good about their investment. You can't argue with the rationale, but looking at it from a micro-perspective, you could reach a different conclusion.

Our experience in Malawi tells us that more than 90% of the population live in a rural environment and that most families will have an average smallholding plot of around a hectare. These smallholdings are an essential provider of foodstuffs for their families. Many of our microcredit clients will in fact reduce their normal commercial activity during the four-month long rainy season in order to concentrate on farming. It is essential for survival, but they do not have the basic skills to maximise on yields no matter what climatic conditions they might face. The microfranchise or socially led franchise approach would be to talk to the poor, understand their parameters and work out a sustainable approach that would combine expertise and self-help. Such an approach could be to establish various recommended scenarios, according to soil types and other conditions such as altitude, and then to develop them through the provision of loans for seeds, fertilisers and irrigation. Irrigation would enable three or four crops a year rather than one. It would also teach them how to see farming with an eye for maximising yield and profitability. Such a package could be built as a social enterprise and then driven through the poor communities using the techniques and skills from microfranchising and microcredit.

Microfranchising is a powerful model. In many respects it takes on board a number of the key elements of microfinance formalised by Muhammad Yunus. To be successful, therefore, a microfranchise operation should be run with a strong commercial focus, just like any consumer- or service-driven company in the developed world, so that it can reach scale. This implies:

- A strong focus on the needs and realities of the poor
- A simple model that can be easily understood and replicated
- A good local business management, driven by social change and performance
- A low-cost operation to maximise the benefits to the poor
- First-rate financial management and control
- Strong and adaptable IT support

- An ability to measure social impact realistically
- Strong partnerships with other supporting organisations

Having strong partnerships requires flexibility from both sides in order to work out the optimum approach. There is strength in saying: 'We know the ultimate destination but we are not entirely sure how to get there.' A typical example is our partnership for selling solar panels with SolarAid. We decided to introduce some of our best performing groups as the initial pilots. The local SolarAid team wanted the groups to concentrate 100% on the solar panels, while the women entrepreneurs wanted to sell them alongside their existing businesses, in case it did not work. So we agreed to adapt to the entrepreneurs' requests and supported them with significantly increased loans to enable the project to develop. The first group is based 30km off the main roads and is developing well. Key to rolling this out across Malawi will be the ability for SolarAid to help our loan managers to carry out the training and to support this with simple diagrammatic materials in the local language.

The glue for success: network marketing

African societies have a real sense of community. Members of communities work with one another, support one another in times of difficulty and have an innate sense of right and wrong. An MLF client responds well if we say, 'Make a success of your business and repay your loan, then we can help someone else in your community.' There is no sense of rivalry and women entrepreneurs, particularly, can see that it makes sense. A number of large-scale international businesses in the developed world have been built in part around this concept, including Amway, Avon, Tupperware, Kleeneze and Herbal Life. These are companies that encourage people to get back to the grass roots and hook up with contacts that lead them to yet deeper roots—in other words, commercially orientated social networking. These companies have in common excellent products and the ability to have tightly focused training knitted in with a system of rewards that encourages people to perform.

Established microcredit operations in developing countries are a natural glue that microfranchisors should take advantage of. We reach deep into the communities. Our combination of loans and training has the potential to release enormous power for good through the establishment of socially orientated businesses, empowering our beneficiaries to become involved commercially. While it will be relatively straightforward for traditional microfranchisors to establish warehouses or key retailers, they are unlikely to have the same reach as well-established, entrepreneurial microcredit operators. Most poor people need to have diversified businesses to be able to weather the natural disasters that regularly hit them. If you have developed a new product in the UK, the easiest way to find distribution quickly is not to sell it yourself, but rather to market it through an established distributor. In developing countries, the best distributors would be the microfinance operators.

As a charity, we believe fundamentally that social enterprise and microfranchising are linked. We see this as a core part of our activity to help the poor in the years ahead. We are keen to talk to potential partners for renewable energy, water and irrigation, farming, health, education, technology, insurance or other enterprises. We know the ultimate goal, but believe that partnership is the best approach in order to maximise social benefit. We are also keen to meet social investors who are interested in taking out a master franchise for our microloan programme in other parts of Africa. Our only concern is not to own the process or charge a fee, but to spread this social mission that is so essential.[2]

2 Visit our website: www.microloanfoundation.org.uk.

8
Creating the market and recruiting microfranchisees

Miguel Ramirez
SolarAid, Kenya

What are the problems with market creation?

As discussed in previous chapters, microfranchising is a tool that applies the proven marketing and operational concepts of traditional franchising to small businesses in the developing world. However, the actual framework can be difficult to set up and retain because of the challenging context in which the microfranchises operate. Households in rural areas are dispersed over large distances; communications, roads and infrastructure are scarce; incomes are low, often below $1 a day; most people make a living from agriculture or from the informal economy; and the market has to be created from scratch. This chapter will look at the implications of this and other issues that affect the creation of a microfranchise. It will start by analysing the problem of market creation: how to generate enough demand for a product so that extremely poor households become willing to pay what is for them significant quantities of cash. It will then look at the issue of franchisee recruitment, particularly how to identify and attract the most entrepreneurial people, and then how to manage, retain and motivate them to sell more. We will look principally at Sunny Money's first microfranchise project in Kenya,[1] and afterwards look briefly at VisionSpring and HealthStore Foundation's approach to management, motiva-

---

1 All information on Sunny Money and SolarAid is based on my experiences working for Sunny Money and SolarAid under the Vodafone World of Difference grant 2008–2009.

tion and retention of their franchisees. Finally, the chapter ends with Nicolas Sireau (SolarAid's first CEO)'s thoughts on branding Sunny Money.

The challenge of market creation

Although there have been some improvements to the quality of life that many Africans experience, extreme poverty is still widespread. In 2007, sub-Saharan Africa's population had reached 800 million[2] of which '315 million people—one in two— survive on less than one dollar per day'.[3] Of these, more than 70% live in rural areas[4] and rely on the rural environment for their livelihood (Mullen 2002: 147), with farming providing sustenance and income (Barnett 2006: 197-98). Both eastern and southern Africa make up some of the 'world's highest concentrations of poor people'.[5] This makes it a particularly challenging context for organisations involved in microfranchising in the region.

Kenya is located in East Africa and is the location for Sunny Money's first microfranchise. An estimated 46.1% of its population live in poverty, of which nearly 50% live in rural areas, 38.8% in urban areas, with the rest in peri-urban areas.[6] Both rural and urban percentages represent recent declines in overall poverty, although it is 'feared that the political crisis of early 2008 is bound to reverse the achievements thus far [made] in poverty reduction'.[7] According to UNAIDS (2008), at the end of 2007 the total approximate population living with HIV/AIDS in sub-Saharan Africa was 22 million, of which more than 11 million were children. In the same year, an estimated 1.9 million people became infected (UNAIDS 2008). As much as 5–28% of adults (aged 16 to 49) within eastern and southern African countries have HIV/AIDS (UNAIDS 2008: 2). HIV/AIDS affects businesses from small to large and can make retaining franchisees difficult over time, especially once the onset of AIDS begins. Compared to the rest of the world, sub-Saharan Africa has borne the brunt of HIV/AIDS, affecting every level of society and business. The last known HIV/AIDS statistics for Kenya (2003) showed that 1.2 million Kenyans were living with HIV/AIDS, with deaths from the disease exceeded 150,000 in the same year (Central Intelligence Agency 2010).

---

2 www.worldbank.org, accessed 11 July 2009.
3 Food 4 Africa, 'Facts on Poverty in Africa'; www.food4africa.org/index.asp?pgid=42, accessed 16 August 2010.
4 Rural Poverty Portal, 'Rural Poverty in Africa'; www.ruralpovertyportal.org/web/guest/region/home/tags/africa, accessed 16 August 2010.
5 Ibid.
6 World Bank, 'Kenya: Country Brief'; web.worldbank.org/WBSITE/EXTERNAL/COUNTRIES/AFRICAEXT/KENYAEXTN/0,,menuPK:356520~pagePK:141132~piPK:141107~theSitePK:356509,00.html, accessed 16 August 2010.
7 Ibid.

Unemployment is another serious challenge. Sub-Saharan Africa and South Asia stand out as 'regions with extremely harsh labour market conditions and with the highest shares of working poor[8] of all regions' (ILO 2009b) Although the trend has been declining over the past ten years, around four-fifths of the employed remain classified as working poor in these regions in 2007 (ILO 2009b). In 2006, 58% of Kenyans lived on less than $2 a day (Yin and Kent 2008). In 2008, Kenya had a 40% unemployment rate (Central Intelligence Agency 2010). It was estimated that the labour force (approximately 17.5 million labourers in 2009 consisted primarily of those working in agriculture (75%), industry and services making up the rest (25% [2007 estimate]) (Central Intelligence Agency 2010). Kenya represents a country that is in dire need of increased investment and employment.

Of Kenya's 37 million people, 'nearly a quarter . . . live on less than $1 a day'.[9] For families in poverty, the ability to afford products that are beneficial is highly unlikely. Furthermore, over time many customers living in poverty but able to scrounge together enough money to buy certain products have had their trust eroded. One reason for this has been an influx of poorly made and often expensive products from China that have degraded people's quality of life instead of enriching it. Such products have no doubt tainted the trust that many Africans have in products from the outside world.

These challenges are all intertwined and make it difficult to create a healthy market. Starting a business of any kind in Africa is difficult. It is only with persistence and dedication that microfranchises such as Sunny Money will help sub-Saharan Africa chip away at these problems.

Sunny Money: a case study

Sunny Money is a microfranchise set up and managed by SolarAid, an innovative and fast-growing charity whose overall mission is to enable the world's poorest people to have clean, renewable power through its micro- and macro-solar programmes. This section shows how, even with the challenges mentioned above, SolarAid has identified a way forward that permits market creation and demand generation to take hold.

SolarAid believes that the two most important threats facing humanity today are global poverty and climate change. The organisation was launched in 2006 as a response to these global issues and now has programmes in Kenya, Malawi, Tanzania, Uganda, Zambia and recently Argentina. SolarAid carries out its micro-solar programme by setting up microfranchises that train people to market and

---

8 'On the basis of new research and information from household surveys, the threshold for extreme poverty has been revised to USD 1.25 a day, while the threshold for poverty has remained at USD 2 a day' (ILO 2009a: 13).

9 www.savethechildren.org.uk/en/kenya.htm, accessed 6 December 2010.

sell small-scale solar products. These products strive to meet the demands of rural people by powering radios, LED lights and mobile phones. SolarAid's macro-solar programme installs large solar systems on community centres, medical clinics, hospitals, schools and community centres. As well as using these solar systems for educational and health purposes, the beneficiaries are taught how best to start up and sustain a business using the solar power generated by the panels. The accrued income helps the beneficiaries to gradually pay back a portion of the total cost of the panels.

SolarAid has seen first-hand how solar power leads to better education, health, safety and income by allowing poor communities to pump water, run fridges, store vaccines, power computers, farm more effectively and light homes, schools, clinics, community centres and businesses. As SolarAid grows, it plans to influence the public and policy-makers in the Western world and abroad as well as educate the public about renewable energy, development and climate change. It is already running a schools programme in London in order to teach children about the links between global poverty and climate change and how solar power is a viable solution.

Because of the above-mentioned constraints to scaling up microbusinesses in Africa and Latin America, SolarAid has adopted a microfranchise system to enhance its micro-solar model. Microfranchising provides the benefits of micro-enterprise, through a proven business concept that serves as a low risk to the entrepreneur/potential franchisee while at the same time giving SolarAid more control over how the business is operated. In order to disassociate itself from typical hand-out aid programmes, SolarAid named its microfranchise Sunny Money.

Sunny Money first implemented its franchise model in Muhuru Bay and North Bungoma, western Kenya. Both regions are difficult to access. The closest electricity grid is more than 45 km away and the closest paved road is more than 60 km away. The combined population of the two districts is approximately 1.4 million. These two areas reportedly have some of the highest HIV infection rates in Kenya. In both regions, Sunny Money's franchise model has remained constant and will be refined and improved gradually as the programme expands throughout the country.

When starting the Sunny Money microfranchise, it was essential to identify and develop partnerships with local NGOs and agencies in order to source potential high-performing entrepreneurs. Sunny Money began in November 2008 by specifically looking for partners that shared its philosophy. This means working with them as a business partner, not as a charity giving aid. The selected partners needed a good understanding of the idiosyncrasies of their local environment, exceptional respect within the community and an open rapport with the key constituents in their area, including the district officers, county officers, senior chiefs and local chiefs. In Muhuru Bay, Sunny Money partnered with an existing NGO in the area, the Women's Institute for Secondary Education (WISER).[10] In North Bungoma, Sunny Money works with the Kibisi Cooperative. Other partners include organisations such as UK-development charity Tearfund, German Technical Cooperation

10 www.wisergirls.org.

agency GTZ and others that can help Sunny Money locate entrepreneurs and help choose new areas for franchise expansion.

As mentioned earlier, an influx of poor-quality products into the developing world has helped create an unreliable market. Sunny Money and other renewable energy advocates have seen many common issues related to meagre products surface such as poor production, a short life-span of anywhere between three and six months and products that carry no warranty or one that cannot be supported or is too convoluted. Sunny Money seeks to do the opposite in its pursuit of bringing dependable and affordable products, with the key goal of providing a reliable and straightforward one-year warranty. The following paragraphs describe how Sunny Money tries to ensure that its products are designed for the rural poor and are able to hold to this warranty. By being able to do the following, Sunny Money has enabled a market to be created and demand to be generated.

Market research

Before Sunny Money begins working in any new country its policy is to hire external market-research companies. Each company is expected to do a survey of at least 400 people, predominantly in rural areas but also in peri-urban areas across multiple regions in any given country.

The purpose of the market research for Sunny Money is to find out through an independent firm how much people spend on, and how often people use, common energy products such as kerosene and candles for lighting, non-rechargeable batteries for radios, and mobile phone recharging—the most basic energy requirements for the average household in rural Africa. This is a prime opportunity for Sunny Money to introduce potential new products and get feedback such as how much someone would be willing to pay for a particular product and how useful the product would be in everyday life. Such research also allows Sunny Money to learn more about the kinds of people it will be selling to. Sunny Money collects a wealth of information, including age, gender, household size, household income, number of incomes, type of employment, how money is spent and knowledge of solar power and other renewables. This builds a pool of information that will be considered when determining product design and product impact. This information when analysed also reveals the challenges that people face in one particular area versus another and where Sunny Money's target customers are located.

Monitoring and evaluation

Sunny Money has extensive monitoring and evaluation (M&E) procedures for all its programmes. Its continued success in creating a market and demand for solar products is partly a result of its M&E practices. These processes look at every level of its microfranchise system, from product design to impact of the product on the lives of the customer and the franchisee. In parallel to the baseline information collected by the market research firms, Sunny Money also collects similar baseline information through its staff and follow-up information from customers and franchisees within the areas where seeding occurs. This information helps Sunny Money determine more precisely what life was like before and after the solar products were introduced—particularly energy consumption patterns—and is compared to the data from the market research firms, increasing the data's reliability. The reason for doing all this research is to determine whether customers are in fact reducing their usage of kerosene lanterns and non-rechargeable batteries for radios, and the amount of time necessary for mobile phone charging. If use of the solar product does lead to this, then the customers will save money, leading then to the question: what is it that their newly found income goes towards? The follow-up surveys look into this in more depth.

The research determines whether franchisees are making enough initial income for the microfranchise to be worthwhile. The data also tells us what they are spending their extra revenue on and if they are beginning to save money in order to expand their franchise in the future. Lastly, the follow-up surveys allow the franchisee to comment on their satisfaction with the franchise.

Along with baseline and follow-up data, Sunny Money assembles focus groups that consist of eight to ten randomly selected customers. This allows Sunny Money to gather qualitative data for donors and verify data found in the follow-up surveys. Likewise, it helps understand more clearly what the impact of the products, the franchisees and the whole Sunny Money experience has been and if customers would continue to buy from Sunny Money in the future. According to Sunny Money, completed focus groups at time of writing have been positive. Sunny Money's continued involvement in this manner within the community undoubtedly has helped customers feel that their opinions matter—cementing further its ability to sustain the market and the demand for its products.

Pricing

Sunny Money's customer research found that many families spend upwards of 15–20% of their income on energy. In Kenya, the mean average of spending per household on batteries, kerosene and mobile phone charging was as follows:

- Average household kerosene consumption equals Ksh844 (US$10.40) per calendar month

- Average household cost of mobile phone charging equals Ksh155 (US$1.91) per calendar month

- Average cost of buying batteries to use for radio playing equals Ksh80 (US$0.99) per calendar month

This gives a total spend of approximately Ksh1,079 (US$13.29)[11] per calendar month. In calculating the total cost once a sale is met while also ensuring the

11 Dollar exchange rates correct at 12 January 2011.

recovery of overheads and a small margin, Sunny Money has been able to price its product at a modest Ksh2,150 (US$26.49) allowing its customers to start saving on energy bills within two months of purchase. This inevitably has enabled them to spend more on items such as their children's education, food and other basic items. Many Kenyan families (made up on average of eight or more members) pool their money to purchase the product. Sunny Money's research states that $5 to $10 is the ideal price for a product in the developing world to be fully affordable by rural poor populations. That is why Sunny Money is developing a product that will be at or close to this price and will guarantee it for a year. Product testing will begin in mid-2011.

In-house product testing

Sunny Money conducts product testing with customers before adding a product to its line. The in-country staff in Kenya, for example, completed a 12-week product-testing period with 15 potential customers in late 2009. It was important that the majority of the testers had no real experience with previous Sunny Money products in order to reduce their bias. The testing consisted of a daily log in which the potential customer wrote down how much time they used the product and for what purpose, such as lighting or charging a mobile phone. After the 12 weeks had passed, the users were asked to fill out a final questionnaire where they could rate their experience of the product, detail what they liked and disliked and give suggestions for how they would improve it. The product testing was a good opportunity to introduce a written and a visually based user guide. Testing the user guidelines is essential as product misuse can confuse the franchisee and the customer.

Sunny Money's warranty

It is the franchisee's task to ensure that the customer understands how to use the product and agrees to the conditions of the warranty at point of sale. Sunny Money has already had customers who have violated the terms of their warranty because they misunderstood the capabilities of the product. Examples of warranty violations include:

- Not charging the product for a minimum of six to eight hours on purchase. The customer tries to operate the product immediately but finds that it does not power a light bulb to its full brightness or is not able to play a radio or charge a phone simultaneously. This creates a misunderstanding between the customer and the franchisee who sold the product. Franchisees in the past have been threatened and physically abused for selling what was thought to be a faulty product or a product that was meant to do more. The customer must walk away understanding the product fully with visual and written guidelines to reinforce this

- Trying to connect other products and devices to Sunny Money's original product. Examples of this include breaking the product open in order to re-wire a 12-volt car battery directly to the solar product's batteries for charging, which can be dangerous and permanently damage the product

In order to honour its one-year customer warranty, Sunny Money has selected manufacturers that work to high quality standards. Nevertheless, the franchise operations manual needs to clearly specify the conditions for the warranty; the franchisee needs visual guidelines to explain the product and warranty to the customer; and the franchisee needs to explain the positive aspects of the product and its limitations. The franchisee should never over-sell the product, which happens frequently. There should also be a clear chain of procedures in order to handle product faults. Sunny Money's fault chain is as follows:

1. A trained franchisee identifies first if a fault exists or if the product is being misused

2. The franchisee communicates this to his or her assigned Sunny Money staff liaison

3. If a component (battery, panel or bulb) is faulty, replacements can be issued immediately

4. If the franchisee does not have the components or feels it requires more technical skills, then he or she can arrange to send the product to Sunny Money's in-country headquarters for repair or replacement

The more organised and confident franchisees feel, the better they can sell the product. Sunny Money wants its franchisees to be known for their professionalism, fairness and customer satisfaction.

The seeding and recruitment process

This section explains how Sunny Money set up its franchise system in Kenya. It describes how the seeding process helps create a market and involves the local community from which it wishes to recruit franchisees.

Respecting rural community authority is paramount. Sunny Money's experience shows that gaining the permission and respect of the local village chief, elders and other authorities is a key factor in rural market creation. Sunny Money uses this opportunity to speak about its mission, introduce the products and explain their benefits and describe the franchisee selection process. As a result of this approach, Sunny Money has received letters from the local offices of the president from North Bungoma and Muhuru Bay, granting free passage within the given territories. On receiving the chief's permission, the next step for Sunny Money is to schedule, advertise and hold community meetings wherever there is the largest concentration of people.

In the case of Sunny Money's first two franchised communities, North Bungoma and Muhuru Bay, the initial three months saw Sunny Money presenting to more than 18,000 individuals split between the communities—the largest presentation having more than 3,000 attendees. Delivering lessons on the uses of solar power, the cost savings for the family and the benefits derived to the environment caused significant excitement within the communities. People immediately began to pre-order from Sunny Money's product line. Sunny Money refers to these initial meetings as 'seeding' the areas because they have the potential to generate mass community interest in the product and a desire to purchase.

The excitement created by the products allows Sunny Money to generate interest from members of the community who want to become franchisees. Sunny Money has a clear process that involves asking the communities to vote for their best candidates as potential franchisees, then interviewing, training and testing them in order to select the best ones. Sunny Money starts by explaining the key qualities that potential franchisees must possess: they must be honest, hard-working, trusted within the community and ambitious and have a willingness and capability to learn. The advantage is that communities tend to choose people with the above attributes. Furthermore, repairs can be made locally and quickly if franchisees live in the communities, saving customers from having to go long distances for assistance. A franchisee who knows the community well is also valuable for Sunny Money as it can benefit from the franchisee's social networks, such as church, vocational and community groups. Likewise, franchisees will have direct contact and rapport with customers, allowing them to report on the popularity of any products. This knowledge is helping shape future product designs.

In Kenya, the initial franchisee election process experimented with an application form followed by election and interview processes that took into account gender inequalities as well as personal integrity. Muhuru Bay and North Bungoma together submitted 1,800 applications from individuals who wanted to become Sunny Money franchisees. Sunny Money narrowed these down to 30 candidates (15 potential franchisees for each area). The applicants were then given a five-day election period during which they had to gather votes from community members. This process entailed walking long distances and knocking on doors to collect signatures and ID numbers from the community members voting for them. Community members could vote for only one candidate. In order to promote gender balance, Sunny Money required that an equal amount of votes were gained from men and women. After the voting verification period, Sunny Money interviewed the 30 applicants, selecting the best five from each region. One candidate, Romanah Omukhobero, from North Bungoma, collected 933 votes, a staggering number considering the distances she had to walk. Today, Romanah is the lead franchisee for North Bungoma.[12] For Sunny Money, the voting exercise proved that the ten selected franchisees were hard-working, industrious individuals who were willing to put in some sweat equity in order to be offered the position.

12 solar-aid.org/entrepreneurs/romonah, accessed 16 August 2010.

Sunny Money does its utmost to ensure that corruption does not take place during elections by working with its partners on the ground, local chiefs, elders and governmental authorities along with having members of its own staff present to evaluate all signatures and ID numbers. Sunny Money also works with Transparency International to ensure that its growing number of staff undergoes anti-corruption training and that all policies regarding this are taken seriously.

Once the election process has finished Sunny Money brings the winning candidates to its head office in Kenya for a five-day intensive training course. They are trained in basic solar theory, proper product usage and multi-functionality, product repair and replacement, sales and marketing, branding guidelines, and administrative and business procedures—all found in Sunny Money's operations manual. After each day an examination takes place that tests their overall working knowledge of the topics learned. Once the franchisees are operational, follow-up surveys as a part of monitoring and evaluation and regular meetings with them allow Sunny Money to continue engaging with its franchisees on a regular basis. This allows franchisees to describe their needs and allows Sunny Money to update them on any system changes, concerns and successes. For instance, franchisees during one meeting with Sunny Money staff said that they wanted to be more visible and professional, with Sunny Money branded polo shirts, caps and business cards. At the same meeting, Sunny Money reiterated that a detailed description of the product sold is necessary for proper receipt-keeping. Sunny Money also discussed the possibility of radio advertisements and when would be appropriate to do some.

Product price and franchisee salary

The retail price for the product is either Ksh2,150 (US$26.49) in a box or Ksh2,500 (US$30.80) in a tailor-made bag with a shoulder strap. Products sold are monitored by receipt books that are reviewed by Sunny Money staff. The franchisee is paid between Ksh275 (US$3.39) and Ksh300 (US$3.70) depending on the product sold.[13] The process is as follows:

- After each sale, the franchisee sends a text message to the Nairobi headquarters with his or her franchisee number and the number of products sold. This results in the quick monitoring of each individual's personal performance and is recorded

- Sunny Money discourages the franchisees from carrying more than Ksh10,000 (US$123.20) of funds owed to Sunny Money and prohibits them from carrying more than Ksh15,000 (US$184.80) owed to Sunny Money as this lays them open to mismanagement of funds or theft. Any franchisees found carrying in excess of this amount could be dismissed

---

13 Product pricing and commissions are from 2008–2009.

- The franchisee pays Sunny Money for the products through the M-PESA mobile phone electronic money-transfer system. The proceeds are then placed in Sunny Money's business account. For each product sold the amount to be sent through M-PESA will be Ksh1,875 (US$23.10) (boxed) or Ksh2,200 (US$27.10) (bagged), which equals the sale price of Ksh2,150 (US$26.49) minus Ksh275 (US$3.39) commission or Ksh2,500 (US$30.80) minus Ksh300 (US$3.70) commission

- The franchisee is expected to pay into the Sunny Money business account once they have sold Ksh10,000 (US$123.20) of product or as often as possible beforehand. This M-PESA transaction needs to come through the franchisee's personal M-PESA account in order to receive credit for the payment. Sunny Money reconciles daily the texts received and payments sent

Franchisee management, motivation and retention

Sunny Money as a first-time franchisor has developed its franchise slowly. This is important as it helped the organisation determine how best to manage operations and franchisees. During its initial set-up, Sunny Money made a point to learn from its experiences and from the experiences of others in order to reach stability and to know how to challenge itself effectively for the future. Sunny Money knew that once a market was created it could be sustained in the long term if management, motivation and retention of franchisees were maintained, which is what this section will focus on. In order to widen the perspective, I also include examples from VisionSpring[14] and HealthStore Foundation.[15]

As mentioned in Chapters 3 and 6, VisionSpring and HealthStore Foundation are prime examples of successful microfranchises within the developing world. Vision-Spring's franchise diagnoses people with minor vision problems and sells affordable corrective eyeglasses within rural areas in Asia, Latin America and Africa. HealthStore Foundation, which began in 1997 and has more than 85 clinics and shops in Kenya and a growing presence in Rwanda, seeks to increase affordable and fair access to much-needed medicines for children and their families.

The operations manual is the most important element for managing franchisees. It holds each franchisee accountable and gives detailed and specific tasks that must be completed. For Sunny Money the creation of the operations manual meant clear structures, guidelines and direction at every level of the franchise. For HealthStore, this meant moving from being run like an NGO to being run more as a business.

---

14 Conversation with VisionSpring's Graham Macmillan on 7 October 2009.
15 Conversation with HealthStore Foundation's Gunther Faber on 1 October 2009.

The evolution of HealthStore was accompanied by an evolving operations manual that has been diligently followed. Indeed, if franchisees do not follow the operations manual, they lose their licence. VisionSpring, however, gives its franchisees flexibility and asks them to follow their operations manual's principles. This is not to say that VisionSpring does not enforce breaches of the operations manual nor does it mean that HealthStore is inflexible; rather it means that a balance needs to be found between the two approaches. The success of both organisations shows that the balance of rigidity and flexibility of the operations manual waxes and wanes. Flexibility with any operations manual is required to a certain degree as each country may have different approaches towards business practices, especially in rural areas that may be more traditional. Insensitivity to this could ruin a market or keep it from flourishing. Equally, any franchisor will agree that clear structures and consequences for franchisees and recruitment processes are essential if a franchise is to be successful. Again it is balance that keeps a franchise afloat.

Good administration comes as a result of clear line-management and organisational structures. Management structures mature over time and need to be re-evaluated regularly throughout the life of the franchise. Sunny Money Kenya, for example, has its country headquarters in Nairobi. Its staff relay policy to a head franchisee who lives and works with other franchisees within a regional group. The head franchisee disseminates policy and advises the rest of the franchisees within the group. The head franchisee is selected for his or her leadership abilities and capacity to communicate within the group. Typically, it is the 'Mama' (female elder) or male elder in the group who emerges as the natural leader. Elders, because of their years of experience and work within the community, tend to be aware of the community's larger needs, know most community members and are familiar with whom to speak to in order to progress the franchise. Sunny Money staff in Nairobi make regular visits each month to the franchisees to conduct monitoring and evaluation exercises; receive direct input from franchisees; discuss and implement policies; deliver products if necessary; and raise Sunny Money/SolarAid's profile via a roving solarised van that can demonstrate solar through new products and solar-powered film screenings.

HealthStore's management structure has franchisees report to local field officers who then report to a regional head nurse, who in turn reports to HealthStore's regional headquarters. The field officer is the first point of contact for franchisees. He/she has a nursing degree and receives marketing and financial training from HealthStore's regional headquarters. Field officers are the first line of evaluation for franchisees who have committed a disciplinary offence. HealthStore's head nurse evaluates the field officer and the franchisees and reports back to headquarters.

VisionSpring's management system set-up has one district coordinator for up to 30 vision entrepreneurs (franchisees). District coordinators and the franchisees work within a 'given sales territory and can directly share in, and influence, [their vision entrepreneurs'] sales activities' (Lehr 2008). VisionSpring's district coordinators and franchisees work together to advertise and sell their services and products within markets. This enables both to benefit from each other's sales.

Professionalism is an obvious necessity at every level, but particularly for the franchisees. Sunny Money, for example, trains its franchisees to clearly explain the details of the warranty so that customers feel that they are buying a product that is backed up by a promise they can rely on. Sunny Money also outfits its franchisees with Sunny Money collared shirts and caps in addition to identification cards and numbers. In order to gain the customer's trust, VisionSpring's franchisees need to be as confident and knowledgeable when doing eye exams as an optician or ophthalmologist, and are trained accordingly.

Sunny Money supervises its franchisees in a number of ways, one of which is through transparency of sales accounts and record-keeping. Sunny Money issues receipt books and financial summary journals to its franchisees. Staff meet periodically with franchisees to review both documents, ensuring that enough product detail is put in receipt books and that financial journals mirror receipt books. Franchisees are trained to fill in each document accurately. The receipt book details the products sold and the product's serial number and has signatures from the franchisee and customer showing that the warranty was explained and accepted. If a franchisee repeatedly fails to provide accurate and detailed accounts, Sunny Money will give two warnings, each leading to a reprimand with fewer products being supplied for the franchisee to sell. In one particular case, a franchisee repeatedly failed to include basic product information, such as the product name and serial numbers, and in two cases did not provide the receipt. Sunny Money retrained the franchisee and warned that such mistakes, especially not giving receipts, would not be tolerated in future and could result in the termination of his franchise. There was then, however, a noticeable improvement in performance.

Motivation and encouragement by the franchisor is crucial if a franchise is to maintain a significant franchisee retention rate. There are many ways to achieve this, for example, through advice on how to increase sales, promises or threats of commission increases and decreases, sales goals, marketing and training. Sunny Money visits its franchisees two or three times a month and is in contact through mobile phone texting at least once a week. Each visit is an opportunity for Sunny Money to ask its franchisees about their marketing needs, review sales strategies, announce new sales goals and of course warn any franchisees if they begin to slip or fail in sales. It also allows the franchisees to provide feedback and hold meetings encouraging all franchisees to share sales ideas, tips and lessons learned. A good example of knowledge-sharing was when franchisees in North Bungoma said they were worried about having too many products on them when selling door-to-door or in open markets by themselves as they did not have big-enough bags. They also felt that carrying multiple products would make them more susceptible to theft. The franchisees got together to exchanges ideas and solutions. After hearing this, Sunny Money agreed to produce a Sunny Money branded bag that allowed the franchisees to carry up to four products. The franchisees also agreed they would bring one sample product to a school, church, market or other social event for demonstration. They would then pass out their phone number to those interested in buying the product with the understanding that once the group was ready with cash at hand they would return with enough products for immediate purchase. This gave Sunny Money's franchisees more certainty about the right number of products to bring and made them feel safer.

One way in which VisionSpring retains good franchisees is by stating the minimum number of sales that must be maintained in order to keep the franchise. The actual target may vary from country to country, but it allows VisionSpring to keep the best saleswomen/men within its growing franchises. From its years of experience, VisionSpring has been able to estimate the quality and longevity of its newly trained franchisees and as a result can push for ambitious sales goals.

For example, out of 100 people:

- The top 20 are likely to be excellent saleswomen/men and sell to virtually anyone

- The middle 40 sell well to friends and family, and with the right sales targets can receive enough income to make selling a positive long-lasting venture. However, they may not be as effective when selling to people they do not know

- The bottom 40 are not able to sell well within the community and are not natural saleswomen/men. They are often the first to leave the franchise either through their own decision or by request from VisionSpring

For HealthStore, 20% of the pay of its staff (field officers and head nurses) is based on performance goals. Furthermore, the more the franchisees sell the more they make, which is one reason why many of franchisees keep their shops open late. HealthStore encourages sales competition between franchisees, and at its annual convention it recognises the franchisees with the best sales. Sunny Money has not been in operation as long as VisionSpring or HealthStore but rewards its franchisees through a base commission of Ksh275–300 (US$3.39–3.70). The commission increases once milestones of 100, 500 and 1,000 plus products are sold. Access to discounted motorbikes and rented public market spaces, as well as support in taking out loans from banks, are possible incentives to continue selling well.

While researching VisionSpring, HealthStore and Sunny Money, the profile of the ideal franchisee began to emerge. The qualities below are found in the most successful franchisees and should be sought vigorously by any franchisor.

According to HealthStore Foundation:

> We need franchisees who are hungry to succeed and have a nose for business. They must have a passion and desire to make money for themselves, which can be seen during their interviews. Ninety-six per cent of our franchisees are women; they are more focused, and are more driven because of family responsibilities.

According to VisionSpring:

> Franchisees need to be able to operate under the franchise model and operations manual. They need to be entrepreneurial and need to look

constantly for and invest in new tools themselves. Franchisees need to have the support of their families. They should also work for the prestige that comes from helping other people improve their eyesight within the community.

For Sunny Money:

We are looking for franchisees who are honest and want to improve their community through the use of solar and other renewable energies. We want franchisees who are just as excited about selling solar as their customers are about being able to afford it. Franchisees need to look to the future and see their village or community no longer dependent on using kerosene to light their homes, burning wood or charcoal to cook their food, or using generators to operate their schools, churches, and community centres. They need to be able to see solar and renewable energies as the key to a better quality of life.

Final thoughts

Creating a market within the developing world context is challenging. VisionSpring and HealthStore Foundation have a wealth of knowledge when it comes to sharing their individual experiences in microfranchising with those just starting out. Sunny Money is following a similarly successful path and is set to build its own franchise and distribution networks while also generating demand for affordable products. Furthermore, Sunny Money is opening up the market for solar lighting and renewable energy with a steadfast commitment to professionalism and high-quality products. Each organisation's dedication to work within these markets will undoubtedly help communities lift themselves out of poverty one product at a time.

Box 8.1 **Branding your microfranchise**

By Nicolas Sireau

While branding as a concept and discipline was developed mainly for the Western market in developed economies, it also has a crucial function in the developing world. Word of mouth is important in developing economies because it is an excellent way of finding out about the quality of a product or service. Hence, reputation—which is at the heart of branding—plays a key role, and a microfranchise needs to have a good, solid and respectable reputation. Without that, it will not be able to sell its products or services, as customers will soon find out that other customers are unhappy with the microfranchise.

The name plays a particularly important role in branding and a distinctive name is crucial for a brand's success (Sireau 2008). It becomes essential that a name is chosen that will reinforce the brand by associating it with the relevant attributes and values that influence buying behaviour (Tan Tsu Wee and Chua Han Ming 2002). Academics have developed a naming spectrum to understand better different categories of names (Sireau 2008). On the one side are purely descriptive names, such as the Royal Institute of International Affairs. These communicate immediately to the consumer, but are less distinctive and protectable (Hart 1998). Next come semi-descriptive names, such as Coca-Cola, which include a partial description of the contents of the product (Blackett 1998). Then come associative or suggestive names, such as Sunsilk, which conveys images of softness and associations with the sun and outdoors. Furthest along the spectrum come freestanding or coined names, such as Kodak, which do not mean anything, take years to fill with meaning in the minds of the consumers, but are much easier to protect legally.

Generating the brand name for the microfranchise

At SolarAid, we used the above concepts to develop the Sunny Money microfranchise brand. Our research and experience in Kenya, Malawi, Tanzania and Zambia was showing that the SolarAid name was detrimental to our work in the field. Indeed, there is such a strong legacy of dependency in East Africa that being associated with the word 'aid' leads people to believe that an organisation is there to provide hand-outs, which is contrary to the microfranchise principle of economic self-reliance. As brand names are short cuts to help people understand the nature of the brand, having the word 'aid' in the name associates an organisation with all the deficiencies, inefficiencies and dependencies caused by the aid system. It also associates the organisation with other NGOs such as Christian Aid, ActionAid and WaterAid that may not share the fundamental same values of market-based solutions to ending poverty.

Hence, staff in each country reported that when operating under the name 'SolarAid', they found it hard to recruit effective entrepreneurs and market products to customers as none of them would understand how an organisation with the word 'aid' in its name could be operating as a business rather than handing out solar products for free. While there is an argument for keeping the name 'aid' in the name in order to help redefine it to a more market-based concept, we did not believe that this was a role for a young and growing organisation. Instead, we decided to rebrand our microfranchise operations under a new brand name that would be more relevant to the African context. We carried out some name generation in order to brainstorm a long list of potential names.

Name generation is a specialist area with clear rules on how to develop, categorise and select potential brand names. We started by agreeing three naming routes—conceptual areas that would help us with our brainstorming. These three routes were: evokes the sun and solar energy; brings to mind enterprise, income generation and business; and evokes Africa. We then carried out the brainstorming using several techniques. First, we carried out group brainstorming, bringing together eight people to generate a long list of names through association exercises (one person says a word and the next person says what instantly comes to mind). Second, we carried out individual brainstorming, with several of us working on our own, using a dictionary, thesaurus and the Internet, to research possible names. Third, we worked with our local entrepreneurs in Africa to brainstorm names with them.

Overall, we collected more than 300 potential names, which we then filtered through Google and an online government trademark registry to make sure they weren't already in use. We then shortlisted them down to 22, based on the following criteria: short; memorable; work across languages as much as possible; flexible: can be used throughout the product range and adapted to each product; support the positioning of the brand; legally protectable as trademarks; not culturally offensive; not an abbreviation and not prone to abbreviation.

We narrowed this list down to three possible names—Sunny Money, Suncatcher and Genergy—and then carried out trademark searches to find which ones were available. This is a crucial part of the name selection process, as you do not want to choose a name and then find out that it's already being used for a similar product and that it is already registered as a trademark. The international trademark system works on a class basis, with each one having sub-categories. For instance, class 16 is for printed matter, newspapers, newsletters, magazines, periodicals, journals, brochures, posters, books, badges, calendars, instructional and teaching materials, stationery items, reports and diaries. We worked with our solicitors at Covington & Burling and White & Case to agree on a list of classes in which to search and then register the trademark. The searches looked for identical or near matches to our suggested names, leading us to eliminate Suncatcher and Genergy, which were already taken by similar products, services or organisations. Sunny Money came out the winner, and was therefore adopted by the organisation as the name for its microfranchise.

Generating the brand identity for Sunny Money

The next stage in the brand development process is to develop a logo—also known as a corporate identity—with branding guidelines on how to use it. For this, we turned to two graphic designers and instructed them to develop a set of logos for Sunny Money that would evoke the sun and/ or money, and would be cheerful, dynamic and easy to use on a variety of materials, from products to billboard ads. A first set of logos was produced as in Figure 8.1.

Figure 8.1 **Sunny Money draft logos**

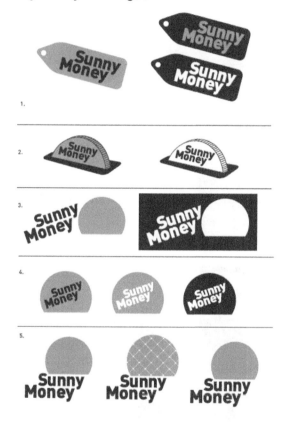

This then led to further work on the logo in order to come up with one that was brighter and more distinctive, leading to the one used in the advertisements in Figure 8.2 being chosen, with the suggested strapline of 'don't burn what you earn' (which we didn't subsequently use) in order to encourage customers to reflect on how much they spend on kerosene and how much they could save by buying a solar lamp instead.

Branding plays a significant role in microfranchising, and organisations that roll out a microfranchise model should pay particular attention to issues such as the name and the corporate identity. But branding goes deeper than this and encompasses issues such as the organisation's values and mission. Sunny Money's values are entrepreneurship, innovation and quality, while its mission is to wipe out the use of kerosene for lighting in Africa by 2020. These are crucial elements of the organisation's brand as they give a sense of direction and purpose. Every microfranchise organisation should spend time thinking through these issues and re-evaluating its brand on a regular basis.

Figure 8.2 **Sunny Money draft advertisements**

9

Social-sector franchising for healthcare

Michael Seid
Michael H. Seid & Associates, USA

After food and clean water, healthcare is the most basic of human rights. Whether a person lives in the slums of Kibera, Nairobi, the inner city of Crenshaw, Los Angeles, or Park Avenue, New York, proper medical care and prescriptive medicine should be available to everyone, regardless of their income or location. People in developing countries deserve what we have given to ourselves: access to services and drugs that meet the standard necessary for effective treatment. This is a human right for everyone, whether they are paying for their own care or receiving subsidised care paid for by others. To be effective, all healthcare, regardless of where it is delivered, must meet certain basic requirements:

- Proper diagnosis of the underlying illness is essential
- The care provided to the patient must be of high quality
- The drugs prescribed must be fresh, appropriate and authentic
- Patient records must be maintained
- The patient must be treated with respect
- Care should be provided within a patient's cultural requirements
- Patient care needs to be provided locally and conveniently
- The cost of patient care must be affordable
- The method of delivering patient care must be sustainable

I do not question that great strides have already been accomplished in providing healthcare to the poor in the developing world. However, regulations to ensure high-quality medical care do not exist or are not effectively enforced there. The care provided to the poor is frequently below what is necessary for effective treatment. Our mission must be to improve access to affordable medical services and drugs that make people well. Developing methods of distribution for the delivery of sustainable and consistently high-quality care, at a low cost, is the reason that true business-format franchising techniques and standards need to be considered as part of the solution. Branded chains of healthcare providers can increase access to healthcare for the poor in the developing world as they have done in more than 120 other industries worldwide in the developed world. To succeed, branded chains must meet certain basic standards:

- Brand standards must be established, monitored, enforced and maintained because this is what spares the poor from needless suffering and death. Brand standards need to define a menu of local products and services available under the brand, customer service standards for delivery of products and services, and benchmarks to measure local performance to the brand promise

- Personnel at the local unit level must be qualified to deliver to brand standards. They must be motivated and have the resources and support necessary to meet these standards

- The delivery system should be structured to ensure that brand standards can be replicated over many outlets. It must be able to achieve economies of scale for the benefit of all system stakeholders, including consumers

- The underlying economic model must be sustainable at all levels, including for the consumer, the unit operator, the franchisor and all other stakeholders such as grantors and social investors

Business-format franchising is one method available to meet the requirements of delivering products and services to the poor in the developing world. As a method of indirect downstream distribution, it has proven to be unequalled in delivering these consistently at brand standards over a large network of outlets. This chapter will explore the requirements for the design, development, execution and management of a business-format franchise system to meet the societal needs of the poor in the developing world, focusing in particular on the healthcare sector. This application of business-format franchising to these societal needs is called social-sector franchising.

The problem

At the 2000 Millennium Summit, the United Nation's Millennium Declaration was adopted, setting goals to reduce poverty and improve conditions in the developing world by 2015. In 2009, I attended the millennium conference at the United Nations' General Assembly, entitled 'Getting Back on Track'. We were now more than midway through the project and each presentation reinforced the fact that the targets that had been set in 2000 have been uniformly missed. Curiously, the rationale presented for the failure to meet the Millennium Development Goals (MDGs) focused almost exclusively on the availability of funds raised with little discussion on whether the funds received were applied effectively. There was little mentioned regarding the lack of measurable results or penalties for the failure to meet targets as the underlying cause of the problem. Uniformly, the discussion focused on the failure of primarily the USA in not meeting its percentage of GDP commitment. The focus on fundraising and the apparent lack of focus on whether or not there are effective standards in place to measure the beneficial application of these funds, in my opinion, is the overwhelming problem with providing basic healthcare and other services to the poor in the developing world.

In discussing the MDGs in 2005, John B. Taylor, then US under secretary for international affairs, is quoted as saying:

> Since we are here to talk about 'getting the Millennium Development Goals back on track,' the first question one must ask is why they are off track, particularly in Africa. In my view, a significant part of the answer has to do with the lack of measurable results. What gets measured gets done, and my experience has been that aid is increasingly being delivered in a way that is disconnected from the results we are trying to achieve. Donors and recipients share responsibility in this. For example, donors are engaging in budget support operations without demanding a serious effort to measure how those resources result in progress toward meeting the MDGs (Taylor 2005).

If there is no immediate change in the delivery methodology to one that is primarily focused on measuring results rather than on measuring receipts, progress will not be made. I believe that the Millennium Project, intended to be a world-class focus on solving the problems in the developing world, is off track for one reason: it was never designed to require accountability on the effective use of the funds expended by grant recipients. This appears to be the inherent weakness in many NGO delivery vehicles that we have reviewed.

It is essential that we begin a process of assessing the current methods of delivering services to the poor in the developing world by measuring the performance results achieved by the recipients of funding. To do less will require us to accept the results that we have witnessed to date. Social-sector franchising is one of the solutions that should be considered, because franchising is a proven method of distribution that at its foundation requires the effective measurement of results in order to keep the enterprise sustainable. For some, mainly those currently providing services in this sector, this chapter may be viewed as confrontational and therefore controversial. That is a natural reaction to any change strategy that challenges the status quo. Arguments have been made by those currently receiving funds that franchise-industry business practices should not be used. They argue that their mission is a social obligation, that healthcare is a basic human right and as such is not suitable for standards of business performance or measure. This belief tends to support the status quo and effectively limits the exploration of improvements to access to healthcare and other social services in the developing world. I fully support the beliefs that healthcare is a basic human right for all people. However, until the standards necessary for effective care and performance measures are applied, then sustainable, high-quality, low-cost solutions will not be possible regardless of the downstream method of delivery used.

Social-sector franchising

As mentioned, social-sector franchising adapts the principals and methods of business-format franchising to solve problems in the developing world. It is not the only solution and should not be considered a panacea to solve every problem or every situation. It is but one of many options. Companies in more than 120 business-to-consumer and business-to-business industries use franchising today. Franchising allows them to license their brand and their operating methodology to independent business owners in exchange for a fee and a contractual promise that the licensee will execute to the franchisor's brand standards. The individual franchisees are trained and supported and have the benefit of profit potential to ensure a consistent quality level of service delivery. They also run the risk of losing their licence should they not perform to the franchisor's standards, which require them to deliver their products and services to the level of the franchisor's brand promise. The success of business-format franchising is based on the careful design and development of each system's unique downstream distribution strategy and is predicated on the franchisees receiving the support they need to enable them to deliver consistently on the system's brand promise to the franchisor's customers.

When structured properly, social-sector franchising also has secondary benefits to the economy in the developing world. Because of the training, standards and support provided by the franchisor, jobs are created, including those in companies set up to support the product and service requirements of the franchise network. This has been a hallmark of business-format franchising in the developed world and is why 15.3% of all private-sector jobs in the USA are with franchisors, franchisees and the suppliers to the franchise industry, according to the Education Foundation of the International Franchise Association (IFA), the leading trade association focused on business-format franchising. The success of business-format franchising is rooted in the system's ability to meet a three-point test, a foundational element evident in all successful downstream distribution strategies, including franchising. First, **the ability to maintain brand standards** at each location, which ensures that the consuming public can rely on the franchisor's brand promise regardless of the location the consumer visits. Second, **the ability to scale operations**, which means that the franchisor can grow its channel of distribution to ensure ease of access to its customers. Third, **the ability to achieve economies of scale**: as the system grows, the franchisor is able to lower the costs for the franchisees for the basic requirements of the business including start-up development costs (construction, furniture and equipment), products, services, disposables and marketing based on the combined purchasing power of the system. The franchisor is also able to leverage the system to reduce the costs for headquarters, field and other support requirements necessary to meet brand standards. The system therefore has the capacity to deliver its products and services to its customers at a lower cost than independent operations. These basic elements are lynch pins for all successful business-format franchisors.

Structuring a social-sector franchise

In designing a social-sector franchise system, the following strategic elements must be considered:

- Establishing standards for the products and services to be delivered to the poor in the developing world

- Establishing the underlying business model necessary to deliver those products and services consistently throughout the enterprise

- Establishing a financial structure to achieve sustainability

- Establishing standards to identify individuals or groups suited to become franchisees and staff at the unit level

- Cultivation of a positive and beneficial relationship between the franchisor, franchisee and suppliers

- Support and, if necessary, an investment in a local supplier base

- Development of the franchise business structure, support and administration to maintain standards and to seek continual improvements to the brand's performance

Each of the design elements above includes a myriad of sub-issues, including but not limited to the following areas.

How to franchise the business:

- The choice of the products and services the individual units should offer to the public
- The financial requirements and realities for the system
- Replicating the company's culture at each location
- The brand promise to consumers
- Requirements for effective operations
- The business drivers
- The system's competitive advantages and disadvantages
- The systems and procedures for the franchisor to execute to brand standards
- The requirements for franchisees to operate to brand standards
- Positioning the brand in the market
- The available conversion opportunities
- The provisions for future enhancements and modifications to the offering and systems
- The availability of a local supply chain or methods to encourage the development of the system

How to structure the franchise:

- Territorial grants and requirements for market penetration
- Site development requirements
- Personnel and training requirements for the franchisees
- Headquarters and field training provided to franchisees, their management and staff
- Other supporting functions including operations, marketing, IT, merchandising and quality control
- Insurance requirements
- System-wide programmes including third-party payment systems to enable customers to access the products and services in a way that expands their availability and enhances their personal dignity
- Purchasing requirements and pricing efficiencies from approved suppliers

- Advertising and other system marketing and consumer education
- Trademark usage and protection
- Internet presence for the franchisees—where possible and appropriate
- In-term and post-term covenants for competition
- Term of the franchise, including the ability of franchisees to enter into subsequent agreements with the franchisor
- Default, cure and termination provisions if franchisees breach their obligations
- Transfer rights and obligations should a franchisee wish to exit the business
- Potential exit strategies for the franchisees and the franchisor

The operational standards:

- Authorised core menu of products and services
- Focus on delivering only those products and services that can be done under the system's methods of delivery
- Product specifications for all products sold or used by the local businesses
- Supply chain and purchasing requirements, including standards, credit terms, inventory levels and restrictions
- Service standards for each of the locations
- Benchmarks of operational competency of franchisor and unit personnel
- Fixtures, equipment and signage procurement for each location: manufacturer, model identification and requirements
- Brand identity
- Advertising, promotion and marketing strategies
- Pricing philosophy and requirements to the consumer
- Customer acquisition and retention programmes
- Communications internally and externally

Franchise network support:

- Types and levels of support to be provided to the franchisees in order to ensure that each franchisee has the ability to operate to brand standards: prior to the opening of the franchised location; during the initial opening period of the franchised business; and as an ongoing function to refresh and update operations

Franchise relations:

- Defining the parameters of a positive relationship policy to create a win–win for franchisor and franchisee
- Identifying dispute resolution methods to be used
- A relationship structure that allows the system to evolve the franchise over time
- Defining what happens when the relationship ends

Financial models:

- Determining the return on investment criteria for the franchisor, its investors and franchisees (while not financial necessarily, it is important to determine the social return-on-investment requirements of the donors to the system)
- Determining the fee structure for each class of franchisee
- Defining the initial investment required by franchisees
- Determining and facilitating the availability of development and operating capital by the franchisee
- Determining the potential of other income opportunities or sources of support for the franchisor
- Anticipating financial performance models for the franchisor, unit level and each selected class of franchisees
- Sensitivity analysis over various performance levels
- Determining the franchise system's cash requirements

Franchise system expansion:

- Determining the appropriate markets for franchisee expansion
- Determining if there are markets more suitable to company-owned or other methods of development
- Determining if there is a necessary blend of locations in primary markets with those in more traditional markets where profits from those locations can be used to sustain the other

- Determining if there will be any additional types of expansion and distribution contemplated and when those will occur
- Determining the types of franchising to be used (single unit, multi-unit, conversion, area representation, etc.)
- Determining the profile of the ideal franchisee (owner operator, investor groups, etc.)
- Identifying the appropriate organisation required for franchise sales
- Identifying the franchise sales lead-generation vehicles to be employed
- Defining franchisee sales-closure and compliance requirements
- Determining the collateral material necessary to achieve expansion goals
- Determining the preliminary growth goals for each class of franchisee
- Determining the marketing budget required

Business structure and administration:

- Determining the type of entity to be the franchisor
- Determining how the operating systems and trade name will be licensed to the franchisees
- Determining the organisation that will be required to grow and protect the brand
- Identifying headquarters and field staff positions and when they should be hired

Each of the above requires research and determinations based on each franchise system's unique requirements. Fungible solutions and strategies rarely are beneficial to the long-term stability and sustainability of any franchise, or for that matter any brand. For example, while there may be similarities between McDonald's, Wendy's and Burger King—three of the world's leading hamburger chains—each of these business-format franchise systems is significantly different in its methods of expansion, methods of support, revenue sources and ancillary products offered.

The challenges

There are unique realities in a social-sector franchise that may not be found in traditional business-format franchising. These include, but are not limited to:

- The culture of a marketplace dominated by NGO-owned, -operated and -financed locations

- The growth of microfranchising, which on the surface may emulate some of the elements of a business-format franchisor but does not measure success by unit output, provide the level of necessary and continual support or meet the basic three-point test of traditional franchising

- Restricted grants that are meant to be beneficial but are not in direct alignment with the social-sector franchisor's brand promise, stated mission or capabilities

Social-sector franchisors, as with any business, must exercise discipline in adding new products and services that do not fit their capabilities or mission. The acceptance of restricted grants, when the resulting products and services cannot be integrated into the franchisor's existing system of delivery, may be one of the largest causes of the lack of performance by current providers of products and services to the poor in developing countries. Social-sector franchisors will compete with microfranchises and other NGO operations for investment and charitable funding. While striving to meet the same consumer needs, microfranchisors and other NGO operations do not generally execute to the same business standards possible in social-sector franchising, including those related to cost, effective control of business and operating standards or general requirements necessary to deliver on the brand promise to consumers.

There are other unique challenges in developing a social-sector franchise system, including but not limited to:

- Qualifications and literacy of potential franchisees, unit management and staff

- Lack of entrepreneurial and brand experience of potential franchisees

- Inability of consuming public to pay the full price or to pay any of the price for the products and services provided by the system

- Poor transportation, road conditions and infrastructure, including lack of running water and electricity

- Poor communications infrastructure and lack of information technology

- Poor supply-chain capabilities in market, including but not limited to counterfeit or sub-standard products

- Inability to use broad-based consumer marketing approaches

- Local management, headquarters and field staff capabilities for franchisor personnel

- Government regulations, interference and corruption

- Donor requirements including restricted grants available for products and services outside the mission or delivery capabilities of the franchisor

Each of these and other issues need to be factored into the strategic make-up of the franchisor for the system to execute to beneficial standards of performance at every level. The failure to develop and execute to pre-determined standards of performance will create an enterprise that does not meet its stated mission or its financial requirements and will result in a business model that cannot be sustained.

Social franchising in the USA

The term social franchising is used today to describe several different structures involving the use of franchising by non-profit organisations. Domestically, the term is used generally to describe the ownership of a business-format franchise by a non-profit organisation where the proceeds from the business are used to fund its mission objectives. Franchisors, with their desire to give back to the community and as part of their growth goals in general, frequently offer community-development corporations and other NGOs reduced initial and ongoing fees when they become franchisees. Some socially responsible franchisors also provide additional support services, including training and field support. Examples of franchisors in this sector include Candy Bouquet, Service Master, Nexcen, KidzArt, Auntie Anne's, Money Mailer, Fantastic Sams, Metromedia and Huntington Learning Centers. To support these efforts, the IFA has established the Minorities in Franchising Committee to educate franchisors and non-profit franchisees and provide opportunities for marketing. There have been approximately 100 social franchises in operation in the USA. While the goals of socially responsible franchisors are laudable, in reality, the performance of many of them has been spotty.

Many of the communities that are candidates for social franchises are outside the core base of most franchisors. As such, there are often misconceptions about the consumers in the market, their buying patterns and their spending on branded products. Many franchisors view these markets as fungible to other similar markets and do not understand that ethnic backgrounds will also have an impact on which products and services will do well in these neighbourhoods. There is a dearth of branded or quality merchants in many of the emerging markets in the USA. The demand for quality and branded products is high, while the availability of local merchants satisfying this demand is low. This results in local residents shopping for branded or higher-quality products and services outside their neighbourhoods. This imbalance leads to a leakage of opportunities from these markets to other ones. While demand is often viewed solely as the population that lives in the market, in reality many emerging markets have governmental organisations and other support organisations that make up additional potential demand. Branded suppliers to satisfy this demand are often rare. For example, many of the branded family-dining experiences that can serve the needs of residents and the lunchtime needs of local business people are frequently unavailable.

During the early 1990s, social franchising began to be considered as a way to re-develop the USA's emerging markets. For some local community development organisations, franchise ownership was used as a tool to bring branded products and services into a community. For others, the ownership of a franchised business was simply a way for the organisation to fund its charitable mission. Since the 1990s, following the success of Magic Johnson's work in bringing theatres to the inner cities, companies such as Pathmark supermarkets, Disney, The Gap clothing stores, 7-Eleven convenience stores, IHOP restaurants and Dunkin' Brands fast-food outlets have entered these markets to meet the pent-up demand. This has had a beneficial impact on those communities, including the creation of local jobs, the development of under-used real estate and the ownership of businesses by residents. These markets are particularly attractive to branded businesses for the following reasons:

- Pent-up demand for certain products and services translates into a captured consumer for those products and services

- The cost of labour is typically lower than in more-developed markets. Where previously residents needed to travel to outlying markets for jobs, local opportunities allow them to work closer to home

- The lower cost of real estate in these markets generally provides opportunities to upgrade it or to develop new real estate in under-used areas

- Transportation: most inner cities have well-developed road systems and mass transit

- Opportunities outside the local neighbourhood: some businesses can be located in the emerging market and provide products and services to more traditional markets at a lower cost. This can best be highlighted by trades franchisees (e.g. plumbing, electrical and handyman offerings) or business-to-business offerings (e.g. printing, janitorial and service providers) that can build a client base outside their neighbourhoods

A tool called a leakage analysis measures local demand against local supply. The difference between the two represents the potential sales by local branded merchants that would be leaking to neighbouring markets. A frequent example cited is the need for consumers in the inner cities to purchase their groceries outside their neighbourhoods because of the lack of a sufficient base of local supermarkets. Because of the experience of Pathmark in New York,[1] this imbalance is slowing being addressed. Frequently, the introduction of social franchises into inner-city neighbourhoods appears to be driven more by the willingness of the franchisor to enter

---

1 Pathmark's Harlem outlet was one of the chain's most successful stores based on sales per square foot.

the market than by what products and services will do well there. Equally, many non-profit organisations do not fully understand the breadth of available products and services offered by franchisors, which frequently reduces the pool of opportunities to select from. These are some of the root causes for the challenges many of these franchisors and franchisees face in doing business in the inner cities. It should not be surprising that many of the leakage analyses conducted revealed that certain products and services are in such high demand that per capita spending is often higher in these markets than in a franchisor's more traditional markets.

There are other more basic problems facing the advance of social franchising in the USA, including:

- **Lowered fees.** Often the costs to support inner-city franchises are higher than in a franchisor's more traditional markets. This can result in a lower return on investment to the franchisor, reducing its desire to grow this channel. This probably lowers the availability of social franchises rather than expands their availability

- **Inexperienced management.** Non-profit franchisees frequently do not have the management or business acumen to operate a for-profit branded location. They view the for-profit business as an extension of their non-profit organisation. In addition, many of the candidates for local ownership do not fit the economic or educational background of franchisor's traditional franchisee candidates. This contributes to these franchises under-achieving when compared to the market opportunity

The solution is evident. Markets require an evaluation based on consumer demand prior to their development in the inner cities. Non-profit and local candidates need to be evaluated to determine what additional, non-standard training and support is required. Financing and insurance need to be made available and returns for franchisor and franchisees need to be determined prior to any universal discounted fees being included in these offerings. At the same time, those brands that have been successful need to have committed to the development of sufficient numbers of locations to create brand awareness in the markets served, just as is done in their traditional markets. Many of the same issues are faced when developing franchises internationally designed to serve the societal needs of the poor.

Microfranchising internationally

Internationally, a growing number of NGOs are adopting franchise techniques. While providing local ownership opportunities for residents in the impacted communities, many of the core elements required for a successful social-sector franchise system do not seem to be well defined, developed or executed. As noted above, social-sector franchising's success is measured primarily by the output of the local franchisees and the ability of the franchisor to manage its core mission efficiently and effectively at a low per unit cost. Microfranchisors typically measure their success primarily on the grants they are able to raise from donors or investors and the number of locations opened. Rather than focusing their core mission on a limited offering of defined products and services, microfranchisors frequently, as required by the restricted grants available, deviate from their core service capabilities. Regardless of whether the product, service or methods of delivery fit the core competences of the organisation, microfranchisors will often justify them based on the available funds and restricted wishes of the granting organisation. This makes the achievement of the three-point test of standards, scalability and economy of scale difficult, if not impossible. As currently structured, operated and managed, microfranchising may not be sustainable until granting organisations understand how to use the inherent structure of a social-sector franchisor appropriately.

Social-sector franchisors need to offer niche products and services. The intended purpose of limiting its products and service to a defined deliverable method enables the organisation to focus on its core consumer while maximising its ability to achieve the three-point test. Examples of this focus can be found throughout franchising and indeed in all successful businesses. The products and service offering of McDonald's differs from that of Ruth's Chris Steak House. While both are restaurants that primarily offer beef, they target a different customer base and use different strategies to achieve their unique goals. Similarly, there are significant differences in the consumer offering and targeted customers of Courtyard by Marriott and a JW Marriott, even though both offer lodging for the business traveller. By understanding their core competences and by focusing on their consumer offering (which by definition requires them to limit those offerings to those that can be delivered to their brand standard and brand promise), business-format franchisors and, by extension, social-sector franchisors are able to meet the three-point test.

Granting organisations often tie funding availability to the grantor's unique mission. Grants tend to come with a set of delivery requirements, including personnel requirements or restrictions. Rather than use the delivery methods employed by the enterprise providing the products or services to the local community, grantors will frequently define the customer to be served, the products and services to be offered, the organisation necessary to provide the service and how performance matrix are measured. This requires the enterprise accepting those funds to change its mission to the wishes of the grantor. By doing so, the core mission and capabilities of the agency are corrupted and it loses the ability to meet the three-point test.

To successfully serve the needs of the poor in developing countries requires an understanding by granting agencies of the structures, capabilities and methods of the operations of the underlying agency's business. For social-sector franchisors this is less of a problem. Prior to accepting any grants or investments, social-sector franchisors need to measure the requirements of those funds against their unique mission and capabilities within their franchise structure. By doing so, social-sector franchisors can achieve a higher effective use of funds. This benefits the grantor, the franchisor, the franchisee and the local population and economy.

CFWshops: a social-sector franchisor

According to the World Health Organisation, nearly 30,000 children under the age of five die each day, and almost two out of three of these children die from common, easily preventable or treatable diseases and illnesses such as diarrhoea, pneumonia, malaria, measles and tetanus and from conditions such as malnutrition. The HealthStore Foundation, already discussed in earlier chapters, was organised to apply the lessons learned from the franchise industry to address the healthcare problem in the developing world. CFWshops are a business-format franchise system operated by the HealthStore Foundation in Kenya and Rwanda. With more than 85 locations, CFW is the largest indigenous social-sector franchisor in East Africa today and a member of the IFA. Because of the beneficial impact that business-format franchising can have in the emerging world, the IFA has recently established a social-sector franchising task force, which I chair. Serving on the task force with me are executives from some of the leading franchised brands in the world and also many of the leading professional experts serving domestic and international franchisors.

The HealthStore Foundation's mission is to harness entrepreneurial talent in Africa in order to improve access to essential drugs, basic healthcare and prevention services for children and their families using business models that maintain standards, are geometrically scalable, and achieve economies of scale. The 25-year goal is to leverage its substantial achievements in Kenya and Rwanda to develop a network of clinics serving 120 million to 150 million people a year throughout the developing world. The strategy is to continue the progressive expansion of Health-Store's social-sector franchise model to new communities and regions, while ensuring continued improvements in the quality and innovation underlying its delivery of healthcare services.

Over the past decade, the HealthStore Foundation (a US tax-exempt 501(c)(3) corporation) has implemented a for-profit franchise network of medical clinics and drug shops operating in Kenya and Rwanda under the CFWshops and more recently the CFWclinics brands. To facilitate funding and to further morph into a methodology better suited for business-format franchising, the board of directors of the HealthStore Foundation has decided to change its corporate structure to one that can accept investments from providers of social venture capital. The business model used by the CFWshops' social-sector franchise system targets the short list of easy-to-treat diseases and health problems (such as malaria, dysentery, respiratory infections and maternal and child health problems) responsible for approximately 70% of illness and deaths in areas where it operates. HealthStore also conducts HIV/AIDS prevention and education activities and treats opportunistic infections in HIV/AIDS patients. There are plans to eventually dispense anti-retroviral drugs under medical supervision. Each franchisee is accountable for upholding the clinical and business standards necessary for effective care and treatment. CFW estimates that it has served more than 2 million patients, customers, and children in school screenings since 2000.

The key to understanding why a social-sector franchise model as used by Health-Store succeeds better than other models is that it meets the basic three-point test used to measure the effectiveness of other business-format franchisors. Just as with traditional franchise organisations, any large-scale public healthcare network wanting to be successful must be designed to reach a large population on a large scale and over time needs to accomplish the following:

- Each outlet in the network must be highly standardised: each location must maintain the franchisor's standards necessary for effective care and treatment

- The network must scale geometrically into hundreds or thousands of outlets over a long period of time. Scale can only be achieved if brand standards are maintained

- The cost of treating each patient must fall as the total number of patients rises. As the network scales, revenue will increase while at the same time the span of control exercised at the headquarters and field level will increase, lowering the per-unit cost of managing the overall franchise system

CFWshops and CFWclinics work because they can maintain high-quality standards over a large network of locations at a lower cost per unit. Still, the underlying issue of the customer's inability to pay has led to significant and continuing issues at CFW. At the franchisee level, the vast majority of HealthStore's clinics are profitable (87% in 2007) for the nurses and community health workers who own and operate them as for-profit medical practices and drug shops. As in any well-structured and well-managed business-format franchise system, each franchisee's enjoyment of the benefits of their business is fully conditioned on their compliance with the franchisor's standards. Franchisees comply with system standards because they value the business more than they value any benefit they might receive by violating system standards. HealthStore Foundation has gathered some of the world's strongest leaders in relevant fields to provide management direction for the organisation. CEO Dr Gunther Faber is the former vice president for sub-Saharan Africa for GlaxoSmithKline. Dr Faber is supported by HealthStore's founder and former CEO, Scott Hillstrom, who chairs a board of directors including major franchise-industry leaders and two international healthcare experts with decades of experience in Africa.

The key to the success of CFWshops and CFWclinics is that it is structured, managed and functions as a typical business-format franchisor and is a true social-sector franchisor. Success is measured by local output, defined as the ability of the individual franchisee to achieve a quality and consistency of offering that attracts and maintains its customer base. Based on CFWshops' and CFWclinics' brand positioning and franchisee execution to the system's brand promise, franchisees have been able to attract and maintain customers. Given that competitors (government- and NGO-operated locations) have subsidised pricing often resulting in free or lower-cost consumer pricing, the success of HealthStore's approach is an indication of the success of a true social-sector franchise model.

Social venture-capital investors are a relatively new source of funding for social initiatives. Social venture-capital investors require reasonable financial returns, which is more that the social returns required by classic donors. Business models that forage at the bottom of the socioeconomic pyramid in basic healthcare, where margins are thin, may not be an attractive investment opportunity for them. Satisfying even reasonable return requirements may require modifications to business models that agree to blend commercial customers into the mission mix of customers to subsidise costs and achieve the necessary returns. Still, there will probably be a need for some continuing subsidies from traditional donors for a period of time as the system achieves necessary scale.

Turning microfranchisors into social-sector franchisors

While there are calls today for the use of microfranchising, most microfranchisor managers have little or no practical experience in business-format franchising and do not seem to recognise the sizeable differences between the two methods. Microfranchisors need to transition to a social-sector franchising model to achieve and establish a sustainable model necessary to meet their beneficial missions. One available avenue to address any deficiencies in the required skill set can be addressed through the IFA. Companies currently using a microfranchise approach to distribution should consider joining the IFA and the social-sector franchising task force. Their perspective and experience combined with that of the current members will create a powerful force for further learning and improvements in execution.[2]

Social-sector franchisors can achieve local brand excellence at a lowered cost per unit for headquarters and field management. This is accomplished through the development and execution of precise standards; headquarters, field and local support systems; a library of operations manuals and training programmes; and measurable performance matrixes for the headquarters, field and local operations. At the unit level, standards are enforced primarily through the support and training provided by the system. Each franchisee executes a franchise agreement that puts the franchisee at risk for their investment should they fail to meet the terms of the agreement, including the franchisor's brand standards. As the social-sector

---

2 For information on the IFA or the work of the social sector franchise task force, feel free to contact me at mseid@msaworldwide.com.

franchise system expands, significant benefits are achieved. These include but are not limited to:

- **Wealth creation.** The ability for individuals to obtain the right to offer a branded line of products or services

- **Job creation.** The opportunity for local members of the community to receive the necessary training to work within the franchise system and the opportunity to use those skills at the franchisee's location. Business-format franchising is the largest provider of entrepreneurial and business training in the world today

- **Development of a local supply chain.** The development of independent businesses to supply the needs of the franchisor and its growing franchise network. This is one of the most beneficial results a social-sector franchisor can provide in the developing world as it creates jobs and opportunities indirectly to the local economy

Other benefits include:

- Access to preferential real estate

- Lower unit development and construction costs

- Lower unit internal and external costs for signage furniture, fixtures and equipment

- Resources for improved research, development and testing of new products and services

- Development and execution of brand and local marketing

- Consumer education to prevent disease

- Influence over government policies

- Reduced costs for merchandise sold or used

- Lower costs for expendables and other system purchases

- Access to financing for franchisees

- Benefits for franchisee employees, including training in managing and operating a commercial business. Employees can be included in the pool of potential franchisees for the further growth of the franchise network. Other benefits include health and other insurance and discounted costs for personal purchases (telephone and Internet service, leasing programmes, capital purchases, etc.)

The operating manual

Each franchisor will have a library of manuals and training programmes for each element of its organisation, including but not limited to:

- Unit operations manual

- Franchisee manual

- Multi-unit franchisee manual

- Headquarters manual

- Field staff manual

- Supply chain manual

- Unit development manual

- Repair and maintenance manual

- Marketing and trademark usage manual

Social-sector franchisors will also require additional manuals, including those related to responding to grant opportunities. Training materials are required for the system's personnel to have the necessary education and knowledge to execute to brands strategy.

The solution

I opened this chapter examining why I thought the Millennium Project goals would not be met. I close this chapter with knowledge that they can be met, but only if those involved in funding and execution understand what needs to be changed and why. Social-sector franchising is a method of distribution and expansion. In developing any downstream distribution strategy, it is imperative to look at all methods available and then adopt those that work in the given situation. Few if any of Michael H. Seid & Associates' traditional business clients today employ one solution, as many operate company-owned locations and offer joint ventures and licences in addition to franchises. In looking at solutions to providing healthcare to the poor in the developing world, social-sector franchising will not be a panacea. It is merely another method to be used when its potentials can maximise the chances for success. However, even where other methods, including facilities owned and operated by government or NGOs, are considered better fits for the market, the tools used by social-sector franchisors, including standards and methods to achieve scalability and economy of scale, should be adopted.

10
Scaling the microfranchise at the base of the pyramid

Ryan Swee Ann Lee
London Business School, UK

While increasing amounts of work are being published on microfranchising and its benefits and various business models, little on the challenges and practicalities of replicating a pilot programme on a large scale has been researched. The majority of microfranchises operated by social enterprises in developing countries tend to operate at the local or national levels. Despite replication being a core advantage of microfranchising, most social enterprises find replication to scale to be a major challenge. Only a few, such as VisionSpring, which started in 2001, have achieved some level of support, partnering and financing at sufficient scale at regional or global levels (see Chapter 8). This seems to indicate that far from being an easy means of replication and growth, microfranchising has unique challenges that need to be addressed. Some hypotheses that could explain why microfranchise businesses are difficult to replicate are:

- The business environments that traditional franchise and microfranchise businesses operate in are different. Microfranchise businesses in undeveloped or developing countries face unique challenges and local conditions. These challenges include low education levels, poor business acumen of entrepreneurs, poor logistics infrastructure and political instability—all of which are not normally faced by traditional franchises. Hence, while traditional franchise concepts, principles and practices are useful, these need to be adapted or changed to suit the unique and harsher conditions that microfranchise businesses face

- Given the low income of customers and diversity of needs in low-income markets, the underlying assumptions and principles of traditional for-profit franchise approaches to marketing and sales may not be relevant. This difficulty is further complicated by the fact that low-income markets, most of which are informal economies with little market information available, are difficult to define and analyse, increasing the risk of investing and expanding a microfranchise business into new territories

- Microfranchise businesses today are run by non-profit entities and social entrepreneurs, who often have to deal with issues such as balancing social and business objectives, seeking funding and grants, and recruiting high-quality business talent to run a proper business. These issues are barriers to growth that have to be dealt with

Despite these difficulties, microfranchising is still a viable way forward for social enterprises to build sustainable businesses to sufficient scale at the base of the pyramid (BoP). With the right strategies, it is possible to grow a microfranchise business, although it may be the case that a microfranchise will never reach the rate and scale of traditional franchises.

This chapter will seek to provide an understanding of the uniqueness and challenges at the BoP, the economic stratum that microfranchises operate at. The intent is to bring out the key design principles, at micro and macro levels, which are critical for operating a successful business. To provide comparative context, I will start by looking at key reasons for franchise success and failure in developed countries. I will then analyse the nature of the BoP and how businesses can operate there. The next part will attempt to marry the insights gained from traditional franchising, microfranchising and nature of business at the BoP to understand the key factors required to build and grow a microfranchise business.

Foundations for franchise success

The strengths of franchises have led many to believe that franchising is a successful formula for growth for the franchisor and a quick way to entrepreneurship for the franchisee. Studies by Shane and Spell (1998), however, revealed that in the USA roughly one-third of franchisors cease to franchise within four years and three-quarters fail within 12 years.

Shane and Spell's study also revealed that the one-quarter of franchisors who succeeded had made a set of interrelated policy choices early in the process—and had stuck to them (Light 1997: 10). The choices made can be described by the following three broad commandments:

1. **Build a brand name.** One of the keys to franchise success is building a recognisable brand name. The challenge for a new franchisor is to grow

quickly in order to minimise the cost per outlet and per franchisee for advertising and promoting the brand name

2. **Let the locals do the work.** Signing up potential franchisees is not easy and is a full-time job in itself. One success factor is to select franchisees who can hit the ground running. Successful franchisors look for prior experience in an industry before signing a contract with a franchisee. Getting people who are willing and able to choose a viable site, negotiate a lease, open the outlet and adapt to local conditions and consumer tastes will free up time for the franchisor to scout for new business

3. **Trust and respect.** Earning trust is not simply a matter of wowing potential investors with tempting figures for projected sales volume. Franchisees, especially those who can be strong local partners, need serious reassurance before providing the money required for an outlet. Franchisors therefore need to take concrete steps to signal the quality and trustworthiness of their operations

Are all products and services franchisable?

The British Franchise Association (BFA) has provided a guide for companies to assess if their business is franchisable.[1] Not all businesses are suitable for franchising, particularly those that have the following characteristics:

- A product or service that is likely to have a market for only a short time

- Gross margins that are too low to offer a return on investment to the franchisor and franchisees

- Skill levels for each operating unit that require long training periods

- Predominantly repeat business customers whose loyalty relates to the individual providing the service and which would be difficult to transfer to a brand

- A geographically defined market that does not have the potential to be repeated in many places

- A business with audit and control requirements that are too critical to involve franchisees operating as separate legal entities

- A business that is failing

1 British Franchise Association: www.thebfa.org/franchbus.asp, accessed 18 August 2010.

A follow-up study by Shane (2005) revealed that franchising is highly concentrated in only 80 industries, out of hundreds, worldwide. The International Franchise Association reports that 18% of all franchise systems are found in fast food and 11% are found in general retail. Other data sources provide similar results. Table 10.1 summarises the percentage of franchisors for the most popular industries for franchising as reported in *Bond's Franchise Guide* (Bond 2004).

Table 10.1 **The most popular industries for franchising**

Industry	Percentage of franchisors	Percentage of franchised units
Fast food	15.2	26.8
Restaurants	7.0	3.8
Automotive products	6.2	5.5
Maintenance and cleaning	5.4	8.2
Building and remodelling	4.9	1.5
Specialty retail	3.8	1.5
Specialty food	3.8	2.0
Health and fitness	3.3	3.5
Child development	3.2	0.7
Lodging	3.1	5.9

Source: Adapted from Bond 2004:14-15

Shane (2005) postulates that the limited range of industries in which franchising operates, combined with the evidence of better franchisor performance in some industries than in others, suggests that an important issue for potential franchisors is to determine whether franchising is appropriate for the industry in which they operate. Shane identifies nine characteristics that make franchising appropriate for an industry:

1. **Production and distribution occur in limited geographic markets.** Franchising works best in industries where products and services cannot all be delivered from a centralised spot. Therefore, franchising is more likely to occur in retail and service businesses than in manufacturing businesses. Franchising also tends to work best where some aspect of operation, such as building the brand name or sourcing supply, is subject to economies of scale, but production and distribution need to take place on a small scale in a variety of different locations

2. **Physical locations are helpful for serving customers.** Franchising is more effective in industries in which the product or service is provided to the end customer at a set location than in industries in which the product or service are provided at the customer's premises. It is harder to minimise conflict between franchisees in such industries. Franchisees are independent

businesses, so they have incentives to compete with each other, a situation that is not present when the same party owns the different locations. While franchising can, and does, occur in industries without set locations for production and distribution, such as online travel services, it requires a vertical organisation in which managers tell sales agents not to compete with each other for customers in order to avoid between-location competition

3. **Local market knowledge is important for performance.** Franchising tends to be more effective in industries in which local knowledge is more important for business success than in other industries. Because the franchisee comes from the local market, he or she can provide information about needed adaptations to the market more cheaply than a centralised company can search for it. Moreover, as owners, franchisees profit from adapting products or services to meet the needs of local markets and thus have stronger incentives to do so than hired employees

4. **Local management discretion is beneficial.** In industries where fixed pricing and a standardised approach work poorly, having managerial discretion at the local level to negotiate with customers is important

5. **Brand-name reputation is a valuable competitive advantage.** As mentioned above, franchising is most effective in industries in which brand-name development is important. This is the case in fragmented industries such as restaurants. In these industries, the development of a brand name is often an important competitive advantage to firms that lack other ways to differentiate themselves from their competition. Because building a brand name relies heavily on advertising, which is influenced by scale economies, franchising provides a mechanism for lowering the costs of building a company's brand. In addition, brand names provide a way for customers who have little information about providers in particular markets—such as tourists looking for a meal—to ensure quality

6. **The level of standardisation and codification of the process of creating and delivering the product or service is high.** Although franchising works better in industries in which local discretion in the process of selling to customers is more important, that does not mean it works well in industries in which products or services need to be customised. Rather, franchising works best in industries with standardised products and services. Standardisation is essential in order to preserve brand name and quality. It also makes it easier to determine the right policies and procedures for monitoring the actions of independent business people (the franchisees), who are serving customers under the system's brand name and using its operating procedures

7. **The training and development of franchisees can be done quickly.** Franchising requires an industry in which an average person can learn the

operation of the business with only the training that the franchisor can provide in a few days or weeks. A prerequisite is that the operation of the business can be codified. One of the critical things franchisees need is an operating manual or written set of procedures for running the business

8. **Outlets are not too costly or risky to establish.** Franchising works best in industries in which outlets are neither very expensive nor very risky for people to operate. Research has shown that industries in which outlets are larger in terms of employment, sales or physical space tend to franchise less than industries in which outlets are smaller. Franchising works poorly in cyclical industries with a high level of risk resulting from factors outside the franchisee's control, such as variation in the general economic environment

9. **The effort of outlet operators is hard to measure relative to their performance.** Franchising works best in industries such as retail, in which measuring the level of people's performance can be done easily and effectively, but measuring their effort is more difficult. For example, franchising works well in fast food because sales, which are easy to measure, tend to increase when people work harder at advertising and promoting a business and when they maintain efficiency and cleanliness in outlets, even though things such as the effort that they expended to clean the outlets or promote the products are hard to measure

The franchise system has proven to be a successful model for businesses to scale and for budding entrepreneurs to start a business with relatively lower risk. However, it is not a formula for assured success. Only a fraction of goods and services are suitable for franchising. Microfranchises could learn a lot from successful traditional franchises and take heed of the success factors described in this section.

What is the base of the pyramid?

The base of the pyramid is the largest, but poorest socioeconomic group in economics. In global terms, the BoP comprises 3.7 billion people who live on less than US$8 per day (in purchasing power parity), typically in developing countries (World Economic Forum 2009: 5). The phrase 'base of the pyramid' is used in particular by people developing new models of doing business that deliberately target that demographic, often using new technology. This field is also often referred to as the 'bottom of the pyramid', but the term 'base' is now preferred to 'bottom' because of the negative connotations of the latter. The phrase 'bottom of the pyramid' was first used by US President Franklin D. Roosevelt in his 7 April 1932 radio address, 'The Forgotten Man', in which he said,

> These unhappy times call for the building of plans that rest upon the for-
> gotten, the unorganised but the indispensable units of economic power
> ... that build from the bottom up and not from the top down, that put
> their faith once more in the forgotten man at the bottom of the economic
> pyramid.

The amount of research and publications today on various aspects of the BoP—strategies, operating principles, business models and protocols, among others—is vast. This research has been undertaken by a wide variety of organisations and individuals, including academics, consulting firms, non-government foundations, and global institutions such as the United Nations and the World Economic Forum. Arguably, the interest in the BoP was sparked by the publication of the article, 'The Fortune at the Bottom of the Pyramid', by Prahalad and Hart (2002), and later by Prahalad's book of the same title (2006).

Since almost all microfranchises operate in BoP markets, the following part will provide an understanding of the uniqueness and challenges of the BoP from the extensive research already done. The aim is to sieve out the key principles required by businesses to operate successfully, and to apply some these to start and grow a microfranchise.

Unique characteristics of the BoP economy

BoP markets are dominated by informal economic activities. The streets of cities, towns and villages are lined by barbers, cobblers, food vendors, garbage collectors, waste recyclers and sellers of myriad non-perishable items ranging from locks and keys to soaps and detergents. According to a study by the International Labour Organisation (Fairbourne *et al.* 2007), the informal economy has grown substantially in all developing regions.

Businesses operating in the informal economy are generally constrained by the following factors (Henriques and Herr 2007: 46-7):

- **Lack of access to credit, working capital and investment capital.** There are frequently inadequate levels of property rights and trademark protection in these economies, and hence lack of collateral for lending

- **Low productivity.** Businesses typically use labour-intensive production methods. Equipment and organisation are basic and awareness of improvements in production technology and methodology is low. Most cannot achieve the economies of scale needed to be competitive

- **Poor working conditions.** Inadequate lighting, insufficient ventilation and low standards of occupational safety and health often contribute to poor working conditions

- **Supply and marketing issues.** Businesses have limited access to resources and technology, as well as to opportunities for bulk purchase of inputs and effective marketing of outputs. There is also a lack of information on, for example, prices and viability of products

- **Lack of education and skills.** There is often no access to formal education and vocational training. Low levels of technology and technical and managerial skills compound problems of low productivity, insufficient innovation and upgrading and low levels of product quality

- **Infrastructure issues.** Poor infrastructure, for example, lack of transport, storage, water, electricity, working premises and physical facilities, has a detrimental impact on business

Corruption in the BoP economies is often rife. The common reason is lack of regulations, legal structures and enforcement, particularly in Africa. The irony is that in countries with proper legal structures and laws, corruption is also a problem. Prahalad (2006) reasoned that there are two main causes. First, countries such as India and Peru have a proliferation of micro regulations, resulting in confusing interpretation of rules by bureaucrats, lawyers and businesspeople. Second, bureaucrats in some countries such as China frequently interpret the law to suit their personal interests. In this situation, business can flourish where bureaucrats have a significant role in businesses and the alignment of interests of the private sector and bureaucracy seems to have worked. However, the poor in villages might be paying a price: many face inconsistent laws that suit the bureaucrats' business.

Ironically, despite the challenges in the informal economies, innovation can thrive at the BoP. The informal economy is arguably the purest form of free market: free-from regulation and other constraints that limit how entrepreneurs can innovate to run their businesses. It is perhaps this innovative nature, coupled with the steeliness borne out of surviving in a harsh environment, which has captured the interest of the developed world in the BoP.

Unique characteristics of BoP consumers

Selling to consumers at the BoP requires a different approach from those at the higher economic strata. While BoP consumers may behave differently from market-to-market, they generally exhibit the following characteristics (World Economic Forum 2009):

- **Low and unstable income.** The burden of low incomes is compounded by the fact that income streams for BoP households are unpredictable. As customers, they resist large upfront outlays and recurring expenses in the form of instalments. In addition, most lack access to affordable credit that would enable essential purchases or business investments. Therefore, companies might look for ways to align their prices and financing for consumers with incomes that ebb and flow. They might also design financial incentives that provide a stable income and encourage entrepreneurship when engaging with the BoP as producers

- **Difficult conditions.** The living spaces of BoP households are typically small. Conveniences that more affluent households take for granted—such as uninterrupted electricity and clean running water—have yet to reach many BoP households. These conditions impose constraints on the type of products that the BoP can produce and consume and their level of productivity. Companies engaging with the poor could strive to deliver business and product solutions that address these constraints

- **Smart shoppers.** Since every cent counts for low-income households, they are unlikely to spend money on products they don't understand or trust. However, they don't necessarily prefer cheaper or stripped-down versions of more expensive offerings. They want high-quality products, even if they have to ration their use. They prefer products that are known to be reliable or are demonstrably superior

- **Unfamiliarity.** They are unfamiliar with many products, technologies and procedures. At the BoP, communication channels are scarce, literacy rates are low, and many consumers are often first-time users. These factors increase the need for consumer education, product trials and demonstrations to explain product benefits and usage. Producers and entrepreneurs also lack crucial information. Companies sourcing from the BoP must be willing to invest in educating their suppliers as well

- **Trusted advice.** They look for trusted advice. Because BoP consumers are new to many products and have limited access to information sources, they are more likely to rely on the opinions of people they know and trust. Additionally, they have traditionally mistrusted large firms and private organisations. Advertisements can help raise awareness, but they seldom address all the barriers to purchasing a product. The experiences (good and bad) of friends and relatives, as well as direct experience through product testing and demonstrations, strongly influence the BoP consumer's choice of products and brands. For that reason, encouraging local groups to advocate products and services to friends and creating networks for educating first-time users are valuable tools in many business models

- **Demand respect.** Surveys of low-income households elicit statements such as: 'We need to be well dressed and look good; otherwise, people will not take us seriously' and 'At school, the teachers will write my children off as poor and not deserving of a good education.' Being treated equitably and with dignity also influences where BoP consumers shop. They often prefer neighbourhood shops—which are familiar and offer personalised service—to supermarkets, which may require more travel time and seem intimidating. Companies should consider such sensitivities and treat the BoP—whether as consumers or employees—with respect

- **Disadvantages.** Because BoP consumers' spending power is limited, and the costs to reach them are high, they tend to be served by inefficient supply chains. This often results in them paying higher prices for inferior goods, compared to wealthier members of their societies—an inequity often referred to as the 'BoP penalty'. This cost dynamic presents a tremendous opportunity for organisations and businesses to offer better-quality and more affordable options to the poor. But realising that opportunity will require uprooting entrenched stereotypes and being open to new ways of engaging with this segment

Basic principles for operating at the BoP

Doing business at the BoP requires unique approaches given the characteristics of the economy and its consumers. Based on the wealth of research that has been conducted on companies that have operated successfully at the BoP, some basic principles have been developed (Prahalad 2006; World Economic Forum 2009):

- **Provide access rather than ownership.** Instead of measuring a product's market potential in terms of the number of people who can buy it, companies should think about who can use the product. This would open up a much larger and potentially profitable opportunity

- **Create the capacity to consume.** To convert the BoP into a consumer market, companies have to create the capacity to consume. Cash-poor and with a low level of unsteady income, the BoP consumer has to be accessed differently. Many subsist on daily wages and have to use cash conservatively. They tend to make purchases only when they have cash and buy only what they need for that day. Single-serve packaging—be it shampoo, ketchup, tea and coffee or aspirin—is well suited to this population. For example, in India, single-serve sachets have become the norm for a wide variety of producers. A similar approach to creating capacity to consume is through innovative purchase schemes, especially for higher-priced products such as appliances. Through a sophisticated credit-rating system coupled with counselling, Casas Bahia in Brazil is able to provide access to high-quality appliances to consumers who could not otherwise afford them

- **Monetise hidden assets.** Many hidden assets, capable of generating economic value, reside within BoP communities. These assets include undocumented capital, which individuals have used historically but do not have formal ownership rights over; personal and community resources, such as community power and personal reputation; and under-used assets, such as civil society organisations and local SMEs. To identify and monetise these assets, companies should mobilise the community by integrating local entrepreneurs into their value chains. Companies should also collaborate with other organisations and possibly even competitors to share community skills, knowledge and training in order to uncover the large human resource potential in the communities

- **Bridge the gap in public goods.** Hard and soft infrastructures enable market activity and value creation, and they are largely considered the responsibility of the public sector. Given that the public sector typically lacks the capacity to provide these infrastructures, companies could overcome infrastructure constraints in two ways: they can form partnerships with the public sector to improve the circumstance of the BoP, or they can find innovative ways—often in collaboration with others—to bridge the gap in public goods. Private intervention can support the creation of public goods, not just for philanthropic reasons, but also to ensure long-term profitability in low-income markets. Interventions in the public domain by many companies around the world have demonstrated that they can add value for customers as well as producers

- **Scale out versus scale up.** To serve customers efficiently, companies often work to reduce the unit costs of products and achieve economies of scale through centralised production in large factories. But this model has two problems when it comes to the low-income market. First, it increases the costs of serving and sourcing since producers and customers live far from central factories. Second, centralised factories often produce standardised products for global or regional markets, which is often not what low-income consumers need or want. The traditional concept of economies of scale often fails when it comes to serving the low-income market. Although demand and supply in this market is potentially large in the aggregate, these consumers buy and sell locally because they live primarily in small, scattered groups. The alternative to scaling up is to scale out: create experiments that can be adapted and rolled out to increasing numbers of markets. This would involve low-income people as producers and distributors, as well as consumers, and would minimise overheads. Companies need to balance scaling up (through centralisation) with scaling out (through localisation) to achieve the right combination of low costs and customised solutions

- **Influence rather than exert authority.** As companies grow, the natural inclination is to exert more control on decision-making and tighten monitoring and audit systems. Yet at the BoP, information gathering and control has to happen through collaboration and with local partners. Given the wide dispersion of villages and communities in emerging markets, it is crucial to retain a high degree of flexibility and decentralisation in order to adapt to local changes and control costs. To reduce the overall costs of monitoring when enlisting the BoP as consumers and co-producers, companies must first align their goals with the community's interests and then introduce local checkpoints. Organisations that have managed to link their interests to those of their local partners have found that they can deliver more value at significantly lower cost. This is also true for partnerships with different organisations. Besides working with local players, businesses can partner with other organisations to create and share assets. But these organisations should be viewed more as a network of peers, rather than vendors

The BoP markets have unique characteristics that require businesses that are used to serving developed markets to adapt their products and service delivery in order to be successful. As players in the BoP markets, microfranchise businesses need to understand the unique characteristics of the BoP economy and consumers. In a way, the microfranchise system, through an innovative way of distributing products and services at the BoP, has addressed some of the market's uniqueness. However, setting up and growing a successful business at the BoP is a challenging task and requires a different approach compared to in a developed market.

The challenge of scale

Reaching scale is difficult for any enterprise. It is even more difficult for an enterprise aiming to serve or engage the poor by providing socially beneficial products and services in a financially self-sustaining way. Microfranchising has been touted as the optimal tool to scale social programmes and businesses quickly at the BoP. Yet empirical evidence reveals that few microfranchises have been able to grow successfully. When they do grow, they do so at rates much slower than traditional franchises in developed markets. According to a study by the Monitor Group (Karamchandani *et al.* 2009), although many microfranchisees are—or have the potential to be—financially sustainable, few have become commercially viable. Franchisors are often dependent on remittances, royalty fees or commission, which are difficult to collect from franchisees, or on donor funds to keep afloat and provide pan-franchise functions. Indeed, financial self-sufficiency is often only a secondary objective in many donor-led efforts (Karamchandani *et al.* 2009). Despite the Monitor Group's study, a few microfranchise businesses such as VisionSpring, Grameen Village Phone and HealthStore Foundation have found ways to replicate and grow their businesses beyond the start-up phase. Analysis of these businesses and interviews with senior management of some of these enterprises reveal that the key challenges of building and growing a scalable microfranchise are:

- Establishing a viable and scalable pilot business or programme

- Seeking additional financial resources to fund growth during the replication phase

- Harnessing organisational resources to manage growth

In the next section, I will describe the challenges of scaling a business through microfranchising and develop a strategy to establish a viable pilot microfranchise business. I will then describe the strategies for overcoming financial and internal resource constraints for replication and growth.

Social enterprises as microfranchisors

Microfranchise relationships are often initiated by social enterprises that recognise the potential for helping the poor by teaching them how to build an income-generating venture for themselves. A social enterprise can find or create a proven business model, develop appropriate systems to guide that business, and then replicate it (Gibson 2007). Social enterprises typically assume their franchisor role in one of two ways:

- **As business creators.** The social enterprise can establish systems, protocols and training that increase the likelihood of successful replication, and then franchise the business model at a reasonable cost to interested parties

- **As investors in an already-operating micro-enterprise.** Instead of creating a business to franchise, a social enterprise may want to create a microfranchise network in an area in which it is already working. The social enterprise will probably know the market conditions and micro-enterprise owners who have good business ideas but whose businesses are struggling. In this situation, the social enterprise can purchase or invest in an established and promising micro-enterprise, strengthen it to the point where it is a viable business, and then replicate it

Whether a microfranchise business is created from scratch or purchased from an existing micro-entrepreneur, social enterprises will need to find funding sources to start the business. More fundamentally, by being involved in business, social enterprises will now have to take care of a new bottom line—business performance—in addition to their social mission. The challenge is to find a financial structure that reinforces the organisation's mission, uses scarce resources efficiently, is responsive to changes and is achievable (Dees 1997).

Related to Dees's social enterprise spectrum, Fairbourne has described a microfranchising spectrum based on three models differentiated by their financing structures (Fairbourne 2007a):

1. **Social microfranchising.** The objectives of social microfranchising are, first, to provide goods and services at an affordable price and, second, to create jobs at the BoP. Social microfranchising operates on a financial model that relies on donations and grants rather than one focused on business sustainability

2. **Sustainable microfranchising.** Arguably, this is the model most social enterprises aim for in their microfranchise business. This model seeks a triple bottom line, which is (1) to create a profit for the microfranchisee, (2) to create financial sustainability for the organisation, and (3) to provide goods and services at an equitable cost. Profits generated are used to create more microfranchises or to assist the existing microfranchisees in increasing their profits through initiatives such as additional training and marketing

3. **For-profit microfranchising.** This model is similar to sustainable microfranchising, with the additional need to return profit to investors. This model works best with multinational corporations and the like because of the much higher start-up capital required to scale quickly and become profitable. People and organisations that pursue this model but lack the financial and technical capacity to see it through run the risk of losing sight of the social aspect and placing an undue amount of emphasis on repaying investors

The choice of the structure for the microfranchise business has huge implications for the immediate and longer-term business and organisational strategies. It is important that the structure be given due consideration as early as possible.

Impetus for growth

Microfranchising is a tool to help bring an underlying social enterprise programme to scale. Why reach scale is a question that should already be answered before an organisation decides to use a microfranchise business model. Based on case studies and interviews, the two main reasons to scale are:

1. **To solve social and economic problems on a large scale.** This is the social goal of the business. Essentially, the social enterprise aims to create a major social impact by creating economic activities in the BoP market. Many of the products that these enterprises sell—such as healthcare, reading glasses and mobile phone services—are lacking at the BoP and there is a need to reach out to as many consumers who need these products as possible

2. **To reach break-even scale in the business.** This is the business goal of any enterprise and one that a traditional non-profit organisation does not usually think about. Social enterprises, depending on which part of the microfranchising spectrum they aim to operate at, typically aim to be self-sustainable or profitable. Reaching this objective requires the business to reach a break-even scale as soon as possible in order to recover costs. The types of products and services sold have low margins, so achieving high economies of scale is essential

Growing a microfranchise

It is useful for social enterprises to understand the typical growth pattern of a commercial start-up business so as to grasp the overall context for managing growth. Many commercial principles and theories are relevant to social enterprises. A company goes through various challenges as it undergoes different stages of growth from local start-up to global company. Churchill and Lewis (1983: 3-9) have proposed a five-stage growth model to analyse the challenge of growing businesses. These five stages are:

Stage 1: Existence

Stage 2: Survival

Stage 3: Success

Stage 4: Take-off

Stage 5: Resource maturity

A company that intends to build a franchise business will thus need to build a viable business model first at stages 1 and 2. After accumulating sufficient financial resources and proving its business model, it could become a franchisor typically at stages 3 and 4 in order to grow its business. The main challenges that this company will face at the different stages of growth through franchising are:

- Building and proving a business model (stages 1 and 2):
    - Obtaining customers and delivering products and services
    - Managing revenues, expenses and cash flows

- Expansion through franchising (stages 3 and 4):
    - Maintaining profitability throughout economic cycles
    - Obtaining financial resources to fund growth
    - Marshalling the company's organisational resources for growth
    - Building systems, processes and new competences to find partners and manage franchisees in new markets
    - Planning and executing business and marketing strategies through franchising

Having a strong foundation from the start is the most critical and challenging step for building a microfranchise business that is scalable. The pilot business must succeed and microfranchisors face additional challenges that commercial franchisors do not typically face. First is the need to design products, services and a business model that will be appropriate for the BoP market. Second is the need to integrate the franchise system into the business model right from the start. Social enterprises usually do not have the luxury of testing the product and services, as the microfranchisees are normally the only route to the market at the BoP. The BoP Protocol developed by the BoP Protocol Project, led by Cornell University, offers a good guide to starting the process of building a pilot business at the BoP. Broadly, the protocol includes (Simanis and Hart 2008: 9ff.):

Pre-field process:

- Selecting the site
- Forming and preparing the team
- Selecting the local partners

In-field process:

Phase 1: opening up

- Building deep dialogue with the community
- Developing the project team
- Developing collective entrepreneurship (including the microfranchisee network)
- Co-creating the business concept

Phase II: building the ecosystem

- Transitioning from project team to formal business organisation
- Building shared commitment
- Developing new capability
- Co-creating the business prototype

Phase III: creating the local enterprise

- Developing organisational and management skills
- Building the market base
- Enhancing collective entrepreneurship and partnerships
- Co-creating the business enterprise

The process is represented schematically in Figure 10.1. The pre-field and in-field stages are where the social enterprise attempts to establish a successful pilot business before it is ready to be replicated. Social enterprises should use the protocol as a guide rather than being a prescriptive tool. The business conditions will be unique for each BoP market and adaptation is important.

Figure 10.1 **The process of starting the BoP business**

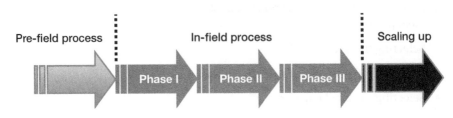

Source: Adapted from the BoP Protocol (Simanis and Hart 2008)

Specific challenges when starting up

Research and interviews reveal, unsurprisingly, that social enterprises face myriad challenges when starting the pilot franchise business. The five key challenges are as follows:

1. Identifying the pioneer market and theory of change

2. Identifying the products and services appropriate for franchising

3. Developing and building the supporting business model

4. Seeking support and partnerships to launch the business

5. Developing and building the franchise system

I will next look at each challenge in turn:

1. Identifying the pioneer market and theory of change

Given the extensive needs for social development and poverty relief in the developing world, a challenging task is to identify in which country and community to establish the pilot microfranchise programme. The questions to ask are:

Which country and community has a market gap that needs to be addressed? Answering this question will require the organisation to analyse the supply and demand of essential public goods and services to be provided. Most critically, it needs to find out why the market gap exists. At the BoP, answering this question is not easy given the lack of market data and information and the nature of the informal economy. Organisations can find the answers through different sources, such as local governments, communities and non-profit entities that are established in the country and community. Compared to normal market research and analysis in more-developed markets, this work will require significant time, effort and network at the local level.

Are the appropriate conditions in place to set up a business in this country and community with minimal risk? Similar to how commercial companies assess market and business risk, the political and macroeconomic conditions in the country need to be considered for suitability to set up a microfranchise operation. The risks of setting up a business in a developing country are inherently much higher than in developed markets. The key risk parameters to consider include:

- Political stability

- Legal system and regulations

- Financial system

- Physical infrastructure

- Purchasing power parity of the population

- Education level

- Social norms

For the setting up of a pilot programme, these risks should be minimised as much as possible. The business viability and sustainability of a pioneer venture need to be considered in conjunction with the social aims. Organisations can assess these risks again through local governments, communities and non-profits that are established in the country and community. Key country information and data can also be found from various open sources such as the United Nations, development banks and the CIA *World Factbook*.

What is the theory of change? Other than meeting market demand and supply, a strong theory of change in the social context needs to be rationalised and articulated. The theory of change helps to clarify the social value of the business for its key constituents: recipients, donors, staff and volunteers. It should reflect the reasons why the business will work and how its activities will produce successful outcomes for its key constituents (Bradach 2003). Being able to communicate this theory of change is crucial to securing initial seed funding through grants or donations.

2. Identifying the products and services appropriate for franchising

Not all products and services are suitable for franchising at the BoP. Suitable products and services typically have the following features:

- They fulfil sustained needs that require repeated purchase

- They provide an adequate gross margin for the franchisee to cover cost and earn a profit

- They are easy to understand and market

- They are good quality with value for money

- They are purchasable in small scale, such as single-serve packaging

- They are sourced or produced locally, or easily transportable from a central source at low cost

It is critical to engage the local partners and communities to identify the appropriate products and services. The process can be time-consuming and resource-intensive, but it is necessary to get it right at the start.

3. Developing and building the supporting business model

The microfranchise system needs to be supported by the larger business value chain. While organisations understandably focus on the downstream microfranchise operations, building strong, sustainable upstream and organisational support—supply, manufacturing, marketing, R&D and human resources—is equally critical.

Given the nature of BoP markets, the microfranchisor has to design a value chain that delivers quality products at low cost, while ensuring the financial sustainability of the business and the profitability of the microfranchisees. Social enterprises operating microfranchises at the BoP will need to address the following challenges across the entire value chain:

- **Supply chain.** Creating efficient supply chains and solving myriad challenges around the movement of goods and monies is particularly challenging in developing countries. Social enterprises could either outsource the supply chain or become supply-chain players themselves. The key consideration is whether they can do it more efficiently at a lower cost than other providers

- **Marketing and branding.** Like traditional franchisors, microfranchisors need to cover most of the marketing and branding of their products themselves. Branding is critical for a microfranchise, building reputation among customers and, more importantly, attracting microfranchisees. This is not an easy task as the brand identity, decor and image must be appropriate for the clients, depending on the location and market. It is a task shared between the organisation's headquarters and country managers and franchisees who understand the consumer behaviour in local markets in order to determine the strategic marketing and branding efforts

- **Supporting activities.** Building the human resources, development expertise and infrastructure at the franchisor level, in order to support the primary activities and franchisee management, will be particularly challenging given the lean sources of most non-profit bodies. The cost of management has to be kept low, particularly for pilot programmes. Organisations could address this by seeking support from philanthropists and commercial companies to fund the project and provide pro bono professional services, or by forming partnerships with other organisations to share the overhead costs of running the project

4. Seeking support and partnerships to launch the business

It is rare for organisations planning to launch a microfranchise business to do so by themselves, given the challenges described. It is critical to seek support and partnerships, but this in itself is a challenge given the vast demand for resources by the large number of non-profit entities around the world. Organisations secure funding, support and partnerships through various ways. Some, such as VisionSpring, were fortunate to be established by an existing corporate sponsor that could provide initial seed funding, network support and business expertise. Others have to build strong proposals and plans to seek funding and support from philanthropists, commercial sponsors and non-profit foundations. Securing support for a microfranchise pilot is particularly challenging, however, given that a business model has yet to be proven. One strategy to address this challenge is to start with company-owned stores or direct sellers to allow time to test the business model and product acceptability and measure the impact before building the case to scale through microfranchising. This approach is typically more suitable for organisations that are able to secure seed funding from established sponsors.

Another strategy, for non-profits that have already been operating social programmes in specific locations but do not have the resources to start a pilot business, is to articulate a strong theory of change of why microfranchising is appropriate to scale their social programmes (Bradach 2003: 20). Enough substantial evidence of success to justify replication has to be provided. What constitutes 'enough' will vary, depending on the nature of the programme, its longevity and the scope of contemplated replication. The organisation needs to reflect its view of why microfranchising will work and its understanding of the activities required to produce successful outcomes for its key constituents.

5. Developing and building the franchise system

Recruiting franchisees is probably one of the hardest and most expensive functions for franchisors. This is no different for microfranchises, although the challenges are unique. Microfranchising is a new concept and potential franchisees at the BoP are difficult to identify and are risk-averse. Research reveals that the profile of a microfranchisee is not the same as that of a microcredit client. The best microfranchisees are not necessarily those who are the most entrepreneurial. The ability and willingness to follow processes and procedures and a desire to learn are more important than having a high risk tolerance or the ability to generate a new business idea (Lehr 2008: 10). Some of the lessons learned include:

- **Community organisations are good sources of leads.** Local organisations, including schools, universities, financial institutions, community-based organisations and other development entities are good sources of leads for finding qualified franchisees

- **The qualifications, skills and characteristics of a franchisee vary according to the types of product and service sold.** Some, such as healthcare and pharmaceutical products, will require a higher level of qualifications. For example, HealthStore's CFWshops can franchise only experienced nurses. In addition to certain skill qualifications, the microfranchisee's motivation, education level and reputation in the community are found to be reliable predictors of success. Training the franchisees is one of the key challenges at the BoP, given that most of them have a low level of education and no formal business training. The microfranchise model has to be simple enough to be understood and managed. Simplicity should therefore be given high priority (Lehr 2008: 8). This will also enable clear and simple processes to be documented, an essential factor to enable scaling subsequently

Another factor to consider is the microfranchisee's sources of financing. Most microfranchisees need an initial investment and working capital of between $75 and $500. Financing may be made available through a microfinance institution (MFI) or bank. The microfranchisor could act as an intermediary between the franchisee and the MFI or bank. Thus, by forming a partnership with an MFI early, the franchisor could help the franchisee overcome the initial financing challenge. For franchisees who are unable to borrow from an MFI or bank, the franchisor will have to offer some form of financial support or create a revenue model that lowers the cost of entering the business. These may include:

- **Sweat equity.** Franchisors that have adequate funding for recruitment and training can consider the option of sweat equity—where the microfranchisee puts in labour and effort. However, the franchisor bears all the financial risk with this model. It will also need a sustainable revenue model that is able to generate a sufficient amount of capital for future recruitment of franchisees and to expand the franchise business

- **Revenue-sharing.** The franchisor could reduce its franchising fees by focusing more on revenue-sharing based on sales. This is an option that could reduce the financial risk for the franchisor and franchisee

The main concern for franchisees is profitability. They need to be convinced that the franchise model will enable them to recoup the initial investment, whether monetary or sweat equity, as quickly as possible. They also need to be convinced that the franchise model is sustainable for them to be profitable, paying more than they could earn elsewhere, for the long haul. Typically, microfranchisees need to earn a profit within six months. If they cannot become profitable, the franchise model will not be sustainable regardless of whether overall operations are subsidised (Lehr 2008: 11). Importantly, even if the microfranchisee is profitable, the business model will need to generate sufficient revenue to cover the franchisor's supply chain, marketing and overall management cost. This is the inherent tension that microfranchisors have to manage through a sustainable franchisee investment and revenue model.

Unlike traditional franchising where an account manager at the franchisor's headquarters usually manages franchisee relationships, microfranchisors have found that the best way is to manage franchisees through a local head office. In a way, the local head office acts like a master franchisee, akin to traditional franchise. This operating model offers several advantages. First, the franchisor could reduce its human resources cost significantly by employing local people. Second, a micro-franchise is a local business tailored to local conditions. A franchise manager on the ground, close to the franchisees, could better manage franchisee issues than one who is thousands of miles away. Third, many BoP consumers still have a deep suspicion of Western organisations, both corporate and non-profit. Having a local office with local employees will help to address this issue and enable trust between the consumers and the brand of product that the franchisees are selling.

Setting up the local office and hiring local employees is a challenging task in itself. For pioneer programmes in new markets, particularly, it is not easy to find a country manager that has the expertise, skills and experience to set up the franchise operation. Partnerships with local organisations and other non-profits may help the franchisor find one. If this is not possible, a non-local with the qualifications will have to be employed. However, it is critical that a local second-in-charge or operations manager be hired as an understudy. This is to prepare the ground for the country office to be eventually localised. Interviews with VisionSpring and Health-Store reveal that there is no shortage of educated local managers in the countries they operate in. The key is to have an experienced person to hold the local managers' hands until they are ready.

The constraints to growth

After establishing a sound business and pioneer microfranchise model, the franchisor will be looking at replication and growth. The BoP Protocol mentioned above has prescribed a pollination process for scaling the business. However, findings from my research and interviews show that the key challenges to the growth of a microfranchise business are typically associated with capacities at the social enterprise (franchisor) level, rather than replicating the franchise system. These two main issues are related to financial and organisational resources.

Several organisational factors, which change in importance as the business grows and develops, are prominent in determining ultimate success or failure. Four of these factors, identified by Churchill and Lewis (1983: 9) are:

- Financial resources, including cash and borrowing power
- Organisational resources:
  - Personnel resources, relating to number and quality of people, particularly at the management levels
  - Systems resources, in terms of the degree of sophistication of information and planning and control systems

– Business resources, including customer relations, market share, supplier relations, manufacturing and distribution processes, technology and reputation, all of which give the company a position in its industry and market

At the level of BoP markets, the diffusion time-frames for products, technologies and concepts to spread can be short compared to developed markets. The result is that microfranchisors at the BoP have to cope with the challenge of rapid diffusion of new products and services. For example, to build a network of 1 million direct distributors in India, Hindustan Lever Ltd in India has to recruit and train 30,000–40,000 people every month. Evaluating applicants and training and inducting them into the system create new demands on the process of management. Few firms around the world, let alone social enterprises, have experience of expanding at this rate. The microfranchisor, in aiming to replicate and scale its business quickly, has to deal with the challenge of harnessing resources quickly to manage growth (Prahalad 2006: 51).

The value of partnerships

Given their status, social enterprises are hugely constrained by financial resources to build their human resources, system resources and business resources to support growth. Research and interviews have revealed that the key to successful replication or expansion into new markets at the BoP is to form successful partnerships with organisations that have financial depth and are established in other markets. One of Prahalad's theses is that 'the opportunities at the BoP cannot be unlocked if large and small firms, governments, civil society organisations, development agencies, and the poor themselves do not work together with a shared agenda' (Prahalad 2006: 2). In many ways, forming partnerships as an expansion strategy is no different from the cross-border alliances and joint ventures that commercial multinational corporations use to access the market knowledge and distribution capabilities of a local company. Many essential functions—such as legal advice, strategic consulting, market analysis and branding—can also be outsourced if strategic partners can be found to provide these services on a pro bono basis. VisionSpring has arguably been one of the most successful organisations to replicate its franchise model across a few regions and countries. Now with distribution networks in 11 countries, VisionSpring has relied on its partnerships with a range of government, non-government and commercial partners to replicate its franchise model and grow its business. Currently, it has partnerships in the following categories:

Strategic partners. Fifteen partners provide a variety of pro bono or joint services, such as funding, business consulting, legal advice, marketing, campaigning, education, business analysis, market entry strategy and market research.

Franchise partners. To reach the hundreds of millions in need of eyeglasses worldwide, VisionSpring licenses its business-in-a-bag model to 12 organisations with deep local roots, established networks, solid reputations and strong infrastructures in order to reach the rural poor. VisionSpring forges partnerships with a wide variety of organisations, from microfinance institutions with large networks of borrowers, to multinational corporations working in some of the poorest regions of the world, to local NGOs providing vital health and economic services in communities. Franchise partners allow VisionSpring to reach people in need of eyeglasses in the world's poorest, hardest-to-reach communities. In return, franchise partners receive a product with social and economic benefit to their constituents, an additional revenue stream for entrepreneurs and the organisation itself, and the transfer of VisionSpring's extensive knowledge, skills, and experience in BoP sales and marketing. Based on its own proven best practices, VisionSpring provides qualified franchise partner organisations with a full VisionSpring franchise, including:

- Business-in-a-bag kits

- Inventory of eyeglasses

- Training and technical assistance

- Management systems

- Support to implement an ongoing, successful eyeglasses sales programme

Referral partners. VisionSpring has partnered with four eyecare clinics and institutes in India and Central America for patient referral and eyecare consultations. The L.V. Prasad Eye Institute, a WHO Collaborating Centre for Prevention of Blindness, also provides training services to VisionSpring's microfranchisees in India.

Wholesale partners. VisionSpring's wholesale channel reaches under-served customers in urban and peri-urban areas through local retail outlets. VisionSpring's exclusive licensing agreement covering sub-Saharan Africa, launched in 2006 with Population Services International, is already reaching tens of thousands a year. Its partnership with Apollo Pharmacies, India's largest pharmacy chain, is making high-quality, affordable eyeglasses available for the first time in urban Indian markets. VisionSpring next aims to develop stylish, affordable eyeglasses and make them available through retail outlets serving the poor throughout the developing world.

Like VisionSpring, Living Goods has also partnered with various organisations to launch and expand its microfranchise business in Uganda. Its microfranchise business in Uganda is a joint venture with BRAC, which started microcredit operations in Uganda in 2007 and has in-depth relationships with the local communities. BRAC's local knowledge was critical to the fast expansion of Living Goods' franchise network into 20 districts within a short period of 16 months. Looking ahead, Living Goods plans to have a flexible business model to partner with other organisations, including government health ministries, to replicate its microfranchise system in other countries. (See Chapter 6 for more information on Living Goods' funding.)

Forming successful alliance and partnerships, however, is not an easy task. The success of cross-border joint ventures and other forms of international strategic alliances in the commercial sector has been mixed. The main problems in the commercial sector arise because the partners are usually also competitors, which causes inherent tensions in the relationships. For non-profit bodies, this is a lesser challenge given that most organisations are not competitors and achieving mutual social goals is the priority. Nonetheless, VisionSpring has already experienced one failure in franchise partnership due mainly to the partner not having the capability and business model to succeed.

The following guidelines are useful to ensure successful collaboration:[2]

- **Due diligence.** Thorough due diligence on potential partners, particularly for unsolicited ones, is critical. Arising from lessons learned from its partnerships, VisionSpring has developed a methodology for conducting due diligence and screening potential partners

- **Management capacity.** Managing cross-border partnerships requires management time and unique organisational competences such as account management and international sales management. The microfranchisor has to build the capacity necessary to manage a portfolio of partnerships and alliances

- **Vision and goals.** Sharing a common vision, social and business goals and mutual expectations is critical. Where possible, a mutually agreed sales target by the franchise partner should be established

- **Trust and respect.** Mutual trust and respect are essential. The partners should bring together unique capabilities and knowledge to create synergy in the relationship. However, they should also respect each other's independence

- **Conflict management.** One common issue is channel conflict within the franchise partner network where the partner distributes competing products. Where possible, a legal contract should be agreed to resolve potentially unpleasant or contentious issues. Once signed, the contract should be put away. If it needs to be referred to, something is wrong with the relationship

- **Flexibility.** It is important to understand that during the course of a collaboration, circumstances and markets change and to recognise the partner's problems and be flexible

2 These are based on interviews with microfranchisors and also extracted from Ohmae 1989.

Conclusion

Microfranchising has been adopted by a number of social enterprises to create social and economic impact in developing countries. The business concept is still in the nascent stage of development, with enterprises innovating in all aspects and an increasing number of academics and foundations conducting research in this field. The future for microfranchising is promising and exciting.

The process of starting and scaling a microfranchise business has, however, proven to be challenging for most social enterprises. Only a handful have arguably been able to build a business of sufficient scale. This chapter has therefore attempted to analyse the challenges faced by enterprises in starting and scaling a microfranchise business at the BoP. The findings conclude that a key external challenge is in addressing the unique characteristics of the BoP economy and consumers. The basic principles for success at the BoP are to create the capacity to consume, monetise hidden assets, bridge the gap in public goods, scale out versus scale up and influence and create partnerships.

Second, franchising is not a secret formula for growing a business after the initial start-up phase. Not all products and services are appropriate for franchising; it is critical to launch the right products and services. Building a successful franchise business by franchisors and franchisees will require strong business fundamentals and acumen, just like any other business. Third, the challenges and focus shift during the phases of starting up and growing the business are crucial factors. During the start-up phase, the key challenges are externally focused on establishing the products, microfranchise system and community relationships. Social enterprises will need to work not only on establishing the microfranchise system, but the whole business model, including supply, marketing and other supporting activities. Additionally, the process of starting a business at the BoP is inherently more complex and challenging given the characteristics of the market. Much research has been conducted in this area and the BoP Protocol developed by Cornell University is a good guide for social entrepreneurs.

As the business grows, the challenges gradually shift inwards to focus on developing management capacity, creating the enterprise structure and getting financial resources for growth. Alternative sources of funding, such as venture philanthropy and debt, have emerged in recent years and could provide social enterprises with financial resources and pro bono professional services to enhance management capacity. Getting investors on board will entail ceding degrees of decision and management control, which means that social enterprises will have to consider the cost and benefits. Strategic and franchise partnerships, akin to alliances and joint ventures in the commercial world, have also enabled microfranchise businesses to grow and achieve sustainability. However, sourcing and building partnerships are not easy tasks, with much due diligence required to get the right partners. Lastly, social enterprises will need to build their capacity to measure and report the social and economic impact of their businesses as a precursor to getting the money and resources in.

Social enterprises need to recognise these changing priorities during these phases and shift their focus accordingly. Building and growing a scalable microfranchise business requires the social entrepreneur to consider a myriad of factors—social, business, economics, organisational, partnering, etc.—throughout the business growth. It is a systemic and complex process. Marrying some of the most appropriate previously developed theories and frameworks described in this chapter, a process framework has been developed as shown in Figure 10.2. It is hoped that this framework will provide a quick map to help social entrepreneurs work through the complexities of building and growing their microfranchise business.

Figure 10.2 **A framework for building and growing a microfranchise business**

Process	Pre-field process		In-field process		Scaling up
Key success factors	• Strong theory of change • Right location and market • Appropriate products/ services and brand name • Appropriate financial structure • Strong local partnerships • Strong donor and corporate support		• Strong brand • Strong local participation • Trust and respect		• Scale out versus scale up • Strong strategic and franchise partnerships • Strong social and business impact
Key challenges	• Identifying the pilot location and theory of change • Identifying the appropriate products and services • Developing and building the business model • Seeking seed funding, support and partnerships • Developing and building the franchise system				• Harnessing organisational resources • Seeking additional financial resources
Main activities	• Selecting the pilot site • Forming and preparing the team • Selecting the local partners	• Building deep dialogue with community • Developing the project team • Developing the micro-franchise network • Creating business concept	• Transitioning to formal business organisation • Building shared commitment • Developing new capability • Creating business prototype	• Developing organisa-tional and management skills • Building the market base • Enhancing collective entrepre-neurship and partnerships • Creating business enterprise	• Reaching out and choosing new locations and partners • Choosing the growth financing mix • Replicating the franchise system • Developing new compe-tencies • Linking the ecosystem • Measuring and reporting social and business impact

11

The scaling bottleneck
Growth challenges faced by social enterprises[1]

Melissa Richer and Nate Heller
Ayllu, USA

Social enterprise has recently gained considerable attention as a poverty-alleviation tool. Around the world these businesses provide market solutions to poverty, offering products and services such as solar lighting and power, low-cost health solutions and information and communications technology. Most of the social and environmental problems faced by a poor community—such as sanitation, energy, education or housing—have a business model somewhere on Earth trying to tackle it. While the social-enterprise field is growing exponentially, it is still at a relatively early stage, with most businesses less than ten years old.[2] The methods employed by social enterprises to deliver their solutions are as varied as the solutions themselves, and they operate in nearly every step of the value chain. Some, such as Barefoot Power, manufacture products that are mainly distributed by other organisations. Others, such as Community Enterprise Solutions, develop distribution

---

1 With research support from Monica Logani and inputs from Greg Van Kirk. Ayllu's database, which we call iuMAP, tracks hundreds of social enterprises worldwide. A public map is available at our website: www.iumap.org. The research for this chapter is based on 30 interviews with leading social enterprises and 112 contextual conversations.

2 Most of the social enterprises on our map are less than ten years old. *Beyond Profit* magazine recently surveyed social enterprises in India and found that 64% are less than five years old (41% are less than two years old and 23% are between three and five years old). See www.beyondprofit.com.

chains for products they source from others. And some, such as VisionSpring, participate in the entire value chain from manufacturing to end-user sales.

Market solutions to poverty are diverse. Although they can be grouped in different ways (point on the value chain, focus on profitability, target population, etc.), each one is unique. Because market solutions are constantly evolving and innovating, the case studies in this essay and our subsequent conclusions can only be understood as a snapshot in time. Despite this, we focus on identifying commonalities in the challenges social enterprises face to scale their impact and achieve financial sustainability. We found that microfranchising is one of the most common ways social enterprises scale, so this chapter focuses on the social-franchising trend. We argue that scaling challenges have as much to do with the social enterprises' business models as with the ecosystems within which they exist. In these ecosystems, many social enterprises are isolated and lack information on best practices and resources that can provide support. We examine a number of cases and offer suggestions on how these challenges might be addressed. Figure 11.1 gives a breakdown of these cases by sector.

Figure 11.1 **Number of social enterprises found by sector**

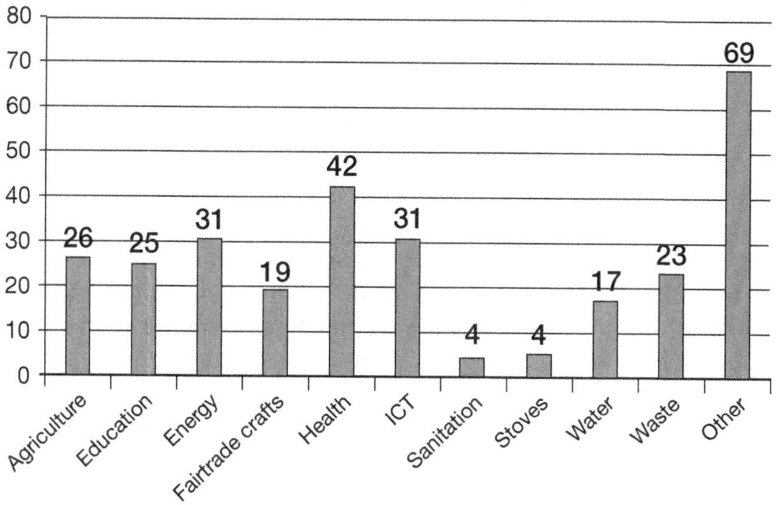

Definitions

We define 'social enterprise' as a market-based approach to solving a social or environmental problem. This chapter focuses only on social enterprises that target and benefit people at the base of the pyramid (BoP).[3] Although these social enterprises are part of the formal economy, they exist in markets where the informal economy dominates. As true hybrids, social enterprises may be incorporated as non-profits, as for-profits, or as both, and many face unique challenges in achieving sustainable profits and spreading their impact by scaling up, replication, or sharing best practices.

We define 'microfranchising' as the systematisation and standardisation of enterprise models for mass replication in low-income markets. The term 'micro' is used because the size of businesses at the BoP is so much smaller than in more-developed countries. Whereas it may cost $200,000 to establish a franchise in the USA, a microfranchise's start-up costs could be between $50 and $50,000 (Fairbourne *et al.* 2007). Most BoP social enterprises are small and medium-sized and microfranchising is a common way for them to expand. There are also a growing number of multinational companies such as Unilever, Nestlé and Danone who use microfranchising to access BoP markets.[4]

Ayllu was founded to make it easier for social enterprises in emerging markets to scale and benefit exponentially more people. As part of our business model, we interview social enterprises about their scaling models and challenges. We have built what we believe is the most extensive map of market solutions in emerging markets. We use the map to collect, analyse and distribute data and our most recent findings are the basis for this chapter. As mentioned earlier, we found that microfranchising is one of the most common tools social enterprises use to scale. This is because a high degree of standardisation and systematisation adapted to the conditions of each market contributes to replicability and resilience in the difficult business environment of BoP markets.

Although microfranchising resembles traditional franchise and direct sales models, it is designed for different market realities. Microfranchising is structured, financed and managed (franchisee–franchisor relationships) differently from traditional franchising or direct sales. It should therefore be viewed as an entity unto itself as opposed to an extension or downscaling of either model. Microfranchising can take many forms depending on the parent company's business model. For this reason we concur with the Monitor Group that, 'although social franchising—and franchising more generally—is often considered a business model [in itself], we see it more as a tool that might help bring an underlying business model to scale' (Karamchandani *et al.* 2009: 53).

---

3 Base of the pyramid refers to the markets made up of the global poor, defined here as the 3.7 billion people who live on less than $8 per day (note that other parameters have been used to define BoP). See also Chapter 10, pages 151ff.. For statistics on world poverty, see www.globalissues.org/article/26/poverty-facts-and-stats, accessed 12 January 2011.

4 An example is Unilever's Project Shakti, which uses village women to sell its products and promote community health.

Why social enterprise matters

Social enterprise could become a key anti-poverty tool because of its potential to achieve massive scale in a sustainable way. If it is able to scale up, through techniques such as microfranchising, social enterprise can have major economic, social and environmental impact by creating jobs, developing market infrastructure and enabling the poor to take control and transform their communities. If the poor are unable to take control of their lives, demographics foretell that traditional aid will become less and less capable of helping people escape the poverty trap.

Global population growth

Market solutions to poverty could play a crucial role in helping to alleviate pressures from the rapidly increasing populations of developing countries. In the next 40 years, the global population is expected to increase at an alarming rate, especially in less-developed countries. Currently, of the world's 6.8 billion people, 1.2 billion live in more-developed countries and 5.6 billion live in less-developed countries.[5] Based on current population growth rates, this disparity is expected to increase greatly in coming decades. Between now and 2050, the population of more-developed countries is projected to increase by 7%, which equates to only 100 million, while the population of less-developed countries is expected to increase by 45%, or 2.5 billion. Therefore *just the increase* in population of the less-developed countries will be over twice *the total population* of the more-developed countries (Haub and Kent 2009).

These statistics highlight the urgency of using aid dollars more efficiently and moving away from a world where less-developed countries depend on aid for their development. If under-developed countries do not become less associated with the vulnerability and lack of basic needs that currently characterise them, it is less likely that developed countries will be able to change that. International development goals must be increasingly achieved in ways that empower people living in poverty to change their own lives by getting jobs and participating in activities that make a difference in their communities.

Efficient use of aid money

Social enterprises are not hand-outs, but businesses that offer affordable, high-quality products and services. Donor funds are intended to buoy up social enterprises until they reach enough people to cover costs through sales alone. The logic is that if beneficiaries cover the costs of service delivery, this reduces the amount of aid money required to deliver those services and increases what can be delivered

---

5 More and less developed are the classification of the UN Office of the High Representative for the Least Developed Countries.

with a given amount of funding. Additionally, because social enterprises rely on beneficiaries for revenue, it is hoped that this makes them more responsive to local needs and demands than many non-profits, which must sometimes accommodate donors' requirements that are out of touch with local realities.

Job creation

Although traditional franchising is acknowledged to be one of the world's most successful business models (Magleby 2007), microfranchising is more early-stage and less proven. Nonetheless, initial results are encouraging. Multinational companies have used the model to generate large-scale employment in BoP markets. For instance, Natura, a Brazilian direct-sales cosmetics company in Latin America, has a direct sales force of more than one million mainly low-income women who distribute their products in Latin America.[6]

Microfranchising is a powerful job creation tool. Franchises provide a degree of stability and security for the poor, who usually lack consistent, stable incomes. Not only do franchisees receive training and mentoring, but they are also protected from market shocks. As Gibson (2007: 24) states, 'The time and mental anguish franchisees save by not having to develop systems on their own enables them to put their full energy into operations from the day they open their business'. Microfranchising also presents microfinance institutions (MFIs) with an opportunity to resolve some of their scaling challenges. Many microfinance borrowers have trouble reinvesting business profits in their enterprises because of household expenses such as healthcare, food and education. This makes it difficult for many microfinance-sponsored micro-enterprises to grow beyond a small size and can limit the number of jobs they create and their impact on economic growth (Hammond *et al.* 2007). Many borrowers are 'necessity entrepreneurs' who would prefer to work for someone else if they could find a job. It is hard for these borrowers to create businesses that stand out, and more often than not their business models simply copy others and crowd the market. Microfranchises not only introduce competitive business models that meet critical social and environmental needs, they also create a deep pool of low-risk, high-growth investments.

Causes of scaling challenges

Most social enterprises aspire to bring their social products and services to millions of customers, but at present they meet only a fraction of global demand. After reaching proof of concept in pilot markets, many face enormous barriers scaling up and achieving the economies of scale necessary to break even. Ayllu's research

6 See www.Natura.com.br.

found that 68% of social enterprises identify scale as a major challenge.[7] These scaling challenges exist for two interconnected reasons. First, social enterprises are spread out around the world and many are isolated in undeveloped market ecosystems. Second, this field is young and there has not been enough time to both understand it and build supportive infrastructure.

Market ecosystems

Social enterprises use hybrid models to operate in BoP markets, where many are isolated from each other and from support. Because they are operating in a field that does not fit within for-profit or not-for-profit boxes, traditional knowledge and support systems are helpful but insufficient. With social enterprises spread out worldwide in different industries using different business models, it is difficult to develop sector norms and supportive infrastructure. Social enterprises may be diverse, but many share similar key challenges because of operating in undeveloped markets. Unfortunately, it is hard to find information about how to overcome these challenges and who can support them in doing so. Social enterprises are often unaware of partners or models that could result in tremendous leaps in efficiency.

Lack of information

Social enterprise is a new field and, as we mentioned earlier, the majority of market solutions to poverty are less than ten years old. As a result, less is known about how to support mature businesses than how to incubate new ones. Given how young this market is, we found that the majority of funding and institutional support targets early-stage ventures. Many social enterprises are achieving initial success in pilot markets, but after this point it can be difficult to standardise their models for scale and replication. They are often pressured and advised to improve their business models without having access to appropriate information or expertise to do so.

The current focus is primarily on individual business models, but social enterprises would benefit greatly if the focus shifted to include aggregated information about the ecosystem such as trends analysis and benchmarking. The Monitor Group, which released an excellent report on scalable models, stated, 'system effects greatly complicate the work of many market-based solutions, since in most cases markets are much less developed and there is no surrounding ecosystem to plug in to' (Karamchandani *et al.* 2009: 115). These effects are outlined by a report on microfranchising by Dalberg Advisors: 'most frontier markets lack the purchasing power, access to capital, legal and regulatory framework and technical advisory services that enable most business format franchises to grow profitably' (Deelder and Miller 2009: xii). In this environment the odds are stacked against social

---

7   Based on a sample of 30 interviews and 112 contextual conversations conducted by Monica Logani, Nate Heller and Melissa Richer.

enterprises, no matter how strong their business models may be. What's missing is quantitative and qualitative information. Social enterprises are not currently under one umbrella, so there is limited information on, for example, how many there are, why they are failing or succeeding, how they measure impact and who they could collaborate with. If it were possible to gather, analyse and distribute information about social enterprises en masse, there could be more learning, better decisions and stronger collaborations.

Consequences of not scaling

The simplest consequence of not scaling is limited impact. Fewer jobs and market solutions are available, so fewer people can access them. A social enterprise can scale its impact in many ways without necessarily scaling its operations massively or replicating its entire business model. Nonetheless, most social enterprises find that scaling operations is an important factor in their success. Even if they do not wish to become large companies, not scaling operations can affect their ability to serve even the people they do reach.

Scaling versus replication

Most social enterprises are designed from the beginning with scale in mind (whether this means scaling the organisation or scaling its impact through replication), and their models are shown, with some adaptation, to 'apply independent of geographic context' (Karamchandani *et al.* 2009: 115). Of the social enterprises we interviewed, 98% were enthusiastic about helping others replicate their models. This would allow them to spread their models without bearing the cost. One example is Grameen Bank (described in Chapters 3 and 6), which encouraged replication to deliver microfinance to hundreds of millions of people. But replication is not always enough. While many social enterprises achieve large impacts even before they scale up, scaling operations is often necessary to reach a break-even point and can be key to these businesses achieving their full potential. Indeed, despite vast replication, Grameen Bank continues to scale up its own operations.

Lack of economies of scale

Scale can be essential not only for maximising social impact, but also for attaining financial viability. Some social enterprises, especially those that deliver services for which most of the costs are fixed, are able to charge low prices to the poor because the cost per product decreases greatly as more and more units are sold. Good examples are Aravind Eye Care[8] and LifeSpring Maternity Hospital.[9] Each additional eye surgery performed by Aravind or baby delivered by LifeSpring costs a minimal amount once the facility and doctor's salary are covered. Another example is Esoko, a Ghanaian software company that provides time-sensitive agricultural market data, as well as other relevant information, via SMS and the web to BoP farmers and agricultural commodity traders in Africa. Due to the high start-up costs necessary to build its business (for software development, office space, salespeople and building enumeration teams, etc.) it will take a number of years of scaling for Esoko to be profitable. Without the scale to cover its fixed costs, these models cannot be viable. In developed markets, industries with high research and development costs, such as pharmaceuticals, charge high prices until these costs are recovered. However, because social enterprises target a population that cannot afford high prices, covering costs depends on reaching large scale.

Isolation lowers impact

Poor communities face multiple problems, most of which are being addressed by social enterprises somewhere in the world. But social enterprises rarely serve the same communities. As Jeffrey Sachs (2005) argues in *The End of Poverty*, if the goal is to help people change their lives and reach the point where they don't need aid, they need multiple solutions that support one another; otherwise each solution is less effective. For instance, a community will benefit less from a health clinic if people are still drinking contaminated water.

Isolation can limit efficiency and profitability. Most BoP social enterprises target remote, barren markets that the private sector has traditionally avoided. Whereas companies normally outsource activities, social enterprises often do not have this choice and have instead 'invented not just a product or approach but an entire business ecosystem encompassing whole value chains', according to the Monitor Group, which also says these are the most exemplary models (Karamchandani *et al*. 2009). When social enterprises need to play a role in entire value chains, end-to-end, from production to point-of-sale, costs and time spent can increase, making it harder to break even and expand into new markets.

Being spread out can also make knowledge-sharing difficult. In the course of our interviews we encountered numerous social enterprises in different industries with similar models. Many of them had never heard of each other. Two examples are Nuru Lights, which sells solar lights in East Africa and trains local shopkeepers/microfranchisees to run rent-to-own pedal-powered machines to charge them, and Sarvajal Water, which sells purified water in India through microfranchisees

8 Aravind Eye Care, based in Madurai, India, uses a cross-subsidisation model to offer affordable cataract surgery to the poor.
9 LifeSpring Maternity Hospital, based in Hyderabad, India, provides low-cost maternity services.

who run rent-to-own purification machines. Even though their models are similar and there is great potential for cross-learning, they were unconnected.

While many social enterprise partnerships do exist,[10] there is a great deal of unfulfilled potential for collaboration. If they were in the same markets, social enterprises could lower costs by sharing channels such as storage, transportation and distribution. Microfranchising is a promising way to make this possible. One example is Community Enterprise Solutions (CE Solutions), which works in Guatemala, Nicaragua, Argentina and Ecuador and aggregates social products from around the world, including VisionSpring glasses, Barefoot Power solar lights, Stefani water filters, Envirofit clean-burning stoves, General Electric energy-efficient light bulbs, and garden seeds from various suppliers. These products are sold through village campaigns by community advisers who buy the products on a micro-consignment model through which the salespeople receive loans in the form of products to sell. CE Solutions helps social enterprises achieve the scale necessary to operate in new markets and aggregates solutions so the poor have access to more products and services. CE Solutions demonstrates how micro-consignment can be used to end isolation and significantly lower distribution costs.[11]

Scaling challenges: case studies

The social enterprise field is on the cusp of a new phase: a wave of businesses have achieved initial success and are preparing to scale. Given that most models are less than ten years old, this is consistent with the scaling horizon found by the Monitor Group: 'no demand-led model targeted at low-income markets is likely to scale in less than 10 years. We would count any time span short of a decade as remarkable, and anything within the 10 to 15 year range as aggressive but realistic' (Karamchandani *et al.* 2009: 33).

The following section examines the most common challenges faced by the social enterprises we interviewed. It presents case studies that, with a few exceptions, use microfranchising.

The challenges fall into many categories, including:

- Access to capital and financing, both for the business to scale up and for customers to purchase products and services

- Sourcing human resources

---

10 VisionSpring has partnered with several other organisations for distribution such as Community Enterprise Solutions, BRAC and Fundación Paraguaya.
11 CE Solutions founder Greg Van Kirk recently published an article about the micro-consignment model CE Solutions developed and how it differs from microfranchising (Van Kirk 2010).

- Marketing and consumer education
- Lack of knowledge and capacity in new markets, including:
  - Distribution and operations
  - Finding appropriate partners
  - Regulation

Financing

The social enterprises we interviewed identified growth capital as one of the most critical barriers to scale. They face difficulties locating capital to pay for market expansion and the start-up inventory and equipment needed for franchisees. Straight for-profit businesses can get bank loans that their profits will pay back, or equity investments because they expect to generate a market rate of return. Because their social goals often make them less profitable, at least initially, social enterprises often cannot access these types of capital and must rely on either grants or subsidised forms of loans and equity, which ask for lower rates of return. This means that their scale is much more reliant on the interest and capacity of donors to cover these subsidies. Norms do not yet exist for financing hybrids, so getting the terms and amounts right is also difficult, especially when a social enterprise is dealing with donors and investors at the same time, who often have different requirements and expectations. Separately, if customers need financing to purchase products and services, which they often do, social enterprises have to set up mechanisms and finance partners in each new market.

Social enterprises require hybrid financing that most donors and private investors are unable or unwilling to provide. Once their funding needs evolve beyond start-up capital, they encounter a missing middle where many funders who provide patient (long-term) capital encourage the social enterprise to diversify its funding base. These funders are a small, mixed group of foundations and investors who are part of the social entrepreneurship community and incubate hybrid ventures. They try to create a flexible, safe environment for social enterprise. However, most make smaller investments that are more appropriate for early-stage ventures. As a result, the more mature a social enterprise gets, the harder it is to access funders who understand how to provide support.

Private investors generally look for greater returns than social enterprises can generate (sometimes as high as a tenfold return on investment within five years), impose interest terms that are unreasonably high or ask for a higher equity stake or dividend than social enterprises want to give or can afford. These investors usually rely on private sector norms to structure investments, which can impose onerous conditions that constrain, rather than encourage, growth.

Lastly, large grant-makers typically fund traditional non-profit entities and are structured to disperse funds in sizes that social enterprises are unable to absorb. The transaction costs of changing their priorities and grant structuring are so high that they lack the incentive to do so. When faced with these choices, social enterprises frequently gravitate toward large grant-makers, because they often cannot generate high-enough returns to meet private sector terms. As a result, they sometimes receive funding as a part of larger projects with broader goals, which can lead to conflicting conditions. There is clearly a large disconnect between the donor world and the social-enterprise world, which is not likely to change unless significant financial motives (such as tax write-offs) are awarded to social enterprise investors.

Legal complications affect hybrids that do not fit with, but must conform to, 'for-profit' and 'not-for-profit' status. A prime example of how legal constraints affect the missing middle is PowerMundo, a Peru-based wholesale distributor of clean energy products and services. According to PowerMundo, it has faced difficulties accessing funding because social enterprise is a new field that is not yet seen as attractive to venture capitalists. At the same time, due to its for-profit status, Power-Mundo is not eligible for many grants from donors who mandate that recipients must be incorporated as non-profit entities. PowerMundo believes the ideal investment would be patient capital that is structured as a reasonably priced loan with deferred interest from a private, socially motivated impact investor.

Another excellent example is CareShop Ghana, a drug distribution franchise that converted several hundred independent over-the-counter drug retailers[12] into a branded network of pharmacies, purchased their drugs in bulk to realise economies of scale and offered training in good practices and hygiene. CareShop began as a project of the Ghana Social Marketing Foundation with some funding from the Gates Foundation, which allocated funds to a third party,[13] which then made a grant to CareShop. Once thought to be a rising star in the microfranchising space, CareShop Ghana ended up going bankrupt.[14] This happened because of contradictory funding requirements. The grant covered training expenses, but required CareShop to borrow money at market rates for all other costs, such as initial inventory purchases. However, the grant also required CareShop to operate in underserved rural areas with a small customer base, which reduced profitability such that CareShop was unable to cover its inventory loans. This was compounded by unrealistic expectations by the commercial pharmaceutical company providing the drugs. Ultimately, CareShop fell victim to conflicting donor and investor demands. Burdened by common challenges faced by social enterprises, such as managing franchisees and building its brand, CareShop was unable to hold out long enough to secure new financing, and it dissolved.

---

12 Officially designated in Ghana as 'licensed chemical sellers'.
13 The third party was a development contractor, Management Sciences for Health.
14 This happened one year after a 'What Works' case study was published about it by the World Resources Institute (Segrè and Tran 2008).

Operating leasing

Many social enterprises need financing for operating leases. Ventures such as Sarvajal Water in India have high per-franchise start-up costs. Initially, they must cover these costs themselves, since franchisees lack upfront capital. Eventually the debt is paid off by franchise revenue, but this could take years. With the old debt still on their books, it is hard to convince investors to finance expansion, especially since more franchisee debt will be assumed. Sarvajal believes that if it could find an investor to purchase and lease back its technology, scale would be rapid. Operating leases are common in the private sector, but not in BoP markets. Sarvajal has a sound business model and one of the best water filtration systems available, but investors are wary because it operates in unstructured, unproven markets.

Customer financing

Social enterprises often have to be creative about helping their customers make initial purchases. Many products such as solar lights, water filters and medical devices generate substantial long-term savings, but the upfront costs are high, and customers are often unable to purchase them without financing. Frequently, MFIs are not suited to providing this financing because the interest rates charged for the financing raise the cost of the products beyond affordability. There has been very little development of financing appropriate for asset purchases either by MFIs or traditional banks, with a few exceptions. SELCO Lights, which installs solar lighting systems in India, was able to obtain less expensive customer financing from traditional banks, and this has been key to making its installations, which cost from $200 to $220 per system, affordable to its customers. While some MFIs have shown interest in product loans, designing them is expensive. Two of the world's largest MFIs, Foundation for International Community Assistance (FINCA International)[15] and SKS Microfinance in India,[16] experimented with product loans in Uganda and India respectively but chose not to continue with them because margins were too low. There are a few initiatives trying to solve this problem, including Frontier Markets,[17] which aggregates social products to create density and designs loan packages for MFIs.

Even when MFIs agree to provide loans, the terms are not always agreeable to both sides. For example, Nuru Lights' microfranchisees want short-term microfinance loans—as short as two weeks—because they are selling their initial inventory so quickly. The MFIs, on the other hand, need a longer loan duration to make the loans profitable. Barefoot Power designed lighting products that do not need the longer-term loans (three to five years) that solar power and minigrids often

---

15 FINCA pursued but chose not to continue with a pilot in Uganda that partnered with Honey Care Africa. More about the market study can be found in a George Washington University study contracted by FINCA (Bracken *et al.* 2006).

16 www.sksindia.com

17 www.frontiermkts.com

require, but instead match the MFIs' preference for 6–12 months. However, MFIs rarely converted initial enthusiasm into action on the ground. Eventually Barefoot Power attracted support from angel investors who now lend money through a company-designed container loan programme. The angel makes a six-month loan for one (or part of one) 6 m shipping container, which houses up to 10,000 solar desk lamps, allowing 50,000 people to get light within six months. According to Barefoot Power, the six-month term is ample time to manufacture, ship and sell the lamps at $10–20 in local markets for cash, without any end-customer loan being required.

When Barefoot Power's importers and distributors similarly could not secure loans from banks and microfinance to fund their inventory, the company did not let a lack of capital stop it from scaling. Instead, Barefoot Power used the angels' loan to extend supplier credit to the full supply chain—to the importer and right down to entrepreneurs that Barefoot Power itself trained. This allowed interest-free 'micro-supplier credit' (also called micro-consignment) to be given more cheaply and efficiently than loans from an MFI. Barefoot Power's initial entrepreneurs were, in some cases, recommended to them by MFIs who were keen to watch the experiment. Now those MFIs are supporting many more entrepreneurs, which has reduced the need for angel investors to fund the supply chain so deeply. Instead, angel funds have been redeployed to other regions where they are more needed. Microfinance investors are also starting to replicate the angel-funded container loan programme as a formal trade-finance fund that delivers containers of micro-businesses to the poor, helping Barefoot Power to scale.

Human resources

When social enterprises scale, the transition to a larger team that has a different relationship with the company can be tough, especially as the number of unskilled staff and franchisees grows.

High-end customers

Many social enterprises we interviewed, especially those with extensive services or wealthier customers, felt that personnel was a critical success factor, and they go to great lengths to ensure high quality when recruiting new employees. SELCO home solar-light systems is a good example. SELCO places a strong priority on understanding the needs of every customer. Its systems are a major investment for homeowners; they cost approximately US$210 and can take three to five years to repay. Therefore, SELCO finds it difficult (and unethical) to make a sale without close attention to the customer's needs and how SELCO can meet them. Employees spend time with customers discussing their energy needs, customising lighting and even redesigning living space for greater energy efficiency. SELCO therefore requires a talented, well-trained and well-managed sales team to build trust and relationships with customers before a sale is possible. The cost of recruiting and developing this team is high, and SELCO feels this is its biggest barrier to expansion.

Digital Divide Data (DDD) employs poor people in South-East Asia to do digitisation work for international clients. DDD faces stiff competition, and it relies on strong managers to make sure the labour force is delivering top-quality work. DDD recruits entry-level staff from a low-skilled workforce and trains them. According to DDD, finding and retaining talented managers in developing countries is quite difficult. When social enterprises like DDD enter new markets, it takes time to train labourers and gain the cultural knowledge needed to evaluate managers.

Franchisees

When social enterprises scale up, relationships with franchisees can become less personal as more layers of communication are added. Managing this transition is not easy, and social enterprises can find themselves continually searching for better ways to ensure franchisee compliance. For example, Sarvajal had to develop a technology for monitoring water meters because franchisees, who pay based on the volume of water filtered, found ways to bypass the system. Similarly, before it went out of business, CareShop Ghana used bulk purchasing to provide drugs more cheaply to the pharmacies in its network, but it found that distributors were breaking exclusivity contracts and making separate deals with pharmacies. CareShop found that private sector companies that stood to gain from this set-up lacked a sound understanding of business and, as a result, undercut everyone's profits. After CareShop closed down, many franchisees realised their mistake and begged it to reopen. If CareShop Ghana had had more time to build trust with its franchisees and suppliers, things might have turned out differently.

Marketing

Need is not the same as demand, and social enterprises frequently struggle with market solutions that can have high upfront costs and are often unfamiliar to customers used to traditional practices. Although these products and services are cheaper in the long run, people do not always understand their value. For instance, a villager may wonder why she should buy purified water when she can drink river water for free, even if river water has higher hidden costs such as illness. LifeSpring Hospital and VisionSpring also struggle with this. People who are used to home births and living without near-vision may not realise the value of a hospital visit or a pair of reading glasses.

In response, social enterprises often have to launch major educational campaigns to enter a new market, and this greatly increases the costs and time needed for expansion. A good example is Envirofit Stoves, which manufactures low-cost stoves that use less wood and produce less smoke than traditional stoves, creating environmental and health benefits for users. When Envirofit enters a new market, it must work with local governments, institutions and retailers to help educate consumers on the dangers of indoor air pollution caused by traditional biomass stoves.[18]

Although converting need into demand can require targeted marketing and education, social enterprises have proven that there is sustained, unmet demand and that the poor have the ability to pay for social products and services. For example, Barefoot Power has successfully convinced tens of thousands of end-users, who currently spend $0.50/week on kerosene, that the purchase of a $5–20 rechargeable light not only has asset value but also pays for itself in as little as three months, and excessive demand for the product has created many large supply gaps that investors have not yet met. If initial challenges can be overcome, social enterprises have a great chance for success once demand is unleashed, but only if investors swiftly respond.

Lack of knowledge and capacity in new markets

Distribution

Social enterprises adjust their microfranchise strategies to accommodate larger scale and adapt to new markets. Though the ways in which social enterprises use microfranchising are diverse, we identified three common methods.

1. Setting up a network and employing distributors themselves (e.g. Vision-Spring in India and El Salvador, Community Enterprise Solutions, Sarvajal and Healthkeepers[19]). This is a common way for social enterprises to start microfranchising. It helps them stay responsive to local realities, including franchisee needs and customer demands. Many of them feel that it is important to maintain an on-the-ground presence to stay in touch with communities and learn from them. Over time, many social enterprises use their on-the-ground experiences to help other networks distribute their products and services. They often find this to be a faster, more cost-effective way to scale their impact. VisionSpring, for instance, retains a small franchisee network that it directly manages, but most of its glasses are sold by franchisees that are affiliated with local partners

2. Partnering with local organisations that have existing distribution networks (e.g. Grameen Village Phone [see Chapter 6], Community Enterprise Solutions in Ecuador, VisionSpring in multiple countries). Social enterprises with standardised distribution strategies can train partners to manage

18 According to Envirofit, indoor air pollution kills 1.5 million people annually, half of whom are children under the age of five.
19 Healthkeepers was a project of the NGO Freedom From Hunger (www.freedomfromhunger. org) in Ghana employing microfranchised community health workers. In 2010 it became an independent organisation.

franchisees. VisionSpring relies on microfinance and non-profit partners to distribute its products and was able to grow quickly when BRAC, the largest non-profit entity in the world, began distributing its eyeglasses in Bangladesh. However, third-party distribution can be challenging. Social enterprises may lose a degree of control, especially if the distributor has competing priorities or an operating model that is not optimal for the product or service at hand. Partners may take a share of margins, may isolate franchisors from franchisees and may have trouble managing the partnership if they are under-resourced and/or under-staffed. For instance, some of VisionSpring's partnerships in the past ended when employees at the partner organisation who were responsible for the partnership left or when the partner switched priorities. Nonetheless, outsourcing distribution can be a great way for a social enterprise to specialise in the supply side, while helping others develop a microfranchise distribution channel. Despite the obstacles, VisionSpring has been able to distribute hundreds of thousands of glasses using this model

3. Conversion of existing businesses into franchises (CareShop Ghana, CDI Lan,[20] Nuru Lights). Conversion franchising can be done in two ways: (1) by absorbing existing businesses into a franchise network (CareShops, CDI Lan); or (2) by inserting a microfranchise strategy into an existing business, as Nuru Lights does by training shopkeepers to operate its pedal-powered light charger. Building and managing a microfranchise network can be labour-intensive, but distribution may be easier because it takes advantage of established micro-enterprises with established customer bases. But these existing channels also pose unique challenges. Each micro-enterprise is set up differently and has its own procedures, so it can be difficult to create standards across microfranchise networks.

Partnerships

Social enterprises often depend on private and public partnerships in their initial markets that are hard to replicate. Unlike large companies, which can negotiate deals with relative ease, social enterprises may struggle to get lower prices and terms of credit, especially when they enter a foreign market. Mi Farmacita pharmacy chain in Mexico was formed as a partnership between a local generic manufacturer and a distribution company, which both wanted to reach poor customers. In exchange for a guaranteed purchase of 10% of the generic manufacturer's output, Mi Farmacita receives heavily discounted prices on its drugs, and these

---

20 CDI Lan is a social enterprise launched by the Center for Digital Inclusion (CDI), a non-profit in Brazil focused on making the Internet accessible to the poor. The Lan project converts independent Internet cafés, known as Lan houses, into CDI franchises with similar branding and services offered throughout the network.

discounts are passed on to customers. Another example is Cinepop, a for-profit Mexican company that travels through small towns to show free family films while providing opportunity tents with BoP products and services. This helps overcome the challenge that companies face when trying to distribute products and services: that it is hard to convene a captive audience. To be successful in a new market, Cinepop must find a partner that can negotiate film rights with distribution companies, forge relationships with local governments to secure free venues to show the movies and work with small and medium-sized companies to sponsor kiosks in the opportunity tent—none of which is an easy task. Other social enterprises, such as Gyan Shala Schools[21] and Drishtee Internet kiosks (see Chapter 4), also benefit from government partnerships. There is no guarantee that business or government deals can be negotiated in other markets, which can limit growth potential.

Regulation

Regulation and bureaucracy can be roadblocks to entering new markets. Over-regulation is sometimes a major obstacle, especially for healthcare solutions. For example, VisionSpring has had great success with the sale of eye drops in El Salvador, but in India, eye drops are classified as a drug, and they cannot be sold by microfranchisees. Healthcare solutions often lower costs by handing over less complicated medical tasks to trained professionals. Unfortunately, in many countries trained professionals are barred from completing tasks, even if they are perfectly capable. Furthermore, heavy taxation is problematic. Without knowing the system well, social enterprises may have to pay prohibitive duties or bribes when they enter a new market. This creates incentives for them to stick to markets they already know, and can keep markets with strong opportunities off limits because the barriers to entry are too high. D.light Design, for example, which manufactures and sells solar lights in BoP markets, said that it prioritises entering markets where tariffs and duties are not prohibitively high, bribery is not absolutely necessary and where government agencies are cooperative. Similarly, because Gyan Shala's schools are predominantly funded by the government, it will only enter a new market if it can get educational accreditation by the ministry of education and if the government is friendly to its model.

Local knowledge

Local knowledge affects all the other challenges listed. Entering new markets can be extremely expensive in terms of capacity and resources. This is especially true for service providers: for example, Gyan Shala Schools, a success in India, estimated it would take three to six months of work to understand the Brazilian education system and labour market. Social enterprises frequently lack information about which

---

21 Gyan Shala Schools is a social enterprise in India offering an improved primary education curriculum in its own schools and in selected government schools.

markets are most suitable and how to adapt their models to local context. They find it difficult to recruit the right staff and franchisees, to handle language differences, to find the right local partners and to market effectively. Social enterprises usually lack the resources to perform in-depth market research, and even if they have the resources, few entities have the expertise necessary to do quality studies. As a result, many great opportunities go untapped.

Solutions to the scaling bottleneck

In trying to address these challenges, it may be helpful to group them based on their underlying causes. We believe scaling challenges can be arranged in three categories:

- Internal capacity of the organisation trying to scale
- Local ecosystems in new markets
- Global ecosystem effects

Table 11.1 maps the different challenges across these categories.

Table 11.1 **Challenges and underlying causes**

Type of challenge	Source		
	Internal capacity	Local ecosystems	Global ecosystem
Financing		*Franchisor:* Lack of financing to start franchises *Franchisees:* Lack of financing for product purchases	• Lack of funder knowledge (donors and investors) about the scope, potential, and risk of market opportunities means they are often wary of investing • Lack of appropriate, flexible capital to support scale
HR	Low management capacity to scale	• Difficulties finding franchisors, franchisees, local managers • Lack of service providers that can help with HR • Often treated by stakeholders as a non-profit, which makes it hard to succeed as a business	

continued over

Type of challenge	Source		
	Internal capacity	Local ecosystems	Global ecosystem
Knowledge		• Little or no information about potential market opportunities • Lack of knowledge about culture and business environment	• Little knowledge-sharing about high-potential markets and best practices
Distribution		• Need for third-party operational support to lessen the need for end-to-end solutions • Environmental problems including crime, violence, resistance to non-profits or women entrepreneurs	
Marketing		• Need to stimulate demand through education about the benefits of social products and services in every new market	
Partner-ships		• Lack of coordination between social enterprises in a particular market • Few links to potential partners in a particular market	• Lack of comprehensive data or information on size of the social enterprise, its performance, needs or best practices
Regulatory		• Onerous, non-transparent regulation • Harsh taxes and import regulation • Restrictions on service provision for healthcare, education, etc.	• Lack of international norms/standards for regulatory policies promoting social enterprises

Based on these categories, we see three focus areas for solutions:

1. Help organisations develop their internal capacity for scaling

2. Develop local market ecosystems to be more transparent and hospitable to social enterprise entry

3. Improve the global ecosystem

1. Organisational capacity

These are internal challenges related to the business model itself. Some argue that internal challenges signify that social enterprises are not ready to scale. The report by Dalberg Advisors (Deelder and Miller 2009) argues that, based on lessons learned in the private sector, a venture should not franchise until the model is ironed out and profitability is achieved. However, traditional franchises have the comfort of waiting for profitability before they scale because they rely on high margins. Meanwhile, most social enterprises have to keep their margins low and can only break even once they scale and achieve high volumes. Social enterprises face a tough reality where scale may be necessary, even if they are not fully ready.

One possible solution is to increase the sharing between social enterprises about organisational challenges and innovative solutions. Another is to help funders understand that social enterprises need more time and require patient capital that is flexible and accommodating. Acumen Fund's founder, Jacqueline Novogratz, explains the role of patient capital in increasing capacity and impact: 'patient capital [is] typically below-market investments that are accompanied by management assistance in enterprises with the potential to reach hundreds of thousands of individuals.'[22]

2. Local market ecosystem development

The markets within which most social enterprises operate are undeveloped, so one course of action is to mobilise stakeholders within these markets who currently play a role in social innovation and can help strengthen market solutions. This includes non-profits, microfinance institutions, local government, forward-thinking companies and, of course, social enterprises themselves. Although this is not easy, it is within reach. The social-innovation community is a small, interconnected network that is both local and global, and includes people from all sectors. If these people can find each other, they can more easily work together to build support systems for social enterprise in local markets.[23]

Social enterprises often struggle to scale because they control value chains end-to-end. This often prevents them from specialising in one core deliverable. For instance, the core deliverable for RedPlan Salud[24] is family planning. For Power-Mundo it is distributing energy products. And for Envirofit it is supplying clean-burning stoves. Controlling whole value chains leaves them with little choice but to take on activities in which they are not specialised. For instance, VisionSpring aspires to focus on being a supplier of low-cost eyeglasses. But in many of its

---

22 SocialEdge interview: www.socialedge.org/blogs/fair-street/archive/2009/10/05/jacqueline-novogratz-patient-capital-and-social-return-on-investment, accessed 19 August 2010.
23 At Ayllu, one of the goals of our map is to increase collaboration and improve support systems for BoP social enterprise.
24 RedPlan Salud is a network of midwives trained to provide low-cost health services in Peru.

markets no other organisation has developed appropriate distribution mechanisms for this product, so VisionSpring had to experiment and develop distribution channels itself. It has now used this knowledge to train other organisations in its distribution methods, but this has been a resource-intensive element of its business model. Another example is Britanica JV, a Ukrainian company that sells machinery for producing roof tiles made from recycled mixed plastic waste. Britanica employs some of the best engineering talent available but owing to constrained resources, the company also relies on these engineers to market and sell its product.

Aggregation of multiple social enterprises within a single market could resolve many of these challenges. The Monitor Group reports that 'aggregating customers or suppliers may be the key to making a market . . . Only aggregation can transform poor people into viable economic entities and thus worthwhile to involve in a supply chain or to target for infrastructure or finance' (Karamchandani *et al.* 2009: 107). Aggregation tackles ecosystem problems in three ways. First, it brings together multiple solutions to create greater, more well-rounded social impact. These aggregated enterprises can learn from each other, do business with one another and share resources such as warehouse space, transportation or distribution channels. All of this can drive down costs. Second, the more businesses that exist locally, the more jobs, wealth and business infrastructure are created. Third, a cluster of social enterprises is more likely to attract specialised support from investors and consultants and to influence outsiders such as policy-makers.

3. Global market ecosystem development

At the global level, the sector needs transparency. Currently, there is little data available on BoP social enterprise. It is not known how many social enterprises exist that can help them overcome challenges or what best practices they have developed. Social enterprises are often unaware of partners and models that, if connected, could result in tremendous leaps in efficiency. Because they lack information, many social enterprises unknowingly reinvent the wheel. Ayllu is working to solve this problem with a global map that collects, analyses and distributes information on BoP social enterprises. We aim to collect essential data that will ultimately drive better decision-making and help develop standards and frameworks to accelerate growth.

Conclusion

Even if many social enterprises are already impacting thousands of lives, the field of social enterprise as a whole is still young, with high potential still to be fulfilled. The Monitor Group captures this well: 'market-based solutions to social challenges are still in their earliest days. Relatively few business models are demonstrably successful and many continue to show more promise than hard results' (Karamchandani *et al.* 2009: 128). When considering the truly enormous challenges outlined in this chapter, it is easy to imagine many social enterprises having limited impact, and even failure, especially when comparing social enterprises to businesses in much more mature markets. Nevertheless, it is important to appreciate that social enterprises are pioneering entirely new paradigms that both blend and defy for-profit and not-for-profit structures. It will take time for this field to mature and to have the structure and depth that is seen in older sectors. When designing financing and support services for social enterprises, it is important to think outside the box, just as they do. In a world where social and environmental challenges mount on a daily basis, new paradigms are essential. The value of social enterprise is its potential to align profit incentives with extraordinary social good in a highly scalable fashion. Social enterprises can realise their potential to impact millions, if they have cross-sector support in making their visions a reality.

12
Conclusion

Nicolas Sireau
SolarAid, UK

As this book has shown, microfranchising is a new area of international development that is still in its infancy, yet growing fast. That is one of the reasons why it is so exciting. It offers a potential for poverty reduction that far surpasses any existing programmes run by the traditional NGOs that control so much of the aid industry. By bringing together market forces with a firm social emphasis, microfranchising offers a scope for major socioeconomic transformation on a large scale. Indeed, that is our experience at SolarAid, where we have seen how the clear processes of microfranchising offer a much-needed path to business success for high-quality franchisees.

Nevertheless, significant progress still needs to be made. First, it is still unclear for which sectors microfranchising works best. While the model is proving itself for areas such as healthcare products, eyeglasses, information and communication technologies and small solar products, further testing needs to be carried out to find out just how widely the model can be applied to other sectors. This will require a number of pilots and access to high-risk funding in order to try out new techniques and assess them.

Second, there is an urgent need to educate funders and investors on the potential for microfranchising. Our experience at SolarAid mirrors that of other microfranchises when we find that few funders and investors understand the challenges of working at the base of the pyramid and the type of patient capital needed to pilot, grow and scale up a microfranchise. Funders and investors are often in a hurry to see significant quantitative results and do not always understand that building a healthy, functioning microfranchise takes time, effort and perseverance. Microfranchises tend to work in geographical areas where there is no infrastructure and hence have to build everything from scratch, which is not something that can be accomplished in a day, a month, a year or even three years. A longer-term view is required.

Third, there is a need for greater collaboration between microfranchises in order to share techniques and learning and ensure quality control. SolarAid benefited immensely from advice early on from pioneers such as VisionSpring and Health-Store Foundation. How-to manuals from Brigham Young University's Microfranchise Development Initiative also helped us. If we want microfranchising really to grow, the sector will have to formalise this assistance, provide training and recommend clear rules and regulations for what can legitimately be called a microfranchise. Otherwise, we could end up as the microfinance sector is today: large and growing, but unregulated and prone to abuse.

Fourth, we need to promote microfranchising as a promising area of social entrepreneurship that can transform the way international development is carried out. As mentioned several times in this book, international development, as done by the majority of NGOs over the past half a century, is failing. Well-intentioned but poorly thought-out programmes just make the situation worse by encouraging dependency and corruption. One of the problems is the endemic anti-market ideology that permeates so many NGOs. While NGO activists are rightly appalled at the excesses of global capitalism, this leads many of them to reject any attempt at using market-based solutions to relieve poverty. An example of this was a senior manager in a development NGO who responded to a presentation I made at a conference by saying that 'there is no link between economic growth and poverty reduction'. Last year, I spent two weeks in Kenya—which is meant to be the economic powerhouse of East Africa—where I witnessed the economic and social turmoil that is engulfing the nation, with rampant poverty and violence despite decades of traditional aid from countless NGOs and donor government programmes. I flew straight from Nairobi to Shenzhen province in southern China, where I was assessing factories to produce a new Sunny Money product. The difference was astounding. When I first visited Shenzhen in 1990, it was as poor as Kenya is today; 20 years later, Shenzhen is experiencing an economic boom, with a higher standard of living than Kenya and an emerging middle class. Economic development in China has led to a significant reduction in poverty without the need for traditional aid and development programmes—although, of course, with serious environmental and social consequences that should not be ignored.

Developing countries will need more than just microfranchising if they want to grow in a sustainable manner in the long term. Nevertheless, small businesses are at the heart of a healthy economy and often provide the jobs that keep families clothed and fed. My hope is that the microfranchising sector will continue to grow strongly over the coming decade, constantly improving and refining its model and techniques in order to make a significant contribution to the fight against global poverty.

References

Armendariz de Aghion, B., and J. Morduch (2005) *The Economics of Microfinance* (Cambridge, MA: MIT Press).

Barnett, J. (2007) 'Environmental Security', in A. Collins (ed.), *Contemporary Security Studies* (Oxford: Oxford University Press): 182-203.

Best, M.L. (2008) 'Reflections on (un)Sustainability: The Sustainable Access in Rural Internet (SARI) Project Nearly One Decade On', paper presented at the *Conference on Confronting the Challenge of Technology for Development: Experiences from the BRICS*, Department of International Development, University of Oxford, 29–30 May 2008.

Blackett, T. (1998) *Trademarks* (Basingstoke, UK/London: Macmillan Press).

Bond, R. (2004) *Bond's Franchise Guide* (Oakland, CA: Sourcebook Publications, 15th edn).

Bracken, E., N. Chao, D. Phaovisaid and B. Slocum (2006) *Microfinance and Microfranchising: A Feasibility Study* (Final Report; Washington, DC: Elliott School of International Affairs, George Washington University; www.gwu.edu/~oid/Capstone/Capstone%20papers/kenya06.pdf), accessed 18 August 2010.

Bradach, J. (1998) *Franchise Organisations* (Boston, MA: Harvard Business School Press).

—— (2003) 'Going to Scale: The Challenge of Replicating Social Programs', *Stanford Social Innovation Review*, Spring 2003.

Central Intelligence Agency (2010) 'Kenya', in *The World Factbook*, Washington, DC: Central Intelligence Agency; https://www.cia.gov/library/publications/the-world-factbook/geos/ke.html, last accessed 16 August 2010.

Chang, Y.Y., A.J. Wilkinson and K. Mellahi (2007) 'HRM Strategies and MNCs from Emerging Economies in the UK', *European Business Review* 19.5.

Churchill, N., and V. Lewis (1983) 'The Five Stages of Small Business Growth', *Harvard Business Review* Reprint 83301 (May–June 1983): 3-9.

Clemminck, N., and S. Kadakia (2007) *What Works: Scojo India Foundation—Restoring Eyesight in Rural India through the Direct Selling of Reading Glasses* (Washington, DC: World Resources Institute).

Deelder, W., and R.A. Miller (2009) *Franchising in Frontier Markets: What's Working, What's Not, and Why* (New York: Dalberg Global Development Advisors, December 2009; www.dalberg.com/PDFs/Frontiers_Markets_content_print_marks.pdf).

Dees, J.G. (1998) 'Enterprising Nonprofits', *Harvard Business Review* 76.1: 55-67.

——, J. Emerson and P. Economy (2001) *Enterprising Nonprofits: A Toolkit for Social Entrepreneurs* (New York: John Wiley).

De Soto, H. (2000) *The Mystery of Capital: Why Capitalism Triumphs in the West and Fails Everywhere Else* (London: Bantam Press).

DeWitt, S. (2008) 'Evolution of Grameen Village Phone: Our Experience in Systemization, Replication, and Scaling of the Village Phone Microfranchise', presented at the *Economic Self Reliance Conference*, Brigham Young University, 7–8 November 2008.

Duckett, B., and P. Monaghan (2007) *How to Turn Your Business into the Next Global Brand: Creating and Managing a Franchised Network* (Oxford: How To Books).

Fairbourne, J. (2006) *BYU MicroFranchise Development Initiative (BYU- MFDI)* (Washington, DC: MicroFranchise Learning Lab).

—— (2007a) 'Why Microfranchising is Needed Now: Introduction and Book Overview', in J. Fairbourne, S.W. Gibson and W.G. Dyer (eds.), *MicroFranchising: Creating Wealth at the Bottom of the Pyramid* (Northampton, MA: Edward Elgar).

—— (2007b) 'Microfranchising', *Marriott Alumni Magazine*, Summer 2007; marriottschool. byu.edu/marriottmag/summer07/features/atwork1.cfm, accessed 20 August 2010.

—— (2007c) *MicroFranchise Toolkit: How to Systemize and Replicate a Microfranchise* (Provo, UT: BYU Center for Economic Self-Reliance).

——, S.W. Gibson and W.G. Dyer (eds.) (2007) *MicroFranchising: Creating Wealth at the Bottom of the Pyramid* (Northampton, MA: Edward Elgar).

Gibson, S.W. (2007) 'Microfranchising: The Next Step on the Development Ladder', in J. Fairbourne, S.W. Gibson and W.G. Dyer (eds.), *MicroFranchising: Creating Wealth at the Bottom of the Pyramid* (Northampton, MA: Edward Elgar): 17-42.

Hammond, A., W.J. Kramer, R. Katz, J. Tran and C. Walker (2007) 'The Next Four Billion', *Innovations* 2.1–2 (Winter/Spring 2007): 147-58.

Hart, S. (1998) 'Developing New Brand Names', in S. Hart. and J. Murphy (eds.), *Brands: The New Wealth Creators* (Basingstoke/New York: Palgrave).

Harvard Business School (2005) *Entrepreneur's Toolkit, Tools and Techniques to Launch and Grow Your Business* (Harvard Business Essentials; Boston, MA: Harvard Business School Publishing).

Haub, C., and M. Mederios Kent (2009) *2009 World Population Data Sheet* (Washington, DC: Population Reference Bureau; www.prb.org/pdf09/09wpds_eng.pdf, accessed 19 August 2010).

Henriques, M., and M. Herr (2007) 'The Informal Economy and Microfranchising', in J. Fairbourne, S.W. Gibson and W.G. Dyer (eds.), *MicroFranchising: Creating Wealth at the Bottom of the Pyramid* (Northampton, MA: Edward Elgar): 43-77.

Hoyt, M., and E. Jamison (2007) 'Microfranchising and the Base of the Pyramid', in J. Fairbourne, S.W. Gibson and W.G. Dyer (eds.), *MicroFranchising: Creating Wealth at the Bottom of the Pyramid* (Northampton, MA: Edward Elgar).

Ikoja-Odongo, R. (2001) 'A Study of the Information Needs and Uses of the Informal Sector in Uganda: Preliminary Findings', *LIBRES: Library and Information Science Research* 11.1; libres.curtin.edu.au/libres11n1/ocholla.htm, accessed 20 August 2010.

ILO (International Labour Organisation) (2009a) *Global Employment Trends: January 2009* (Geneva: ILO; www.ilo.org/wcmsp5/groups/public/---dgreports/---dcomm/documents/publication/wcms_101461.pdf).

—— (2009b) 'Unemployment, Working Poor and Vulnerable Employment to Increase Dramatically due to Global Economic Crisis', press release; www.ilo.org/global/About_the_ILO/Media_and_public_information/Press_releases/lang--en/WCMS_101462/index.htm, accessed 16 August 2010.

Interplast (n.d.) *The Forgotten Global Health Crisis of Burns* (Mountain View, CA: Interplast; www.interplast.org/about/gfx/fs09_burns%20factsheet.pdf, accessed 19 August 2010).

Jones Christensen, L., H. Parsons and J. Fairbourne (2010a) 'Building Entrepreneurship in Subsistence Markets: Microfranchising as an Employment Incubator', *Journal of Business Research* 63.6: 595-601.

——, D. Lehr and J. Fairbourne (2010b) 'A Good Business for Poor People', *Stanford Social Innovation Review*, Summer 2010.

Karamchandani, A., M. Kubzansky and P. Frandano (2009) *Emerging Markets, Emerging Models: Market-Based Solutions to the Challenges of Global Poverty* (Cambridge, MA: Monitor Group; www.mim.monitor.com/downloads/emergingmarkets_full.pdf, accessed 19 August 2010).

Karlan, D., X. Giné, T. Harigaya and B. Nguyen (2006) *Evaluating Microfinance Programme Innovation with Randomized Controlled Trials: An Example from Group versus Individual Lending* (ERD Technical Note Series 16; Manila, Philippines: Asian Development Bank Economics and Research Department).

Karnani, A. (2007) 'Microfinance Misses its Mark', *Stanford Social Innovation Review*, Summer 2007; marriottschool.byu.edu/selfreliance/wiki/UserFiles/2007SU_feature_karnani.pdf.

Khanna, T., K.G. Palepu and J. Sinha (2005) 'Strategies That Fit Emerging Markets', *Harvard Business Review* 83.6.

Lehr, D. (2008) *Microfranchising at the Base of the Pyramid* (Working Paper; New York: Acumen Fund; www.acumenfund.org/.../Microfranchising_Working Paper_XoYB6sZ5.pdf).

Light, D. (1997) 'Briefing from the Editors: Franchising, Getting It Right From the Start', *Harvard Business Review*, May–June 1997.

Littlefield, E., J. Morduch and S. Hashemi (2003) *Is Microfinance an Effective Strategy to Reach the Millennium Development Goals?* (Focus Note 24; Washington, DC: Consultative Group to Assist the Poor).

Magleby, K. (2005) 'Microfranchises as a Solution to Global Poverty'; www.cybermissions.org/icafe/theory/Microfranchising%20by%20Magleby,%20Nov.%2005.pdf, accessed 10 January 2011.

—— (2007) 'Microfranchise Business Models', in J. Fairbourne, S.W. Gibson and W.G. Dyer (eds.), *MicroFranchising: Creating Wealth at the Bottom of the Pyramid* (Northampton, MA: Edward Elgar): 133-48.

Moharana, T.R., N. Mohapatra and S. Pattanaik (2009) 'Microfranchising: A New Business Model to Empower Rural India'; www.indianmba.com/Faculty_Column/FC968/fc968.html, accessed 12 January 2011.

Montagu, D. (2002) 'Franchising of Health Services in Developing Countries', *Health Policy and Planning* 17.2: 121-30.

Mullen, J. (2002) 'Rural Poverty', in V. Desai and R. Potter (eds.), *The Companion to Development Studies* (London: Arnold): 143-46.

Ohmae, K. (1989) 'The Global Logic of Strategic Alliances', *Harvard Business Review*, March–April 1989.

Porter, M. (1985) *Competitive Advantage* (New York: Free Press).

Prahalad, C.K. (2006) *The Fortune at the Bottom of the Pyramid: Eradicating Poverty through Profits* (Upper Saddle River, NJ: Wharton School Publishing).

—— and S. Hart (2002) 'The Fortune at the Bottom of the Pyramid', *Strategy + Business* 26: 54-67.

Ratan, A.L., and M. Gogineni (2008) 'Cost Realism in Deploying Technologies for Development', presented at the conference on *Confronting the Challenge of Technology for Development: Experiences from the BRICS*, Department of International Development, University of Oxford, 29–30 May 2008.

Sachs, J. (2005) *The End of Poverty: How We Can Make It Happen in Our Lifetime* (London: Penguin).

Segrè, J., and J. Tran (2008) *What Works: CareShop Ghana: Improving Access to Essential Drugs through Conversion Franchising* (What Works Series; Washington, DC: World Resources Institute; pdf.wri.org/whatworks_careshop_ghana.pdf).

Shane, S. (2005) 'Is Franchising Right for Your Industry?', FT Press, 14 January 2005; www.ftpress.com/articles/article.aspx?p=360649, accessed 19 August 2010.

—— and C. Spell (1998) 'Factors for New Franchise Success', *Sloan Management Review*, Spring 1998: 43-50 .

SIDA (Swedish International Development Cooperation Agency) (1999) *Health Profile Uganda 1999* (Stockholm: SIDA).

Simanis, E., and S. Hart (2008) *The Base of the Pyramid Protocol: Toward Next Generation BoP Strategy* (Ithaca, NY: Cornell University, 2nd edn).

Sireau, N. (2008) *Make Poverty History: Political Communication in Action* (Basingstoke, UK/ New York: Palgrave Macmillan).

Slaughter, S. (2008) 'Living Goods: A Sustainable System for Defeating the Diseases of Poverty, Combining the Best Practices in Microfinance, Franchising, and Public Health', presented at the *Economic Self Reliance Conference*, Brigham Young University, Provo, UT, 7–8 November 2008.

Stacey, J., and J. Parker (2009) *Listening to the Voices of Women and Children in Malawi: A Report for the MicroLoan Foundation*; www.microloanfoundation.org.uk/What-we-do/ SocialImpact, accessed 11 January 2011.

Stanworth, J., S. Price, C. Porter, T. Swabe and M. Gold (1995). *Franchising as a Source of Technology Transfer to Developing Economies* (Special Studies Series 7; London: University of Westminster Press).

Tan Tsu Wee, T., and M. Chua Han Ming (2002) 'Leveraging on Symbolic Values and Meanings in Branding', *Journal of Brand Management* 10.3: 208-18.

Taylor, J.B. (2005) 'Statement on Getting the Millennium Development Goals Back on Track', John B. Taylor, Under Secretary for International Affairs, United States Treasury, Davos, Switzerland, 27 January 2005.

Tharoor, I. (2006) 'Paving the Way Out of Poverty', *Time*, 13 October 2006; www.time.com/time/world/article/0,8599,1546100,00.html, accessed 19 August 2010.

Trelstad, B. (2009) 'The Nature and Type of "Social Investors" ' (New York: Acumen Fund, April 2009; www.acumenfund.org/uploads/assets/documents/KFP-impact-investing-1_5HgFXhoh.pdf, accessed 19 August 2010).

Tushabomwe-Kazooba, C. (2006), 'Causes of Small Business Failure in Uganda: A Case Study from Bushenyi and Mbarara Towns', *African Studies Quarterly* 8.4; web.africa.ufl.edu/asq/v8/v8i4a3.htm, accessed 19 August 2010.

UMI GDLC (Uganda Management Institute Global Distance Learning Centre) (2005) 'Urban Informal Sector in Uganda', presented during the *Key Labour Market Issues Course*, at UMI GDLC, Uganda, April/May 2005; info.worldbank.org/etools/docs/library/211247/ Uganda_Urban%20Informal%20Sector.pdf, accessed 12 August 2010.

UNAIDS (Joint United Nations Programme on HIV/AIDS) (2004) 'A Global Overview of the AIDS Epidemic', in *2004 Report on the Global AIDS Epidemic* (Geneva: UNAIDS; www.unaids.org/bangkok2004/GAR2004_html/GAR2004_03_en.htm#P237_35114, accessed 16 August 2010).

—— (2008) 'Status of the Global HIV Epidemic', in UNAIDS, *2008 Report on the Global Aids Epidemic*: Ch. 2; data.unaids.org/pub/GlobalReport/2008/jc1510_2008_global_report_pp29_62_en.pdf, accessed 16 August 2010.

UNDP (United Nations Development Programme) Uganda (2008) 'Strengthening Small and Medium Enterprises (SMEs)', UNDP Uganda; www.undp.or.ug/projects/34, accessed 19 August 2010.

—— and WHO (World Health Organisation) (2004) 'Joint Statement on Indoor Air Pollution: World Rural Women's Day 2004'; www.who.int/mediacentre/news/statements/2004/statement5/en/index.html, accessed 19 August 2010.

Van Kirk, G. (2010) 'The Microconsignment Model: Bridging the "Last Mile" of Access to Products and Services for the Rural Poor', *Innovations* 5.1: 101-27.

WHO (World Health Organisation) (2008) *A WHO Plan for Burn Prevention and Care* (Geneva: WHO).

World Economic Forum (2009) *The Next Billions: Unleashing Business Potential in Untapped Markets* (Geneva: World Economic Forum).

Yin, S., and M. Kent (2008) 'Kenya: The Demographics of a Country in Turmoil' (Washington, DC: Population Reference Bureau; www.prb.org/Articles/2008/kenya.aspx, accessed 16 August 2010).

Yunus, M. (2003) *Banker to the Poor: Micro-Lending and the Battle against World Poverty* (Cambridge, MA: PublicAffairs).

—— (2007) *Creating a World without Poverty: Social Business and the Future of Capitalism* (Cambridge, MA: PublicAffairs).

About the contributors

Harry Andrews is one of the founders of Barefoot Power and has over ten years of experience in the renewable energy sector. Harry worked in the early days of Barefoot Power in raising series A financing, product development and field trials. Over recent years, he has managed the set-up and expansion of Barefoot Power's operations in Africa, with particular focus on its subsidiaries in Kenya and Uganda. Prior to Barefoot Power, Harry worked as a project manager for various feasibility studies on small to medium-sized renewable energy projects in Australia and the Pacific, including managing a rural electrification master planning project in Papua New Guinea. Working for Tasmania's state government, Harry managed project assessment and funding under Australia's federal Remote Renewable Power Generation Program.
harrya@barefootpower.com

Jason Fairbourne is the CEO and founder of Fairbourne Consulting Group; he is the Peery Social Entrepreneur Fellow at the BYU Marriott School of Management. Jason was the previously Director of Business Solutions for Development, and founder of the microfranchise Development Initiative at the University. Jason has consulted many organisations, both non-profit and for-profit corporations on designing and/or growing businesses in emerging and developing markets. Jason is industry-agnostic; he is more concerned with meeting consumer demand by designing efficient BoP businesses. He is the author of *MicroFranchising: Creating Wealth at the Bottom of the Pyramid* and he has written several pieces on microfranchising, including the 'MicroFranchise Toolkit', a guide to systematising and replicating microfranchises. His work is being implemented around the world. Jason has presented his work at numerous international conferences on five continents and has conducted several Learning Labs. Jason has an MSc in Development Management from the London School of Economics and Political Science, and has spent the last 11 years of his life working in developing countries.
jason.fairbourne@byu.edu

Nate Heller is the chief operations officer Ayllu. He has worked with a variety of social enterprises around the world, including VisionSpring and Pratham Books in India, Conversion Sound in Nigeria, and Somos Mas in Colombia. Previously, Nate worked primarily in West Africa, with the United Nations Food and Agriculture Organisation, the Institute for

Transportation and Development Policy, and the US Peace Corps. Nate holds an MBA from the Yale School of Management, an MA in International Relations and Economics from Johns Hopkins University (SAIS), and a BA in Philosophy from Connecticut College.
nate@aylluinitiative.org

Kurt Illetschko left his native Austria in 1968 and has since settled permanently in Johannesburg, South Africa. His involvement with franchising started in 1975. After moving through the various facets of franchising as a franchisee, a franchisor and a franchise consultant, he established himself as a franchise writer and lecturer. Kurt has written books on franchising and small business topics for several publishers including Hodder Education (UK), Butterworths, Troupant, Frontrunner and the Franchise Association of South Africa. He has had numerous articles published and contributes to two leading franchise websites. On the commercial front, Kurt writes operations manuals, disclosure documents and other franchise-related documentation for leading franchisors across Africa. Kurt is an honorary life member of the Franchise Association of South Africa.
franchise@intekom.co.za

Lisa Jones Christensen is Assistant Professor of Strategy and Entrepreneurship at the Kenan-Flagler Business School at the University of North Carolina at Chapel Hill. In addition to microfranchising, her research interests include sustainable enterprise in the USA and developing economies, corporate social responsibility, leadership, change management and change implementation. She has initiated projects studying microfinance and entrepreneurship education in developing countries and the public health outcomes of microfinance. With co-authors and with support from Procter & Gamble, Lisa is researching the motivation, opportunity and ability variables that relate to behaviour change among the poorest consumers in developing countries. She has an MA in International Development and an MBA from Brigham Young University. Before graduate school, Lisa held senior sales and marketing positions at multiple Silicon Valley firms. Subsequently, she co-founded HELP-International, an incubator for social entrepreneurship. Most recently, she has consulted for Acumen Fund, Jamii Bora Trust and Procter & Gamble.
lisa_jc@unc.edu

Ryan Lee contributed his chapter as a Sloan Fellow at London Business School, when he took a one-year sabbatical to transit to the private sector after an 18-year naval career. Ryan is a mechanical engineer by training and a Leadership in Energy and Environmental Design Accredited Professional. He is currently the Director of Corporate Development at Elmich Pte Ltd, a Singapore-based company specialising in providing architectural and landscape engineering products to the global construction industry. Ryan hopes to start a social enterprise to tackle environmental and poverty problems in South-East Asia in the near future.
lsweeann@gmail.com

David Lehr is an international development consultant and Adjunct Lecturer at UNC's Kenan-Flagler Business School with over 15 years of experience creating both social and for-profit businesses. His focus is on sustainable approaches to international development that create employment and economic growth. David has written about his work for the *Stanford Social Innovations Review*, and teaches on Market-Based Approaches to Poverty Alleviation and Corporate Social Responsibility. He is also a committed proponent of microfranchising, and leveraging cell phones/Internet access to achieve scale. David has held senior management positions at Adobe Systems and Mercy Corps, and was one of the innovators behind Reuters Market Light, a commercial venture that delivers customised market data via mobile phones to farmers in the developing world. He has consulted for several non-profits including the

Gates Foundation, World Vision, Save the Children, REDF, Linked Foundation, Acumen Fund and TransFair USA, and has lived and worked in several countries in Asia. David was a Fellow at Stanford University, holds a Master's from the University of California, San Diego, and a BA from the State University of New York at Albany and speaks Mandarin Chinese.
lehr.david@gmail.com

Miguel D. Ramirez attained Bachelors' degrees in Psychology and Philosophy at the University of Texas at Austin and an MA in Conflict Resolution at the University of Bradford's Peace Studies Department in the UK. He undertook research in Sierra Leone on the efficacy of aid agencies, the difficulties in post-conflict reconstruction, and environmental insecurity felt by rural populations, which led to a specialisation in Human Security and HIV/AIDS, Post-Conflict Reconstruction, and Mediation. He has undertaken internships at Human Rights Watch, the Coalition to Stop the Use of Child Soldiers and SolarAid, in the latter further developing SolarAid's macrosolar model for schools and community centres as well as undertaking solar product research and development. He was awarded the first Vodafone World of Difference Foundation's grant. Miguel's work evolved to evaluating and coordinating the Kenya and Zambia programmes, and latterly managing the SolarAid Kenya programme in Nairobi. In Kenya Miguel is engaged in developing and managing SolarAid's microfranchise model in rural areas and also their macrosolar model to both medical clinics and schools. At time of writing Miguel and his team have trained 101 entrepreneurs and have put 27 solar systems in rural schools and clinics throughout Kenya.
miguel@solar-aid.org

Melissa Richer is the founder and executive director of Ayllu, which provides critical support to social enterprises in emerging markets to scale their impact. Melissa launched Ayllu in 2007 while she was working for Ashoka: Innovators for the Public. She has worked on international development projects in Africa, Europe, the Middle East and Latin America that include education, maternity care, conflict resolution, immigration, and minority rights. Melissa is a graduate of Duke University. She lives and works in São Paulo, Brazil.
melissa@aylluinitiative.org

Dr **P. Clint Rogers** holds a doctorate in instructional psychology and technology, was the first to teach web analytics at a university, and has developed world-class web promotional strategies for various organisations. Clint has specific interests in synergistic cross-cultural collaboration, innovation, global virtual teams, fostering human potential, international business and education, and the impact of media and technological diffusion on international development. He is active in consulting, teaching, travelling and research. Clint is coordinating the Consortium of African and European Universities (ICT 4 Development), and supervising dissertations in the IMPDET programme (International Multidisciplinary PhD Studies in Educational Technology: www.impdet.org).
clint.rogers2008@gmail.com

Peter Ryan was educated at Kelly College in Devon, UK, and then took a year off to travel before obtaining a BA (Hons.) in International Marketing at Greenwich University, London. His initial career was focused on marketing consumer goods products and toiletries such as Old Spice, Imperial Leather Soap and Duracell Batteries to Africa and parts of Europe. This experience triggered an interest in gaining a better understanding of the realities of Africa and in particular the lives of the poor who would never be able to afford the products that he was marketing. He then started a number of businesses in the food and IT sectors before founding the MicroLoan Foundation in his spare time—a project that has now become the full-time focus of his life.
peter.ryan@microloanfoundation.org.uk

Michael H. Seid is the founder and managing director of Michael H. Seid & Associates (MSA), a domestic and international franchise advisory firm. He has more than 25 years' experience as a senior operations and financial executive or consultant for companies within the franchise, retail, restaurant, hospitality and service industries as well as having been a franchisee. MSA is a member of the International Franchise Association's (IFA) Supplier Forum and Michael currently serves as chairman of the IFA Social Sector Franchising Committee, as a member of the IFA's Finance Audit and Budget Committee and on several other IFA committees. Michael is a member of the board of CFWshops, a franchisor established to provide clinical services and essential medicines to the poor in rural Kenya and Rwanda. He is also co-founding Healthguard (Uganda), an innovative franchise approach to indoor residual spraying that can reduce malaria rates by up to 80%.
mseid@msaworldwide.com

Dr **Nicolas Sireau** was founding Executive Director of SolarAid, an award-winning non-profit organisation that promotes the use of solar power in developing countries. SolarAid launched and runs Sunny Money, a microfranchise programme that identifies, recruits, trains and manages a growing network of solar entrepreneurs in East and southern Africa. Nicolas started his career as a financial journalist before moving to mainline church charity CWM, then as Director of Communications for international development agency Progressio. Nicolas is a fellow of the Ashoka Network of Social Entrepreneurs. He has a PhD in social psychology from City University, London. He is the author of *Make Poverty History: Political Communication in Action* (Palgrave Macmillan, 2008) and a contributor to *The Mediation of Power: A Critical Introduction* (Routledge, 2007). He now devotes the majority of his time to running the AKU Society, a medical charity set up to find a cure for AKU (short for Alkaptonuria), a rare disease affecting his children. He is also a non-executive director of bioinformatics company GenSeq and continues as an advisor to SolarAid.
nick@sireau.net

Dr **Robert C. Wolcott** is founder and executive director of the Kellogg Innovation Network (KIN) at the Kellogg School of Management, Northwestern University, USA. The KIN is a network of senior executives dedicated to driving sustainable innovation. He teaches corporate innovation and entrepreneurship in the USA, Hong Kong and Latin America, and has been a visiting professor at the Keio Business School (Tokyo, Japan). Robert is an adviser to the Nordic Innovation Centre of Nordic Council of Ministers, Oslo, Norway. His book, *Grow from Within: Mastering Corporate Entrepreneurship and Innovation* (McGraw-Hill), with Dr Michael Lippitz, was launched in 2010. Robert's work has appeared in the *MIT Sloan Management Review*, the *Wall Street Journal*, *Advertising Age*, *BusinessWeek*, the *Financial Times* (UK/European Edition) and the *New York Times*. Robert received a BA in European and Chinese History, and an MS and PhD in Industrial Engineering and Management Science, from Northwestern University, Evanston, Illinois.
r-wolcott@kellogg.northwestern.edu

Index

For Product Safety Concerns and Information please contact our EU
representative GPSR@taylorandfrancis.com Taylor & Francis Verlag GmbH,
Kaufingerstraße 24, 80331 München, Germany

Printed and bound by CPI Group (UK) Ltd, Croydon, CR0 4YY

01/05/2025
01858457-0001